Plateau Indian Ways with Words

Pittsburgh Series in Composition, Literacy, and Culture

David Bartholomae and Jean Ferguson Carr, Editors

Plateau Indian Ways with Words

The Rhetorical Tradition of the Tribes of the Inland Pacific Northwest

Barbara Monroe
Foreword by Scott Richard Lyons
Afterword by Kristin L. Arola

University of Pittsburgh Press

Portions of chapters 3, 6, and 7, in slightly different form, appeared in Barbara Monroe, "Plateau Indian Ways with Words," *College Composition and Communications* 61, no. 1 (September 2009): W321–342. Copyright © 2009 by the National Council of Teachers of English. Reprinted with permission.

Material by Nipo Strongheart in chapter 4 is reprinted with permission of the Yakama Nation Library.

All meeting minutes in chapter 5 are located in the Relander Collection, housed at the Yakima Central Library. Relander material is reprinted with permission of Yakima Valley Libraries. Revised portions of chapter 7, in slightly different form, appeared in Barbara Monroe, *Crossing the Digital Divide: Race, Writing, and Technology in the Classroom*. New York: Teachers College Press. Copyright © 2004 by Teachers College, Columbia University. All rights reserved. Reprinted by permission of the publisher.

Published by the University of Pittsburgh Press, Pittsburgh, Pa., 15260
Copyright © 2014, University of Pittsburgh Press
Manufactured in the United States of America
Printed on acid-free paper
10 9 8 7 6 5 4 3 2 1

Library of Congress Cataloging-in-Publication Data

Monroe, Barbara.
Plateau Indian Ways with Words: The Rhetorical Tradition of the Tribes of the Inland Pacific Northwest / Barbara Monroe.
    pages cm. — (Pittsburgh Series in Composition, Literacy, and Culture)
Includes bibliographical references and index.
ISBN 978-0-8229-6306-6 (paperback)
1. Indians of North America—Northwest, Pacific—Languages—Rhetoric. 2. Indians of North America—Columbia Plateau—Languages—Rhetoric. 3. Indians of North America—Great Basin—Languages—Rhetoric. 4. Indian students—United States—History. 5. Persuasion (Rhetoric)—History. I. Title.
PM217.M66 2014

497'.412—dc23   2014012667

TO ANITA,
PEGGY,
AND STEVE

without any one of you,
this book would not have happened.

Contents

Acknowledgments

This book was ten years in the making. But I could not have completed this journey without the aid, advice, and support of so many people along the way, from start to finish.

The starting point, the Writing Across Cultures project, was funded by CO-TEACH (Collaboration on Teacher Education Accountable to Children with High Needs), a federal grant secured by my colleagues in the College of Education at Washington State University. The generous support, both financial and moral, of co–principal investigators Tariq Akmal and Dawn Shinew, in particular, launched this project. Two sabbatical years, as well as the Buchanan Scholarship, funded by the English Department at Washington State University, cleared my schedule, giving me the mental space and time to read, research, and write.

Of all the institutional support I have received, none has been more important than that from Trevor Bond and Cheryl Gunselman from Manuscripts, Archives, and Special Collections of Washington State University Libraries. Trevor Bond not only helped me navigate the McWhorter Collection; he also schooled me in the whole point of curating: providing context for artifacts that would otherwise be as meaningful as a box of photographs and papers under a stranger's bed. To Cheryl Gunselman, I owe a debt of gratitude in securing permissions to quote so extensively from that collection. Thanks are also due to the anonymous librarians at the National Archives, both in Washington, D.C., and in Seattle, as well as at the Yakima Central Library, which houses the Relander Collection—all of whom assisted me in retrieving archival material on multiple visits. I would not have known that this collection even existed had it not been for Debby DeSoer, director of the Ellensburg Public Library, who introduced me to that library's historian-in-residence at the time, Milton Wagy, who in turn pointed me to the Relander Collection.

Patricia Bizzell, Helen Fox, and Victor Villanueva wrote letters of support for grant applications, and in Victor's case, multiple letters; I am so honored that you endorsed my work. Other colleagues at Washington State University and tribal colleges gave me invaluable feedback on my ideas, as they started to make their way into writing, either in grant applications or in early drafts of articles and chapters; these colleagues include Will Hamlin, Debbie Lee, George Kennedy, Lisa Johnson, Crag Hill, Laurie Johnson, and the blind reviewers at *College Composition and Communications,* Teachers College Press, and the University of Pittsburgh Press. Others heard me speak in public forums or in private conversations, asking questions that I was not always able to answer at the time but that continued to nag me like a bad tooth. This book answers those questions. Todd Butler, Augusta Rohrbach, Elizabeth Siler, and Laurie Johnson: thank you for asking them.

Special thanks to my colleagues Lynn Gordon, Nancy Bell, and Michael Hanley, all of whom helped me with issues of linguistics and translation; and Deirdre Black, a linguist who has lived and worked with the Flathead for many years, who introduced me to William Leap's *American Indian English,* a brilliant piece of scholarship on Native languages that transformed my own understanding of the abiding impact of one's ancestral language. I want to acknowledge the support of the Plateau Center for American Indian Studies, most especially Barbara Aston, Mary Collins, and Kim Christen: Barbara, for introducing me to Native educators and for mentoring me through cultural expectations of those relationships; Mary, for so enthusiastically embracing the project of recovery that my work represents; and Kim, for making me mindful of the problems inherent in white researchers curating Native materials. Colleagues from other departments, including Orlan Svingen (history) and Judy Meuth (critical culture, gender, and race studies), increased my bibliography, source material, and Native contact list, all taken to heart and rigorously pursued. To Brian McNeill and Laurie "Lali" McCubbin, co-directors of the Pacific Northwest Center for Mestizo and Indigenous Research and Outreach, I owe the notion of "cultural congruence" that I explore in chapter 7.

Several graduate students worked with me over the years, assisting in various capacities: scanning hundreds of papers, driving to remote reservations, attending meetings, listening to my reasoning. Some students were writing dissertations themselves on American Indian topics, which also kept me thinking. Thank you, especially Heather Kimmel, Michael Jordan, Pam Chisum, Shawn Lamebull, and most of all, Jeanette Weaskus. Jeanette and I were mutual sounding boards for each other for several years running.

Also important were the many casual conversations with friends and colleagues over the years. When asked, "So what's your book about?," I had to articulate an answer, trying out various synopses in twenty-five words or less. My responses to these people met with instantaneous, enthusiastic validation, some leading to extended or multiple conversations. These conversations, individually and collectively, kept me keeping on. Thank you, Jerry Bopp, Sally Brownfield, Jay

Dennison, Samantha Dennison, Jack Duffy, Helen Fox, Phyllis Frus, Chris Frye, Ruth Monroe, Marta Restrepo, Susan Romano, Becky Rosenberg, and Jessye O'Connell Schmitz. It was my beloved Stevan, though, with whom I had the most of these casual conversations. During meals, in the car, on vacation, over the telephone, in bed at night—for more than ten years, Steve would ask or just listen at every juncture in this long process and praise and urge and hound me to keep writing, keep writing.

To the administrators, teachers, and students who participated in the Writing Across Cultures project, I acknowledge the greatest debt of gratitude. Please forgive me for omitting your last names; I do so only in an effort to protect your anonymity as well as that of your schools and your students involved in the project. Anita, Carol, Frank, Jim, Karen, Kelly, Lavinia, Lorraine, Lynn, Marilyn, Marion, Mary, Paige, Peggy, Rainbow, Rick, and Teresa—to you especially, I offer lifelong thanks for sharing your students' work and your professional lives with me. I have never met educators more dedicated to their students, their schools, and their communities.

Finally, I have to thank all the editors at the University of Pittsburgh Press, but especially Cynthia Miller for her early and patient support of this project since 2009.

Foreword
Scott Richard Lyons

A s far as we know, the first Native American to publish writing in the English language was the Mohegan preacher Samson Occom (1723–1792). Occom is primarily remembered today for his autobiography, "A Short Narrative of My Life" (1768), the first of many Native autobiographies to come, and for his *Sermon Preached at the Execution of Moses Paul* (1772), the first Native-authored text to see publication. Life writing and death writing: one might suggest that Native writing in English has dealt in serious business from the very start. One might also remark, as many have, purely on the basis of these two texts, that Samson Occom was "assimilated"—and perhaps that was the price that Indians paid to write their way into the public sphere.

But, in fact, Occom wrote a great deal more than those two oft-anthologized texts, as seen in the fine anthology edited by Joanna Brooks, *The Collected Writings of Samson Occom, Mohegan* (2006). There we find that in addition to the "Short Narrative" and *Moses Paul,* the Occom archive also includes four occasional essays, seventy-six letters, thirteen petitions and tribal documents, nineteen sermons, plus a large assortment of journal entries and Christian hymns. The range of subjects that Occom addressed—from New Light Calvinism, to the abolition of slavery, to matters of what would now be called tribal sovereignty—is broad and engaged. Occom was, to put it accurately, a committed public intellectual and fairly successful indigenous activist, but one might not draw that conclusion by reading only his two best-known pieces in isolation from the rest of his corpus. As Brooks has explained, on the basis of those two famous texts "a consensus view once developed of Occom as a missionary apologist for Christian imperialism" (9). That view couldn't help but take Occom for a dupe instead of seeing him as a formidable intellectual with a sharp critical perspective who navigated his world and spoke truth to power using the best tools at his disposal: his education, his access, and his literacy.

Since Occom's time, Native American writers have written extensively—and, I'll add, consistently—about matters of life and death, including concerns related to imperialism, using those same tools, but until quite recently most of that work was lost to archives soon after publication. It wasn't until the civil rights movement of the 1960s and 1970s and the subsequent rise of what American Indian studies scholar Kenneth Lincoln has termed the "Native American Renaissance" that Native writers started being recovered, reread, and reconsidered. At that point in history—decades after the anthropologist Franz Boas popularized what is now known as cultural relativism—scholars and critics of Native American writing assumed that Native cultures were "oral." While orality was clearly more authentically Indian than literacy, neither orality nor literacy was inherently better or more advanced than the other. In fact, many critics said, Indian writing of the Native American Renaissance was not a departure from but rather a continuation of oral tradition by other means. To evoke the title of one critical study from the period, Indians were "writing in the oral tradition." This was quite the sea change from the attitudes of the previous century. For example, in 1847, when the Ojibwe writer and preacher George Copway felt compelled to explain to his readers that "the mind for letters was in me, *but was asleep,*" he credited Christianity for waking up his latent literacy in a way that strikes me as logically the opposite of writing in the oral tradition. Both characterizations of Indian writing assume that orality and literacy are (1) dramatically different from each other, even opposed, yet (2) somehow existing inherently inside the subject—asleep, perhaps, but now in the process of being dramatically (re)awakened.

What thinkers across history, from Occom's time to our own, seem to have in common is a "great leap" theory of the movement from orality to literacy—the idea that, as classical literature scholar Walter Ong famously put it in *Orality and Literacy: The Technologizing of the Word* (1982), "writing restructures consciousness." Substitute the words "culture" or "identity" for "consciousness," and suddenly Samson Occom seems assimilated. Indians, according to this great leap theory, do not write; it is not their culture or tradition, and if they do write, well, it seems they have become a little less Indian—unless of course we flip the script entirely and see them becoming *more* Indian, a feat that the Native American Renaissance writers somehow managed to pull off, at least according to their contemporary critics who saw oral traditions on the page.

But what if none of this is quite the case? What if it has never really been true that Indians who wrote changed in some radically interiorized way through the act of scribbling their marks on a readable surface? What if all we're really talking about is not a vast restructuring of consciousness, culture, or identity, but rather the use of a powerful and important human tool—no more and no less than that? And what if Indians used this compelling, complicated tool to advance their interests, to promote an idea, to rethink (or reclaim) their values; what if they wrote simply because they enjoyed their literacy, as so many human beings have done before and since? What would happen if we conceived of Indian writing as having fewer cultural or identity claims at stake in its basic genetic makeup? Might it not actually seem all the more powerful a communication technology—a tool for survival instead of assimilation?

Barbara Monroe has written an insightful and compelling book that starts from these latter questions rather than scouring the Native text for signs of oral traditional resistance or, conversely, proof of assimilation. Her subjects, Plateau Indian students, use alphabetic writing in English in ways that do not threaten their identities or cultures so much as protect and even advance them in the way of a tool. From school essays to hip-hop lyrics, the Indian writers she discusses here are engaged in survival, not tragic assimilation or defiant resistance to the written word. In this sense they resemble their great Plateau Indian (Salishan) predecessor Christine Quintasket (1885?–1936), who in the early twentieth century published fiction and nonfiction under the pen name of Mourning Dove and became a celebrity in eastern Washington. In her posthumously published autobiography, *Mourning Dove: A Salishan Autobiography* (1990), Quintasket, a collector (and thus preserver) of her tribe's folklore and the author of the important novel *Cogewea, the Half-Blood* (1927), wrote of her appearance in school: "I was anxious to learn more English and read."

The young people discussed throughout this book carry on Quintasket's legacy, and Monroe makes sense of it all for her readers. The results are extremely interesting and productive, and because the writers discussed here seem more focused on life than death, they give me no small amount of hope.

Scott Richard Lyons

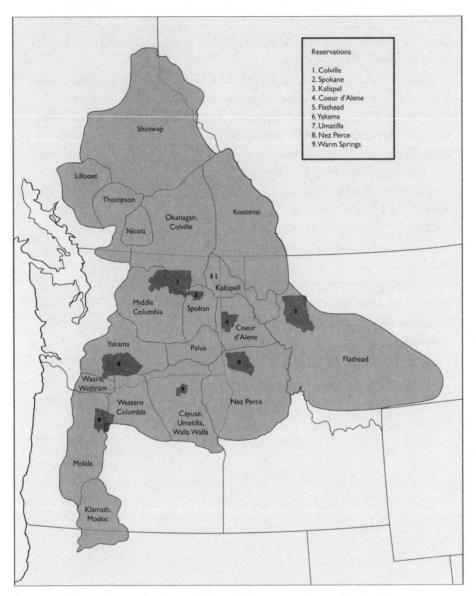

FIGURE 1. Ancestral grounds of some Plateau Indian groups (in gray) and contemporary reservations (in black). Spellings of tribal groups and their respective reservations do not always correspond for historical reasons.

Sources: "Contemporary Indian Reservations of Northwest Coast and Plateau Cultural Groups" and "Key to Tribal Territories," Digital Collections, University Libraries, University of Washington. Adobe illustration by Monreaux Monroe.

Introduction

In 1870, in anticipation of the removal of several Plateau Indian tribes to what would become the Colville reservation, the superintendent of Indian Affairs dispatched sub-Indian agent William Parkhurst Winans to northern Washington state to collect census data, among other particulars. At the tribal council, Winans asked his Indian audience if they would like to have teachers and preachers to guide their vocational and religious training. His question elicited this response (excerpted here from a longer speech) from Wee-ah-pe-kum (Okanagan):

> When you see my Boy working for the Whites, ask him, "Did your Father send you?" if he says no, send him home; for, when he comes home at night I will say to him, "My son, I am thirsty, go and get me some water to drink," and he turns around and says, "You God damned Indian how much will you give me"; or if you see my daughter prostituting herself for money, ask her, "Did your Father send you to earn money in this manner?," then, take a whip and drive her home, for when she comes back, her Mother will tell her to get some wood to cook her Father's supper, she will turn around and say, "You damned old Bitch pay me for my trouble." All this they have learned from the Whites.[1]

Even in this brief excerpt, Wee-ah-pe-kum's words nonetheless embody many of the principles of an indigenous rhetoric that, I argue throughout this book, continues to exert a discursive influence on the writing of Plateau Indian students today.

That conclusion has been a long time in the making. In my capacities as an English professor training future English teachers and as a coordinator of a federal grant targeting schools in high-poverty communities in Washington state in the early 2000s, I often heard a common comment from English teachers working in multiethnic classrooms with Indian minorities as well as in Indian-only schools: There is something special about Indian student writing, teachers often said, but were hard-pressed to explain exactly how, much less why. To determine how, I collaborated with two schools on one Plateau Indian reservation, collecting about 940 papers written from 2001 through 2004. To determine why this writing might be special, I looked at possible historical and cultural roots from archival sources; to this material, I then employed the methods of critical discourse analysis. Working primarily at the intersection of American Indian studies and rhetoric and composition, I drew additional insights from contrastive rhetoric, sociolinguistics, and new literacy studies. The title of this book pays homage to Shirley Brice Heath's ground-breaking ethnography, *Ways with Words: Language, Life, and Work in Communities and Classrooms,* published in 1986. Although my methodology and disciplinary background differs from Heath's, it was her work that inspired me as a young scholar and, unbeknownst to me then, set my research agenda for the rest of my career.

My project is also one of recovery. To authenticate the Plateau Indian rhetorical tradition as both distinctive and indigenous, I sought out primary source materials that report Indian words *verbatim* (either spoken in English or spoken in Native languages and then translated) as well as material written by Plateau Indians. Of necessity, I took what I think of as a post-hole approach, digging deep when I hit rich soil; much has been lost, but enough has survived to establish where the fence must have run. As luck would have it, I found large caches of primary material at roughly twenty-five- to forty-five-year intervals, from 1855 to 2001. Besides outlining a historical evolution, the selected material allows examination of different genres and modalities (oratory, correspondence, petition, telegram, lecture, State Supreme Court brief, General Council deliberations, newspaper letters to the editor) and consideration of different audiences (intergroup and intragroup). While two chapters focus on one Plateau tribe, one chapter draws material from different tribes across the Plateau, showing how those productions still work from common rhetorical premises. Throughout, I found that Plateau Indians spoke and wrote and deliberated primarily to a single purpose: to reassert tribal sovereignty. And they did so using an indigenous rhetoric that crossed languages, genres, and generations. That rhetoric has preserved and renewed cultural values and identity into modernity.

I focus on the arts of persuasion and public deliberation in part because storytelling and literary narrative have received much scholarly and popular attention, but in larger part because these are the modes that most closely align with those inscribed in high-stakes testing and essayist literacy in school and college, sites dominated by Euro-American rhetorical traditions. As evidenced in Wee-ah-pe-kum's words excerpted earlier, the Plateau Indian rhetorical tradition privileges the use of experiential knowledge as supporting evidence re-created through performance-like techniques, such as hypothetical dialogue and humor, often in the form of sarcasm and irony; suspended thesis, either delayed or unstated altogether, coupled with suspenseful arrangement; and situated elaboration marked by the use of highly selective detail. Such "strategies of personalization," as I term them, run counter to those of Euro-American academic argument, which distrusts and devalues "subjective" supporting evidence, "emotional" techniques, and implicit theses, among other discrepancies.

Not coincidentally, the writing of Plateau Indian students scores lower on standardized tests and on school and college assignments than the writing of their white counterparts. Certainly, the reasons American Indian students meet with failure at all levels of the educational system are multiple and complex. As much previous scholarship has shown, one issue is assessment itself, because typical measures are based on Euro-American norms. This book adds yet another angle to the scholarship on the so-called achievement gap, making the case for the first time that Plateau Indian students write from a different rhetorical tradition driven by different values—a tradition that has not yet been formally recognized, much less honored in school and college assignments and assessments.

When rhetorical worlds collide, how should educators respond? Different approaches have been advocated, based variously on models of deficiency and deficit, assimilation and accommodation. Expanding the conversation beyond these usual binaries, I advance instead the idea that faculty need to seek out points of cultural congruence, selecting methods, assignments, and assessments where culturally marked norms converge, rather than collide, thereby giving all students the opportunity to succeed. This stance breaks from common practices and customary arguments. The pedagogy of poverty, which focuses strictly on basic skills, and the pedagogy of power, which focuses on the goal of assimilation, are typically justified in the name of educational and financial success. I strongly advocate another option, for yet another reason: educators should honor American Indians' right to rhetorical sovereignty, in the name of nationality and nationhood.

In so arguing, I am following the theoretical path laid down by indigenous studies scholar Scott Lyons, who first called for American Indians' right to "rhetorical sovereignty": "the inherent right and ability of *peoples* to determine their own communicative needs and desires in this pursuit, to decide for themselves the goals, modes, styles, and languages of public discourse."[2] More recently, Lyons has pointed out that it is land that gives all nations, including Indian nations, the basis for identity. A people who inhabit or who identify with an ancestral land is a prerequisite of nationhood as well as nationality—or *ethnie*. The connection to ancestral land provides both the theoretical and the literal territorial grounds for national autonomy, worthy of the "recognition, respect, and rights" afforded sovereign nations.[3] Lyons challenges scholars in American Indian studies to trace the "unbroken line of descent" from mythical to modern times in all domains of

Native life, thereby "modernizing the *ethnie*," showing how distinct tribal cultures, as defined by their land base, maintain tradition by adapting it to modern conditions, just as all living cultures do.[4] While specific traditions may change or fade, the values that make a culture adhere as a culture in the first place are carried forward, taking on adapted but still recognizable forms.

This book responds to Lyons's charge in several regards. I attempt to trace an unbroken line of descent in the Native domain of rhetoric, but specific to the Plateau Indians, whose ancestral ground centers on the high plateau drained by the Columbia River in the Pacific Northwest, stretching from Canada and down into eastern Washington, northern Idaho, and eastern Oregon. My study confines itself roughly to the tribes south of the international border and between the Cascades and the Rockies. Generally little known on the national scene except for author Sherman Alexie (Spokan/Coeur d'Alene) and Chief Joseph (Nez Perce, Wallowa band), whose "I will fight no more forever" surrender speech is frequently anthologized, Plateau Indian tribes include the Cayuse, Coeur d'Alene, Colville, Flathead, Kalispel, Klamath, Mid-Columbia, Modoc, Nez Perce, Okanagan, Palus, Umatilla, Sans Poile, Spokan, Walla Walla, and Yakama, among many other tribes, clans, and bands; some of these are large confederations of yet more clan-based groups (see figure 1). Besides geography, the Plateau Indians hold in common culturally marked practices and values, having traded and intermarried for countless generations before Lewis and Clark first reconnoitered the area in 1805. Among those shared practices is a distinctive rhetorical tradition.

Chapters 1 and 2 lay the theoretical groundwork: the first, within the context of American Indian studies; the second, within the field of rhetoric and composition. Chapter 1, "'Real Indians' Don't Rap: Theorizing Indigenous Rhetorics," proposes grounds for authenticating what counts as Native. The twin issues of authenticity and identity have long preoccupied federal Indian policy, which found its legal backing in three decisions handed down by the Supreme Court under Chief Justice John Marshall in the early nineteenth century. Invested in the ideological complex of scientific racism, the white bio-logic of *being* an Indian ultimately supplanted the Native cultural logic of *doing* Indian-ness. The Marshall court also eroded the legal meaning of sovereignty, opening the door for breaking treaty terms, justifying policies of ethnic cleansing, and constructing Indian Country as colonial spaces. My methodology, critical discourse analysis, exposes these discourses, even as they continue to be played to and against in modern productions, largely by using the resources of an indigenous rhetoric, as a close reading of one student's rap poem illustrates. Chapter 2, "Defining Principles of Plateau Indian Rhetoric," offers a thick description of this rhetorical tradition, which might be broadly characterized as one premised on strategies of personalization. I situate this description within the long-standing conversation in composition and literacy studies on cultural differences, while also attempting to understand this rhetoric in terms of its own values, the most central of which is respect for personal autonomy. This value is multiply refracted in Plateau Indian lifeways, including traditional political organization and child-rearing practices, the two domains that have the most direct bearing on Native education.

Chapters 3–7 examine Plateau Indian ways with words in multiple genres, with representative documents from major periods in the conquest history of the Pacific Northwest. Historicized within the treaty period, chapter 3, "Speaking Straight in Indian Languages, 1855–1870," examines seven speeches in full, with additional speeches quoted in part, from four different Indian-American councils on the Plateau. These speeches were first spoken in various Indian languages and then translated and transcribed into English. Without question, much was irretrievably lost in translation, especially at the syntactic and semantic levels, thus obviating the validity of any close readings. What does translate across languages and across generations, however, is broad discursive moves. Analysis of early Plateau Indian oratory points to some of the foundational premises of Plateau Indian argumentation to this day, with striking parallels to their descendants' writing for the next seven generations—and counting—as subsequent chapters show.

While chapter 3 examines the oratory of Plateau Indian leaders, who might be viewed as extraordinarily noble by the white public of the nineteenth and twentieth centuries, chapters 4 and 5 consider ordinary Indians, writing either to whites or deliberating among themselves at tribal meetings. Focused on early activism of one Plateau tribe, the Yakama, chapter 4, "Writing in English, 1910–1921," showcases how the discursive principles of the spoken ancestral language base survived the crossover into English and literacy in both private and public domains during the allotment period. This indigenous rhetoric also crossed over into Euro-American genres on a wide swath of issues, including draft registration, liquor sales on the reservation, water rights, hunting and fishing rights, and citizenship. These early writings document that ordinary Indians embraced literacy and English not to assimilate to white culture but to insist on their sovereign rights as guaranteed by treaty.

Unlike previous chapters that analyze intergroup communications, chapter 5, "Deliberating Publicly, 1955–1956," examines intragroup deliberations of one tribe at the height of the tribal termination movement. The minutes of eight meetings on the Yakama reservation in 1955 and 1956 offer fresh insights into intragroup interaction, argumentation, and public deliberation. Plateau Indian political processes are both inherently and historically contentious, in part because of traditional interactional protocols that encourage dissent and confrontation, but in larger part because of federal Indian law policies that have bred factionalism. A closer look at the processes both for airing conflict and for building consensus sheds light on the expectations and experiences of argumentation that students bring to the classroom.

Chapter 6, "Writing in School, 2000–2004," culls student writing collected from two reservation schools, documenting the unbroken line of descent in rhetorical practices from the Treaty Council at Walla Walla in 1855 into the next millennium. At once resilient and resourceful, Plateau Indian students attempt to reconcile the demands of school with the communicative practices of home and community. In so doing, they are modernizing the rhetorical *ethnie*, carrying forward strategies of personalization, implicitly reasserting their right to rhetorical sovereignty. The last chapter explores the implications of my study for educators at all levels. Chapter 7, "Reassessing the Achievement Gap," investigates the achievement gap qualitatively and also critically from the standpoints of discourses of Indian-ness, exposing other kinds of gaps in its construction, including a data gap and a culture gap. Closing the achievement gap is tantamount to closing the culture gap, for most educators agree that the keys to Native achievement are cultural relevance and positive Native identity. But I question what is culturally relevant today, for which Native identity, and within what educational context: Native-run schools and colleges, public schools on or near reservations, white-dominant schools, and white-dominant universities. In closing, I offer examples of cultural relevant pedagogy that honor Native students' rhetorical sovereignty even as they promote Native achievement in each of these educational contexts.

This book makes a contribution not only to the long-standing conversation on cultural differences in education but also to the growing field of American Indian rhetorics. Although I purposefully make no pan-Indian claims, there may nonetheless be points of convergence with the rhetorical traditions of other tribal cultures; the challenges of mapping those convergences remain for scholars of non-Eurocentric rhetorics. This book also builds on the scholarship on the rhetorics of survivance, which typically demonstrates how Native rhetors subversively accommodated white audiences by using white frames of reference and white discourses to revise the audience's notions of Indian-ness. My own project does that, too, but I call attention to the traditional rhetorical resources that Plateau Indians also bring to bear. Ultimately, establishing a rhetorical *ethnie* requires modernizing it. The line of descent is unbroken, but it is unbroken because it is highly adaptive while remaining true to the values that that rhetoric embodies, specific to a group of tribes, a tribe, a distinct discourse community. And describing the *ethnie* always entails acknowledging the diversity *within* Native communities as well as individual innovation—which are both traditionally valued—lest tribal rhetorical traditions become monolithic, fossilizing Indian-ness once again.

Plateau Indian Ways with Words

"Real Indians" Don't Rap
Theorizing Indigenous Rhetorics

et me begin by saying that I am not an Indian, "real" or otherwise. I am a white female English professor whose research focuses on the cultural rhetorics of U.S. minorities. In 2001, I embarked on a five-year collaboration with two schools on a Plateau Indian reservation in Washington state. The project entailed collecting hundreds of papers written by Plateau Indian students, grades 7 to 12.[1] From this collection came the rap poem that I discuss later in this chapter. As a test of an indigenous rhetoric, this rap poem raises several theoretical questions, all of which are foundational to the study at hand. First, questions of what constitutes indigeneity and how it should be authenticated need to be theorized in a manner that does not essentialize identity or culture or tradition. Second, without necessarily negating similarities to other rhetorics, the notion that indigenous rhetorics are somehow distinct also needs to be explored to determine how and why they differ, in rhetorician Malea Powell's words, from "The Rhetorical Tradition," the Eurocentric tradition dating from the Greeks.[2] But we also need to look at how these indigenous rhetorics differ from other tribal-specific rhetorics, lest an "idealized American Indian Rhetorical Tradition" be erected to represent and reify Indian-ness, once again disappearing the diversity among and within Native societies.[3] A close reading of the student's rap poem illustrates how both issues—indigeneity and rhetorical traditions—are inextricably intertwined in practice.

That reading succinctly demonstrates my own methodology throughout this book: critical discourse analysis—a method that makes accessible the discursive formations that have defined Indian-ness since the days of Columbus. American Indian historian and activist Vine Deloria has said: "To be an Indian in modern American society is in a very real sense to be unreal and ahistorical."[4] Arguably, critical discourse analysis is the only way to get past that representation, to open up the many possibilities of the "postindian," in American Indian studies scholar Gerald Vizenor's terms, who is "real" and historical. Besides having the right to move into, and within, modern times, Vizenor's postindians also have the right to their own rhetoric, or what indigenous studies scholar Scott Lyons has famously called "rhetorical sovereignty": "the inherent right and ability of *peoples* to determine their own communicative needs and desires in this pursuit, to decide for themselves the goals, modes, styles, and languages of public discourse."[5]

Although rhetorical sovereignty is sometimes invoked today in conversations about how to respond to or encourage the culturally marked written practices of any U.S. minority, the phrase holds special resonance for American Indians and should be reserved for that context only, in deference not only to the Native-specific history of sovereignty but also to the Native-specific history of education, a subject I return to in chapters 6 and 7. The word "sovereignty" is a particularly loaded word in Indian Country because of its convoluted, contradictory history in federal Indian law grounded in nineteenth-century scientific racism, from which most of the discourses of Indian-ness derive. A brief summary of that history helps explain how federal policy and colonialism continue to override Native ways of authenticating identity. After analyzing the student's rap poem and evaluating his expressed attempt to "reinvent the rez," I again turn to Lyons, this time for his idea of modernizing the *ethnie*. This term describes the principle of maintaining a sovereign nation's ethnicity while carrying that nation forward into the future.

Sovereignty and the Marshal Trilogy

Three Supreme Court decisions in the early 1800s, commonly called the Marshall Trilogy after presiding Chief Justice John Marshall, laid the foundation for dispossessing Indian nations of their lands and their sovereignty. These court decisions ultimately legitimized removal policies, constructed Indian Country, and provided the legal groundwork for colonization for the next hundred years and beyond. At question in the first case, *Johnson v. McIntosh* (1823), was whether or not Indian lands could be sold to private individuals. The Marshall court found that such a transaction was not legal on grounds that the federal government, not the Indian nations, held absolute title to Indian lands. Indians nations were "subject to the sovereignty of the United States," and state and federal statutes could rightly "treat them as [an] inferior race of people, without the privileges of citizens, and under the perpetual protection and pupilage of the government."[6] Imposing Western concepts of individual property rights onto Indian concepts of inalienable, communal land, Marshall rationalized that communal land might be understood, in effect, as a corporate holding. With each individual of the tribe owning equal shares, the chief had the authority to sell those collective shares and redistribute the proceeds back to the individual tribe members (50). The ruling therefore started the process of redefining the key concept upon which Indian political economy rested: land as infungible property.

The second Marshall decision, *Cherokee Nation v. the State of Georgia* (1831), triangulated and tested the relative sovereignties of Indian nations, the states, and the federal government. The Cherokee Nation sued the state of Georgia for violating its treaty that ensured Cherokee sovereignty by enacting, and enforcing, the Indian Removal Act (1830). The court found that the treaty was invalid because the Cherokee were not a foreign, independent nation but a "domestic dependent nation" (51), and therefore they could not sue the state of Georgia. The federal government, however, held ultimate sovereignty over both (the Cherokee Nation and the state of Georgia), by virtue of the European "doctrine of discovery" (51) that had been in force since the time of Columbus. To prevent competing claims and war among imperialist powers, the doctrine held that whoever had arrived first had first claim to a newly discovered land. Legitimizing the breaking of treaties, the *Cherokee Nation v. the State of Georgia* decision also cleared the way for the Trail of Tears (1831–38) and future removal policy—or what Assistant Secretary of Indian Affairs Kevin Gover in the official apology 170 years later rightly called "ethnic cleansing" (53). The decision reemphasized the legal status of Indians as, in Marshall's words, "pupilage," their relationship to the United States "[resembling] that of a ward to his guardian" (51). Even though all Indians were officially granted citizenship in 1924, this trust relationship continues to this day for enrolled Indians and Indians living on reservations.

The third Marshall decision, *Worcester v. Georgia* (1832), qualified the previous two decisions, limiting states' power while reasserting a measure of tribal autonomy. This time Marshall reasoned that tribes were "distinct political communities, having territorial boundaries, within which their authority is exclusive, and having the right to all the lands within those boundaries, which is not only acknowledged, but guaranteed by the United States" (102; Eric Cheyfitz's emphasis is omitted here). Another justice's concurring opinion sought to temper Marshall's language, however, clarifying that although Indians did have distinct political communities that had many "attributes of sovereignty" and possessed the right of self-government and the rights of occupancy, the soil nonetheless belonged to the federal government (102). The *Worcester* decision set the precedence for establishing the plenary power of Congress to govern Indian affairs (later clarified in *Lone Wolf v. Hitchcock* [1903]), even in violation of treaties if Congress deems that in so doing, the best interests of both Indians and the U.S. government are served (as if Congress could serve as neutral judge of that criterion) (54).

Over and beyond the legal impact of the cases themselves, the language of the written opinions bears witness to the discursive processes by which Indians were dispossessed and impoverished. Descriptions of Indians as warlike, uncivilized "savages" and land as uncultivated, uninhabited "wilderness" partake of New World imperialist discourse. Also striking is the definitional downgrading of Indian political status: from "foreign nations" to "nations-within-a nation" to "domestic dependent nations"; from "distinct political communities" to communities with "attributes of sovereignty"; from "nation" to "tribe"; from "sovereign" to "wards" under "pupilage"; from "treaty" to "agreement."[7] This is "rhetorical imperialism" in action.[8] Left unspoken were the historical forces behind this devolution: settlers' increasing demand for land, unbridled capitalism, and massive military might, as detailed in chapter 3.

Before and after the Marshall decisions, Native rhetors resisted, and continue to resist today, racist constructions of Indian identity even as they reassert their rights as sovereign peoples, as much previous scholarship has pointed out. Today, in the context of Native nationalist projects, the word "sovereignty" may be inflected to connote political status as "distinct political communities" (recalling the *Worcester* decision) or economic self-determination or even "intellectual sovereignty."[9] This reassertion of the word signals a return to traditional philosophy and research methodologies untainted by Western paradigms, such as postmodernism and postcolonialism—two terms particularly ill-suited for Native studies, as critics have rightly countered. "Postmodernism" leapfrogs over Indian efforts to reassert control over defining Native identity and the right to modernity, while "postcolonialism" overlooks the fact that the federal government still occupies Indian Country in a trust relationship that is colonial in nature.[10] Postcolonial and postmodern analyses also run the risk of losing sight of sovereignty, a right exclusive to Indian nations as political and legal entities, while celebration of postmodern hybridity may divert attention from the realities of reservation life and the very real consequences of colonialism.[11] What counts as authentically indigenous in modern times? Addressing that issue requires reviewing two key concepts—identity and culture—and the role of discourse in shaping and sustaining both.

Being an Indian

The issue of identity is particularly, and painfully, vexed when it comes to American Indians. The oft-heard remark "Funny, you don't look like an Indian" reveals the pervasiveness and persistence of the Hollywood stereotype, which fails to recognize that phenotype varies widely across tribes and that most Indians have intermarried with other racial groups.[12] No other racial/ethnic category has been so plagued by ethnic fraud, so easily, and to such consequence as that of American Indian. Much is at stake in establishing one's Indian identity, including affirmative action hiring, federal resources to officially designated tribes, and tribal benefits, such as health services, education, reservation land ownership and inheritance, and voting rights.[13] More important, questioning a person's authenticity denies that person the heritage and connection so crucial to identity formation itself.

So how can Indian identity be authenticated? The most common measure is official enrollment in a federally recognized tribe. But most enrollments are based on various base rolls dating from the allotment era, starting with the General Allotment Act of 1887, or the Dawes Act. The Dawes Act attacked Native identity formations on multiple levels. Building on the legal precedence set by the Marshall Trilogy, the act effectively translated communal land into fungible property and Indians into individual property holders. Tribal lands were to be divided up among Indians in lots ranging in size from 40 to 160 acres, depending on the age and household status of the individual, with the so-called surplus to be sold to settlers. Indians had to register as members of a tribe to lay claim to their share. As part of the enrollment process, Indian kinship-based family names were replaced with Euro-American names, further displacing Indian communalism. With the Burke Act (1906), the federal government started factoring in blood quantum to establish degrees of Indian-ness. Thus the notion of the mixed-blood was officially institutionalized.[14] The problem for Indians today is that if a person's ancestors did not enroll during the allotment period (and many had good reason not to), she cannot enroll now; therefore she is not an Indian. But there are other "authenticity markers," the most important being kinship relations.[15] Kinship claims might be established not by official rolls but by stories, oral histories, known networks. Finally, the case has been made for "affiliation claims" that require both authenticity and accountability markers, the latter involving active participation in maintaining tribal traditions and cultural practices.[16]

Although the notion of affiliation claims is a relatively progressive and recent idea, that criterion still rests on blood lineage documented either by tribal enrollment or by oral histories. As such, all of these markers participate in colonial discourse by conceding the terms of the debate set by that discourse: identity as biologically based rather than socially and culturally constructed. Like all discourses, colonial discourse has its own history, dating as far back as Columbus, whose invasions of the continent first raised the question: "What is an Indian?" This set up the binaries not-human/human and savage/civilized.[17] Nineteenth-century scientific racism shifted the question from "What is an Indian?" to "Who is a (real) Indian?"[18] It also shifted the terms of the authenticity debate, defining it in terms of blood quantum and racial categories derived from animal husbandry: half-breed, mixed-blood, full-blood—terms that freely circulated in discourses from legal to popular even in the antebellum period. Blood quantum deeply informed the long-standing savage/civilized binary, its logical extensions coupling biology and culture: the more Indian blood a person had, the less likely he could be civilized, converted, educated, learn English, stand legally competent to handle his own affairs, including manage his resources and own title to his land. In short, he was a child, a ward, a dependent of the U.S. government, the Great Father who controlled all aspects of his life.[19]

Under this totalizing colonial condition, the "bio-logic" of blood quantum fairly quickly displaced the cultural logic of identity as practiced by many traditional Indian communities, which more commonly saw identity in terms of proximity and behavior.[20] If a person lived among Indians and adopted community ways, he was recognized as an Indian—even if he intermarried, even if he was originally a captive.[21] Thus kinship was not restricted to blood relatives; Indian-ness was something someone *did*, not something a person *was*. Observable behaviors were identity markers because they indicated adoption of the group's way of life: culturally marked practices like childrearing, food production, housing, clothing, music, cooking outside, and ceremonial rituals. The specific practices were always historically contingent and dynamic, not stable and inflexible. Most Indian groups were actually quite adaptive and responsive to change, but only insofar as that change sustained, or could be adapted to sustain, the group's larger belief system. Traditional constructions of identity and culture were very pragmatic, supporting continuity even as they accommodated change, thus ensuring group survival in all senses of the word.[22] Culture was a verb, not a noun. It was colonialism that reversed that grammar.[23]

Doing Indian-ness

The bio-logic of identity has become the standard for official enrollment in most tribes today. Almost all require one parent documented from a base roll, and about two-thirds mandate blood quantum as well.[24] Unofficially, however, traditional Native cultural logic of identity is still evident. I have heard teachers on reservations and graduate students recognize Indian-ness in ways that suggest traditional logics of identity, although mixed with bio-logic markers. If need be, they will identify a person as simply an Indian or a white, the latter sometimes further distinguished as Hispanic (rather than Latino), depending on context. If Indian, they will often identify the specific land formation from which that person's ancestry derives or the specific branch of Native language he speaks: for example, a "river Indian" who speaks "river" or a "mountain Indian" who speaks "mountain."[25]

Commonly absent are indications of federal tribal affiliations, where they tend to identify others on the basis of local natural features of that group's homeland or that group's traditional livelihood: "buffalo people," "whale people," and so on. These localized identifications recall traditional ways of locating one's identity in terms of land and the lifeways and language that land formations presupposed them to. Kinship has less to do with blood than behavior, as individuals are often referred to not by their personal names but by affinitive terms like "brother," "sister," or "auntie" regardless of actual blood relation, family more broadly understood as a mutual support system, which includes extended clan networks interconnected through marriage but not exclusively. Within each network, each person's contribution is expected and respected and valued.[26] These networks, in turn, collectively define the communal, to whom the land "belongs" not as property but as inalienable ground—the literal and figurative ground for identity, personal and communal. Or as an old adage expresses the relationship: "The land don't belong to us. We belong to the land."

Among my Indian contacts, identity may be referenced in two other ways, both of which seem to reassert a cultural logic of identity rather than the bio-logic: (a) a white person may be "Indianized," indicating that person's acculturation in, and alignment with, Indian values; and (b) a person may be an Indian by blood but not by behavior. For an example of the latter, on one occasion when a graduate student and I were talking about a mutual Indian acquaintance who spoke like an academic, he remarked: "She looks like an Indian, but when she opens her mouth and all that theory starts coming out, she sure don't sound like an Indian." The graduate student's assessment speaks to the distinction between blood and discourse as different determinants of identity. It also attests to the critical role of what literacy scholar James Gee has called "recognition work."

That recognition work hinges on the question, Who is a "real Indian"? I use this term advisedly, as does Gee, always enclosing it in quotation marks, however redundant and cumbersome that practice may be, in recognition that only Indians can and do use it. Following intercultural communications scholars D. Lawrence Wieder and Steven Pratt, Gee explains that a "real Indian" is identified as authentic when other "real Indians" recognize him as such.[27] The initial qualifying criterion is kinship with other "real Indians" but biological ties are not enough. *Being* an Indian also requires *doing* Indian-ness (24). This *doing* entails enacting a Discourse, with a capital D: who you are when you speak or write or otherwise interact and what you are doing when you do speak or write or otherwise interact. Thus enacting a Discourse involves "a great deal more than 'just language.' It means acting-interacting-thinking-valuing-talking-(sometimes writing-reading) in the 'appropriate way' with the 'appropriate props' at the 'appropriate' times in the 'appropriate' places" (26). Acting-interacting-thinking-valuing-talking-writing-reading in the right way at the right time in the right place constitutes "cultural competency" (24) or what sociolinguist Dell Hymes has termed "communicative competence."[28] This actually reconstitutes across generations and across language, a point I explain more fully in chapter 2. Akin to Noam Chomsky's notion of linguistic competence as knowing intuitively when one's grammar is acceptable, communicative competence refers to knowing what is an appropriate utterance in a given situation. In fact, Hymes argued, a native speaker's intuition of grammatical acceptability is inextricably tied to her sociocultural sense of situational appropriateness. Acquired through interaction and early childhood socialization, communicative competence means that native speakers share the same ends and meanings of language use; in that process they transmit culture.[29]

Native communicative competence is often quite distinctive from that employed by other cultural groups in similar situations, and Euro-Americans typically misunderstand this competence, their evaluations usually flawed by the emic fallacy: comparing "cultures as if they were operating from the same meaning template as one's own."[30] Gee details several examples of such emic misreadings. "Real Indians" have a distinct disinclination to speak to strangers not because they are unfriendly, as Euro-Americans might think, but because to do so would establish them as nonstrangers, and friendship carries with it reciprocal, ongoing obligations to each other's welfare. "Real Indians" love verbal sparring and "razzing," often larding this repartee with sexual innuendo, a practice that some Euro-Americans find shockingly inappropriate in mixed-gender groups, public settings, and formal occasions. "Real Indians" avoid confrontation not because they are stoic or timid but because they do not want to immodestly put their ideas above others.[31] In school contexts "real Indians" know how to behave in class, showing attentiveness by avoiding eye contact and remaining silent because asking questions is considered rude and immodest (224–25). In all these instances, to do otherwise would cast aspersions on a person's Indian-ness, regardless of blood quantum. That some of Gee's examples do not hold true for Plateau Indians, as chapter 2 explores more fully, points to the fact that communicative competence is in fact tribe-specific not pan-Indian.

Further, communicative competence is neither static nor ahistorical. Gee emphasizes the provisional and continuous nature of such competence and thus of the recognition work involved in authenticating it as "Indian": "The circumstances under which these features are employed emerge over the course of a developing history among groups of people. They are employed always in the context of actual situations, and at different times in the life history of groups of people" (25). Who is or is not a "real Indian"—or a "real" feminist, yuppie, regular at a bar, or Catholic, Gee points out—is always "settled provisionally and continually, in practice, as part and parcel of shared histories and ongoing activities" (25). To "pull off" a Discourse, one must perform it in a way consistent enough with past performances to be recognizable; at the same time, it can be just different enough to change and transform the Discourse itself over time (27).

Gee's dynamic notion of identity as recognition work—intersubjectivity enacted through discourse(s)—is not without problems. First, while Gee acknowledges the importance of "shared histories" in intragroup recognition work and references philosopher Michel Foucault, he understates the role of power and the history of power relations in intergroup communications generally and Indian communities specifically. The enormous power differential between the U.S. government and Indian nations in the nineteenth century ensured that treaties were not really negotiated. Words like "discovery," "contact," "encounter," and "settlement" mask the brutal violence and death toll effected by invasion and genocidal policies. Many Plateau Indians more aptly refer to this history as "the Conquest." As always, the victor names the age, thereby controlling the historical narrative thereafter in supposedly neutral language: the Treaty Period, the Allotment Period, the Self-Determination Period, and so on. Gee also overstates the fluidity and ease with which one can move into and out of identity. Certain discourses are off-limits to American Indians in particular.

As Lyons has pointed out, American Indians can speak as "protestant ethnics" (for "protest" serves the purpose of demonstrating that the status quo allows for dissent, as Gramsci might argue), but they are disallowed "prophetic discourse," unless they accommodate their mainstream audience by using rhetorics of survivance.[32] One such case in point is that of American Indian author and activist Ward Churchill, who unaccommodatingly argued that the terror attacks of 9/11 were the result of U.S. imperialist policies. Not only was he stripped of tenure, he was stripped of his Indian identity, which he could not document through biological descent (29). More generally, when an Indian gets up to speak, he is "expected to say something about the following: *culture, tradition, heritage, land, the circle of life, colonization, resistance, suffering at the hands of the white man, whether or not gaming is good thing*, and/or *whether or not mascots are a bad thing*" (29; emphasis in the original).

Apparently, even the *educated* Indian presents an incongruity that needs be reconciled, the seeming oxymoron recalling the savage/civilized binary. For example, at least some literary critics have argued the Indian-ness of *Cogewea, the Half-Blood*, the first major Indian novel published in 1927, written by Mourning Dove, the pen name for Christine Quintasket, a Plateau Indian (Salishan). They have often claimed that her white collaborator and editor Lucullus McWhorter did most of the writing. But they fail to recognize that Quintasket herself experienced both a Native upbringing and a formal boarding-school education and spoke least three languages; she was well versed in the oral tradition and well-read in the conventions of the novel.[33] Not only does Indian-ness get essentialized and ossified in and by discursive restraints, it also gets romanticized and idealized: Indians are not just *savages*, but *noble savages* who cannot be educated. Exotic, nostalgic, mythological—these adjectives come to characterize and constrain Indian-ness. All draw on colonial discourses that continue to deny Indians modernity today.

Modernizing the *Ethnie*

Keeping in mind these very important caveats on Gee's understanding of discourse as it applies to "real Indians," I would still argue that certain discursive practices are recognizable as specific to certain Indian groups and that those practices provide a mechanism for cultural transmission as well as cultural revitalization. Critical analysis of those practices entails first singling out the *nationality* or *ethnie* for recognition. Recognizing the *ethnie*, including indigenous rhetorics, is the kind of "recognition work" (to recall Gee's term) that character-izes the Native nationalist project today. Breaking from both the traditionalist movement (with its emphasis on "pure" culture) and global indigenism (with its emphasis on political revitalization), Native nationalists marry political economy with cultural values, with projects such as ecological sustainability and collective land rights.[34] They stress both *nationality* and *nationhood*, the former a prerequisite of the latter.

Nationality is what nationalism scholar Anthony D. Smith calls *ethnie* (from the Greek term *ethnos*, from which the word *ethnic* derives), which Smith defines as "a named human population with a myth of common ancestry, shared historical memories, elements of shared culture, and association with a specific homeland."[35] *Ethnie* is foundational to nationhood because it retrieves cultural heritage, not to police identity or even just to revitalize culture but to legitimize and inform all aspects of a modern community to one end: to better the lives of its people. *Ethnie* provides cohesion even as it supports modernization, for it restores those vital historical and territorial connections that make a people, a people. As Lyons explains:

> Modernizing the *ethnie* involves a great deal more than simply agitating for
> a state or seeking rights on the level of nationality, and it transcends acts of
> cultural resistance or focusing purely on the level of nationhood. An effective
> nationalism must function on political and cultural levels simultaneously. It will
> reveal to both the interior population and the exterior world *an unbroken line of
> descent connecting an ethnie to a modern community distinguishable from others
> and hence deserving recognition, respect, and rights.* An *ethnie* that has been
> modernized won't resemble its cultural ancestors down to the smallest details.
> . . . It is the memory of the *ethnie* that gets modernized by a nationalist, and it
> can happen in different locales and in different ways. . . . For an *ethnie* to become
> a nation, its old cultural memories have to be publicized: depicted, displayed,
> and shared, so nationalists must always wear their cultures on their sleeves.
> [Emphasis mine][36]

In other words, modernizing the *ethnie* entails recovering the cultural practices and distinguishing them as belonging to a people who are tied to a specific homeland. Recovery of the modern *ethnie* includes not just histories but also indigenous rhetorics marked by characteristic moves, purposes, values, epistemology—rhetorics distinctive not only between Indian groups but also differentiated within a group. That work, of course, has already begun, largely focused on rhetorics of survivance. It is now time to recognize and recover "tribally specific rhetorical traditions . . . in their own right," providing the specific *territorial grounds* for national recognition and autonomy.[37] What does a modern *ethnie* specific to one Indian group look like? By way of example, I now turn to a piece of writing by a Plateau Indian student.

Reinventin' the Rez

Obviously rap is not an indigenous art form like the ceremonial chant or origin narrative or trickster tale, but neither is it a Euro-American form, such as the autobiography, novel, or personal letter. Thus rap is not easily categorized as a colonized form, drawing as it does from the expressive history of another oppressed minority, African Americans, thereby introducing a complicated third term to the usual binary of red/white. Traditionally, "real Indians" don't rap, as authenticity is popularly reckoned in terms of a mythologized precontact past. But in real life, in practice, many young Plateau Indians (mainly males) can and do rap, mirroring the trend worldwide, where most hip-hop practitioners are ages twelve to seventeen.[38] In the rap below the Plateau Indian rapper re-presents himself in an art form that resists colonial domination but otherwise remixes traditional tribal values and reinvents life on the rez in a modern world:

— [Tribe's name] Nation comin up out this Rez
— just some Native Boys bein put to the test
— They say keep it real, Rhymes tight like a seal
— But on this deal, its like a zip-lock
— End of the Trail is what fuck we rock
— End of the Trail just can't be stopped
— Even if our raps an caps might be off the wall
  we never stall
— Always ready when that bugle calls
— Like some soldiers with big ballz.
— M[rest of word illegible] [illegible word] big or tall, I aint scared at all
— Wanna fight me Let me get my gloves
— Meet me in the ring to see whats up
— do it up, then shake hands or whatever the fuck
— grew up like a rat or similar to something
  like that, was never strapped
— But boxed to put myself on the rez map
— for the rakiki-mish bustin out already gaining
  much clout

— just the beginnin an ain't even begun to shout
— sayin what you bout?
— Lyrical artillery, don't pull it, just do it,
 or move it, just cool it, write your own shit
 an come back with some bullets
— Takin all comers, I couldn't be dumber
— lyrical warfare so hot it could be summer
— Believe me I can't stop representin this
 reinventin Indian world rez, thats right
 what I said
— ain't no Clinton or Bush, just a hungry Native Soldier
— but I aint smoking coosh
— Clean head thinkin straight always on debate.[39]

What makes this poem authentically Plateau Indian? It is an indigenous production, I would argue, because it was penned and probably performed by a Plateau
Indian, so recognized by his community by any number of standards, solely or in
tandem: his tribal enrollment, his extensive kinship (family and friends) network
on the reservation, and—perhaps most important of all—the traditional values
he reasserts in ways consistent with the discursive practices of his community
and its forebears. As such, the rap can be productively understood within a rich
dialectic of discursive processes, necessarily historically and culturally bounded.
What this male teenaged rapper expresses and in what ways and within this
specific context (as a student at a tribal school whose mission is to indigenize
education)—all of these issues complicate easy binaries between white/Indian,
civilized/savage, written/oral, individualistic/collectivist—binaries largely constructed by colonialist discourse. The poem also bears witness to the intergenerational transmission of an indigenous rhetoric and the values it embodies of the
Plateau peoples, implicitly helping to establish "the unbroken line of descent," to
recall Lyons's words, thereby modernizing the rhetorical *ethnie.*

The writer's portfolio almost completely consists of rap poetry; he obviously
feels a deep affinity for the genre. Although rap originated in African American
expressive culture, globalization of the form has led to distinctive national ver-
sions (in, for example, Germany, Sri Lanka, and Somalia, among other countries);
thematic types (such as lovers' rap, gangsta rap), and different U.S. regional types
(East Coast, West Coast, Midwest, and Southern style, with additional subsets
within these regions, such as Dirty South).[40] Rap has also become a popular art
form particularized on reservations of the Pacific Northwest. In Indian Country,

as in other countries, rap's appeal cannot be chalked up to a simple identification with African Americans as another oppressed group. African Americans and American Indians have had very different histories with white America. Whereas the civil rights movement sought equality within American society, Indians seek recognition of their sovereignty, literally grounded in their ancestral land.[41] As the history of the American Indian Movement (AIM) might suggest, even political solidarity across Indian groups is a difficult proposition, in part because super-structural political organization runs counter to historical clan autonomy, but also in part because colonialism has thrown Indian groups into competition for limited resources. In addition, rural Indians of the Pacific Northwest have little to no contact with African Americans, urban or otherwise. This lack of contact not only forecloses group affinity; it also fuels racist stereotypes of black people on the reservation. Rap has become a global youth phenomenon not necessarily because of identification with African Americans, but because the genre allows for local themes and identity work, even for white, middle-class conservative German rappers.[42] Still, no matter the locale, rappers generally are preoccupied with issues of authenticity and survival. Their mantra is "keep it real"; their project: to "(dis)invent" identity and stereotypes.[43]

Appropriately enough, rap has proven adaptable to Plateau Indian culture and rhetoric in several ways, at least some of which are evident in this student's poem. The rap is written down but intended for performance, validating both the genre's oral and literate values. The literate values, however, are clearly not those associated with school. The rapper's group of Native Boys are ready to rap "like some soldiers with big ballz"—his spelling of "ballz," like his word inventions ("rakiki-mish") and the dropped g's on the suffix –ing's—reproduce hip-hop influence on the grapholect.[44] Such convergences not only break down the oral/literate divide; they also implicitly question Native relationship to literacy as encoded in noble-savage discourse, where nobility confers upon the illiterate savage a kind of natural eloquence.[45] In both oral and literate forms, rap urges performance and presence. Predicated on highly contextualized audience interaction, performance intends to entertain and to instruct, but to instruct indirectly and interactively, implicitly inviting the audience to question the speaker as well as their own sense of the world, further pondering these potential meanings after they leave and live their everyday lives.[46] Native texts, whether written or oral, are best understood as social acts, not just aesthetic objects.[47] The last three lines of the student's rap may be variously interpreted, concluding with a kind of inconclusiveness requiring audience interpretation:

— ain't no Clinton or Bush, just a hungry Native Soldier
— but I aint smoking coosh
— Clean head thinkin straight always on debate

The student rapper may be modestly acknowledging that he is "just a hungry Native Soldier" with no political power—not on a par with Clinton or Bush anyway—but implying that he has the power of words; nor is his claim drug-induced bravado ("I ain't smoking coosh"). The rapper may also be saying that he is a drug-free Indian, attributing his verbal power to sobriety, an implicit acknowledgment of the wide-ranging social problem of alcoholism and drug abuse on the reservation and perhaps a subtle allusion to his own ongoing battle with drugs, as his home audience would know.

While certain kinds of rap infamously flaunt misogynist attitudes, boast sexual bravado, and glorify drug use and violence, historically its purpose was to divert street violence into nonviolent verbal encounters, drawing from "playing the dozens"—a speech event with West African roots. The student rapper seems to draw on rap's nonviolent tradition as "battle rhymes" when he advocates "lyrical warfare" to show "what you bout," the dropped "are" common to both African American language and Plateau Indian English.[48] More important, he recalls and revises colonial discourses on Indian-ness. He references the Hollywood westerns with phrases like "end of the Trail," itself an example of Tonto-speak (oversimplified Indian English demoting that variety of English to baby talk), to suggest both Indians' inefficiency with English and, by implication, their lack of education and intelligence. Interestingly, the rapper and his friends stand ready "when the bugle calls / Like soldiers with big ballz /. . . . big or tall," clearly identifying with the American army in western movies, not the Indians. This misaligned identification—a common one among Indians growing up watching westerns—speaks to just one of colonialism's legacies.[49] True to the nonviolent roots of rap but also to Plateau Indian traditional belief in pacifism, the rapper advocates sparring with words, using "lyrical artillery" instead of live bullets. He is also ready if called out to physically fight, but with gloves on and in a ring, referencing a favorite sport on the reservation: boxing.

More generally, the poem is a modern remake on the way of the warrior, effectively countering colonial discourse rife with comment about warring savages. As far back as 1777, in his *History of the Discovery and Settlement of North America,* which quickly became the standard reference on Indians through the mid-nineteenth century, William Robertson maintained that Indians waged war not for glory (deemed too abstract an idea for Indians to grasp) but strictly for tribal and clan vengeance.⁵⁰ Chief Marshall, in the *Johnson v. McIntosh* (1823) case discussed earlier, draws the same portrait of the noble albeit ungovernable savage, living in wild(er)ness: "But the tribes of Indians inhabiting this country were fierce savages, whose occupation was war, and whose subsistence was drawn chiefly from the forest. To leave them in possession of their country, was to leave the country at wilderness: to govern them as distinct people, was impossible, because they were as brave and as high spirited as they were fierce, and were ready to repel by arms every attempt on their independence."⁵¹

For the student rapper the warrior's way involves more than physical bravery (as credited by Chief Marshall) or even verbal skill (as the rap tradition itself celebrates). It is also defined by mental toughness and persistence. The student boxes and raps to establish his reputation as a man on the reservation even as he alludes to his hard-won sobriety ("I aint smoking coosh"), offering a glimpse of reservation life that sounds more urban than rural and more civilized than savage:

— Wanna fight me Let me get my gloves
— Meet me in the ring to see whats up
— do it up, then shake hands or whatever the fuck
— grew up like a rate or similar to something
   like that, was never strapped
— But boxed to put myself on the rez map

Thus the student rapper revises clichéd understandings of Indians as close to nature, largely by redefining nature, not as wilderness or wildness but as a specific ancestral land, even as he reasserts his special, spatial relationship to that land, putting himself on "the rez map." Redeploying nontraditional activities (boxing and rapping) to carry forward traditional values, the rapper enacts Indian-ness— *doing* rather than just *being* an Indian—demonstrating a dynamic understanding of identity as intersubjective recognition work, an ongoing process that authenticates his multiple identities as a young man among other young men, other adults, other Indians, other Americans in the armed forces, and even other rappers worldwide:

— Believe me I can't stop representin this
   reinventin Indian world rez, thats right
   what I said

This recognition work entails constantly "representin this reinventin Indian world rez," in part to counter colonial discourses but also in part to modernize what it means to be an Indian in the twenty-first century. Indians not only have a right to modernity; by reestablishing that right, they also expose the lie of the Vanishing Indian.

Recognition Work

Nor have indigenous ways with words vanished. Discussed briefly here but at length in chapter 2, and substantiated in later chapters, the discursive moves that typify Plateau Indian arts of persuasion and argument might be collectively characterized as multiple strategies of personalization, all privileging experiential knowledge as well as presence and performance. Such strategies carry tribal-specific values, the wellspring of which is the nexus of land and kinship that nonetheless honors individual autonomy, the contradiction between collective and individual interests more apparent than real.

Indicative rather than all-inclusive, the student's rap embodies many, although not all, features of the indigenous rhetoric of the Plateau peoples. Neither a narrative nor an argument in the Euro-American sense of those terms, the rap nonetheless makes the student's point largely by way of self-location, a phrase that Lyons uses off-handedly but that I have taken up officially: self-location in relation to his own life, to the land and life on the rez, and to his audiences.[52] Complicating polarized understandings of Indian-ness in terms of collectivism/individualism and modesty/self-display binaries, the student rapper alludes to his own struggles with drug abuse but also speaks *of* his friends and ultimately *to* his friends—another commonality with global rap, which typically speaks of and to the "crew," a kind of extended chosen family sustaining loyalty among its members.[53] Breaking from rap tradition, though, the student does not speak *for* his friends. The first stanza celebrates Native boys ("we") who have this lyrical power to rap and cap, but the rest of the poem is actually a boast of the speaker ("I") ready to fight "all comers" in the boxing ring. However, he balances this brag with self-deprecation: "I couldn't be dumber." The hip-hop genre conveniently allows him to use his rap to support his rep, but he instructs others to also "write your own shit," respecting personal autonomy, both his and that of others— a value that deeply informs the Plateau Indian political principle of direct democracy (discussed at length in chapter 5).

But one rap poem, obviously, does not an *ethnie* make. Discursive moves stand out as typical only when substantiated over time, over several pieces, across different types of writing. My approach is not ethnographic nor is it "ethnographic-formalist."[54] Both of these approaches have been criticized as looking for authenticity, defined as those moments when the effects of Eurocentrism are least in evidence.[55] Nor do modern Indians have to live in two separate worlds and find ways to reconcile them.[56] Not only does the two-worlds metaphor reify Native and Euro-American cultures as separate; it also sets up a different emphasis, shifting the critical discussion away from the political struggles of American Indian communities and onto an ahistorical cultural identity and individual psychology, as Natives find ways of assimilating into a multicultural United States, just as all minorities must do.[57]

The student's rap holds implications for Indian education. Tradition necessarily entails re-presenting it in terms of modern Indian life. American Indian studies scholar and author Greg Sarris cites one example of older students developing a *Pomo Supernaturals Coloring Book* for younger students, where they pictured, among other things, Coyote as a low-rider.[58] Re-presenting tradition may mean taking the senior class motto from Dr. Seuss's *Oh, the Places We'll Go!,* as a Plateau Indian tribal school did one year. At other times, re-presenting tradition means upending colonialist notions of Indian-ness, as the following prank illustrates. As told to me, two Native educators attended a regional series of workshops on multiculturalism, at the end of which all participants were to share something of their culture with the group. The two educators decided to demonstrate the round dance. After seating their audience in a circle and solemnly explaining the significance of the round dance in their culture, one started up a recording of the "The Twist" covered by Chubby Checker as the other started doing the twist. The audience was taken aback when they realized the joke. The two educators broke out laughing to the dismay of the workshop organizers, who brusquely told them to sit down. One then explained to the organizers (and I paraphrase here): "I grew up in the fifties and sixties, and twisting was a part of my culture. It is my round dance."

The prank was more than a cultural expression; it was also a political one, a point not completely lost on the displeased workshop organizers. The two educators played along with the multicultural premises of the workshop, a paradigm that fixates on cultural difference as a marker of authenticity, subsuming Indian political struggles for autonomy as just a matter of civil rights, even as it legitimizes the national mythology of tolerance and equality.[59] The multicultural paradigm also fails to recognize Indians' right to history—not just past history of white oppression and violence but also present and future history, not just as individuals but as nations. And as Indians have done since the Conquest, as historian Philip Deloria has pointed out in his book *Playing Indian,* seeming to participate "in white people's Indian play, assisting, confirming, co-opting, challenging, and legitimating the performative tradition of aboriginal American identity," the Native educators reasserted their right to control their own representations as well as their right to modernity.[60] Indians performing the twist or a rap poem counters the bio-logic discourse of the Vanishing Indian, locked in the past, losing purity of blood and tradition, ultimately facing "statistical extermination."[61] Such Plateau Indian adaptations are akin to the process of "Hopification" among the Hopi: "Whether dealing with peach trees, burros, sheep, or cattle; governors or elected councils; tribal constitutions or legal codes; writing systems or schools, the Hopi have endeavored to fit new things into an overarching system of Hopi meaning."[62] Or as American studies scholar David Murray has explained: "True intellectual sovereignty is practiced in the ability to choose eclectically from other areas while still retaining Native traditions and communities."[63]

Modern productions open up discursive spaces for Indian identities *plural*, giving expression to diversity within Indian communities and allowing for individual agency and innovation, while at the same time staying true to a people's *ethnie*, including certain rhetorical practices selected to carry forward the values that have sustained a people through time. Recognizing that unbroken line of descent is crucial to establishing rhetorical sovereignty. It is also crucial for opening up our scholarship as well as our classrooms, in Lyons's words, making them "more relevant to and reflective of actual populations of this land"—in a phrase, real Indians.[64]

2

Defining Principles of Plateau Indian Rhetoric

In chapter 1, I theorized how and why a rhetoric might be identified as indigenous, situating that discussion within the context of American Indian studies. In this chapter I describe the indigenous rhetoric specific to the Plateau Indians, situating that description within the context of rhetoric and composition. In so doing, I resuscitate the sociolinguistic roots of the field of cultural rhetorics, a move that allows me to reconsider many of the major conversations in rhetoric and composition of the past several decades, such as the debates on orality and literacy and on cognitive orientations. Although those issues have long since been resolved in rhetoric and composition, they continue to plague scholarship in indigenous studies as well as in Native education.

I use applied linguist Robert Kaplan's "five terrible questions" to organize this chapter's discussion.[1] That framework seems appropriate, given that Kaplan was the first to formalize the idea that rhetorics are culturally marked. He coined the term "contrastive rhetoric" in 1966 to distinguish it from the comparative linguistic studies at the time.[2] Kaplan's work specifically and cultural rhetorics generally are oft criticized for essentializing culture, insofar as that work portrays culture as a static object rather than a dynamic process that is both resilient and responsive to change. Isolating key features of any rhetoric always entails, to a certain degree, making it hold still for a moment in order to pinpoint and describe those features. A return to the sociolinguistic roots of cultural rhetorics aims to offset that problem, repositioning it more squarely within the history of new literacy studies (NLS). As literacy scholar James Gee has explained, NLS was one movement among many that took a "social turn" with "the view that reading and writing only make sense when studied in the context of social and cultural (and . . . historical, political, and economic) practices of which they are but a part."[3] Among the many other movements that partake of this same social turn are analyses of conversation and interactional protocols and the ethnography of speaking, fields from which I also draw. An early example of NLS is Shirley Brice Heath's *Ways with Words,* whose critical orientation inspired and deeply informs my own work. The title of this book pays respect to that debt.

According to Kaplan, speakers and writers not working from monocultural assumptions about communications are faced with five terrible questions:

1. What may be discussed?
2. Who has the authority to speak/write? Or: Who has the authority to write to whom under what circumstances?
3. What form(s) may the writing take?
4. What is evidence?
5. What arrangement of evidence is likely to appeal (be convincing) to readers?[4]

Kaplan's questions serve well as touchstones, if not mainstays, for understanding the cultural boundedness of all communicative tasks—a term that emphasizes "interactive intentions" and requires "interpretive judgments" in communications between and among people.[5] In using these questions, albeit in different order, as my organizing framework, I am both respecting and updating the field of cultural rhetorics, implicitly recognizing how far it has evolved since its inception in the 1960s, while keeping true to Kaplan's focus on educational consequences. Other more terrible consequences can result, however, regardless of how blended the discourse or powerfully poetic the language, even as adjudged by Euro-American standards. At the Treaty Council at Walla Walla in 1855, for example, Plateau Indian rhetors made meaning in culturally consistent ways, but in a world where Euro-American meanings already prevailed. Blending their rhetoric to accommodate the American military would not have changed the outcome: the illegal dispossession of Indians' ancestral land, forced removal to reservations, subsequent impoverishment, and the intergenerational trauma of conquest.

Retrieving Plateau Indians' habitual ways with words is not a formalist exercise; it is a project of recovery with an activist agenda. Before the rhetorical sovereignty of Plateau Indian students can be honored, their characteristic discursive practices must first be recognized as distinctive and historical. And what counts as appropriate discursive behavior by whom is always dynamically arbitrated by a historically situated discourse community that has both interpretive and generative power.[6] This authentication process preserves even as it modernizes—or modernizes in order to preserve—the rhetorical *ethnie*. What discursive practices define the parameters of the indigenous rhetoric of the Plateau Indians? In brief, Plateau Indian rhetors employ multiple strategies to personalize their arguments, to wit: experiential knowledge as supporting evidence; the use of high affect techniques in retelling that experience; suspended thesis and suspenseful arrangement; and situated elaboration with the use of highly selective detail. Taken together, these strategies embody the centralizing value of Plateau Indian culture: respect for personal autonomy, a value that is multiply refracted in all domains of Plateau Indians' lifeways. An examination of two domains that have direct bearing on Native education—political organization and childrearing practices—reveals this value in action.

Experiential Knowledge as Supporting Evidence

What is evidence? Kaplan's fourth question suggests that what counts as convincing evidence is culturally bounded. Perhaps the most striking feature of Plateau Indian persuasive texts is the use of personal experience, often in the form of narrative, to support an argument—a strategy of personalization that might be called "arguing-with-story." As opposed to "telling a story" or, alternatively, "storytelling"—terms closely associated with fictive narrative or the oral tradition—arguing-with-story in the context of nonfictive persuasion usually entails relating an autobiographical experience but not necessarily always and not necessarily with factual accuracy. Sometimes the rhetor may cite the experience of someone he knows, either firsthand or secondhand, always mindful of attribution. Or she may tell a hypothetical story, if she deems that more effective in persuading an audience to her viewpoint. In either case, the rhetor does not want to just retell a story; he wants to re-create a good one.

What constitutes a good story, however, is defined by culturally bounded conventions and interpretative processes of a given discourse community. In her study involving forty Greek and American subjects retelling a film narrative in speech and in writing, sociolinguist Deborah Tannen found that Greek oral retellers showed a strong tendency to interpret the narrative largely through detail selected to support an unstated point. While American retellers in writing tended to report information in their retellings, the Greek retellers "reported as fact what was conjecture."[7] The American writers showed more interest in getting the story correct, but the Greek retellers seemed to be more interested in telling a good story. These differences suggest that the oral retellers had a greater "recognition of speaker/hearer interaction and involvement" and a heightened awareness of presentation-of-self.[8] The Greek oral retellers were more interpretive, less informative, and more self-aware and audience-aware than the American writers retelling the same film narrative.[9] Similar to Tannen's conclusions, sociolinguist Frederick Erickson's analysis of an extended conversation among African American male adolescents found that participants "stitched together a series of narrative anecdotes" selected to support a point that had been left unstated.[10] They used specific concrete detail not just to vivify their stories but to establish the connections between the speaker's knowledge and the audience's own. Themes were left unstated not because participants could not think in abstractions but because abstractions for these participants would be less persuasive than their highly selective use of concrete details.[11]

Telling a good story is not just a way of supporting arguments; it is the way "of gaining and conveying knowledge, of doing philosophy."[12] Therein lies the cultural conflict: with its foundations in classical rhetoric, academic discourse generally discounts, if not disallows, experience-based support on grounds that such support is subjective and therefore unreliable. Even Plato, who valued speech over writing in *The Phaedrus,* would ban poets from his Republic for appealing to emotion and soul, which he saw as exerting a corrosive influence on objective reasoning. As one of my colleagues once complained during a doctorate oral exam infused with the student's personal experience, how does one argue with someone's experiences? In my colleague's view the subjectivity and the implicit emotionality of this kind of support forecloses argument rather than, in his words, "problematizes" it, as would be appropriate in academic discourse. Ironically, a Plateau Indian rhetor might agree, at least up to a point: personal references enact the *limits* of the speaker's perspective, precisely for the purpose of allowing the audience its own.

Although spontaneous interjections are allowable while the speaker still commands the floor, more commonly the audience will mull over the significance of the speaker's words in their own lives for several moments, days, even months later. The rhetorical purpose of a good story is not just to dramatically re-create identification between speaker and audience, but rather to suggest the limits of such identification.[13] As intercultural communications scholars Ronald Scollon and Suzanne Wong Scollon have established, for Athabaskans (a northern Plateau Indian culture in Canada and Alaska), "sense-making is a joint rather than a single-handed adventure."[14] The speaker re-creates her story for a specific audience but leaves its point unstated or understated; therein lies the audience's opening to make and take away their own meanings. What is under consideration is not so much the speaker's position but positionality itself.

Consistent with this process of shared meaning-making is a common discursive move: what indigenous studies scholar Scott Lyons has called self-location, where the speaker identifies his kin, his kin's locale, past and present, thereby establishing possible points of connections to his audience.[15] Besides establishing connections, this move might be seen as establishing *ethos,* credibility, authority to speak, even authenticity, but within the context of Plateau Indian culture, it is more likely an act of modesty or, paradoxically, self-promotion. Frequently the speaker says, in effect: "I'm just a poor Indian; what do I know?" These gestures of deference recur not just in intergroup contexts, where they are commonly read by scholars as politically contingent or simply puzzling.[16] As American studies scholar David Murray has pointed out, the typical "self-abasements" in Indian texts are often coupled with grievance, rendering the move deeply subversive.[17] Statements of humility, ironically, call attention to the speaker, demonstrating a heightened awareness of presentation-of-self, just as the Greek story-retellers did in Tannen's study cited earlier. Self-location not only locates the speaker; it also orients the audience. In establishing her footing, the speaker is constructing a relationship with her audience.[18]

As Sarris has pointed out, the absence of a first-person narrator—or, conversely, the presence of an anonymous, authoritative voice—adds to school-children's difficulties in reading and their difficulties in writing. The distance between speaker and audience is both disorienting and silencing, implicitly telling them to "shelve personal experience," and with it their own customary ways of knowing and learning.[19] As rhetorician Patricia Bizzell has pointed out, many composition theorists have argued that distancing in academic writing allows learners to think about their own thinking.[20] I posit that a lack of distance can also create conditions for doing the same, depending on the discourse community. From the viewpoint of Plateau Indian rhetoric, the objectivity achieved from distancing is viewed with suspicion, for it separates the speaker from his audience, destroying the egalitarian dynamic of meaning-making so central to Plateau Indian ways of doing philosophy (to recall American studies scholar Eric Cheyfitz's words). Distancing in academic writing is linked to "enthusiasm constraint," a lack of affect suggesting that the information conveyed is objective and therefore less assailable.[21] But in Plateau Indian culture lack of affect is understood as a lack of conviction, a point I return to later in this chapter.

Self-location foreshortens the distance between the audience and the message, helping them understand how the message applies to them personally. For example, as one graduate student related to me, his preacher might say, "Some of us right now are checking out the hotties in the room instead of paying attention," without naming names but looking straight at the man in the front row. And someone in the audience might interject, "He ain't the only one," followed by other one-liners and rounds of laughter. This sort of improvisational personalization ensures that sermons, speeches, and the like are never accurately repeated, or rather, they are always repeated with a difference, keeping them relevant to those present. These listener-centered productions are not designed to embarrass or isolate the listener but to include her and to personalize the argument.[22] The same process of meaning-making also characterizes the Plateau Indian oral tradition when passing along stories. As one mother told me, in the bedtime story ritual in her home, she retells Coyote stories at bedtime, recontextualizing the stories that her own grandmother had told her but in terms of her own children's lives. Thus accuracy of detail is sacrificed for more time-bound details for the sake of imparting a larger, timeless truth.

Notice, too, that preacher's remark might be characterized as direct and indirect at the same time. Such examples demonstrate the emic fallacy of the directness/indirectness scale so often invoked in the fields of intercultural communication and contrastive rhetorics generally, where indirectness gets read as deference or politeness or even political expedience. Typically delaying the thesis, if stating it at all, Plateau Indian rhetors are showing tolerance for other perspectives and honoring their audience's right to draw their own conclusions, not wanting to impose their views on others. This is persuasion but in a noncoercive way.[23] At the same time, indirectness cannot be read as equivalent to deference, for Plateau Indian rhetors bravely and bluntly state their point, however delayed, regardless of political expedience. In fact, speaking directly—or "speaking straight," as the Plateau Indians repeatedly enjoined during the Treaty Council of 1855 (discussed at length in chapter 3)—is highly prized. Speaking straight means speaking truthfully, at least as one has experienced the truth, speaking directly from one's own knowledge of the world, and not others' knowledge, unless one knows those others personally.

When citing others' experiences, speakers carefully attribute those sources, often pointing out how they or the audience knows them, a process that authenticates the source even before citing the evidence. Citing unknown others or even distant relatives is uncommon, if not nonexistent; to do so is simply unconvincing, given the privileged status of experiential knowledge in this interpretative community. These principles governing supporting evidence and attribution hold profound implications within the context of teaching academic writing, premised on the equation of distance = objectivity. Plateau Indian students often personalize their essays, their seminar papers, their dissertations, drawing supporting evidence from their own life experiences or their family stories. And just as regularly, they are told to state their points explicitly and cite outside expert sources to support them—in other words, to distance themselves from the communicative task at hand.

High Affect

The characteristic high affect of many Plateau Indian texts partially addresses Kaplan's third question: What form(s) may the writing take? Arguing-with-story not only personalizes a point; it dramatizes it. The use of high-affect techniques, such as first-person point-of-view and performance cues, counters the lie of the stoic, laconic Indian. As American Indian studies scholar and author Greg Sarris has pointed out, in face-to-face settings, Pomo speakers will typically modulate their voices to impersonate various characters.[24] The same holds true for Plateau Indian speakers. In like manner, high-affect cues in written texts (such as fictionalized dialogue, sarcasm, capitalized and underlined words, and so on) re-create a story as an oral experience.

I use the term "oral experience" to distinguish it from "oral tradition" or "oral history," both of which have received much popular and scholarly attention. That attention has not served modern Indians very well. The oral tradition has become ossified as imagined scenes of Indians gathered around a campfire sharing stories. It has also been universalized in terms of the Homeric tradition, even though oral narratives vary greatly across cultures, as Scollon and Scollon have shown with the Northern Athabaskan oral tradition.[25] In like manner, oral history is often glamorized for its accuracy, even though genealogies, for example, have been shown to be heavily revised to reflect contemporary political realities.[26] By sentimentalizing Indians, such a view of oral history also fails to take into account that "doing history" itself is culturally bounded, doing different kinds of intellectual work in different societies and in different forms. In contrast to "oral history" and "oral tradition," I use the phrase "oral experience" to expand attention to the many speech events that Plateau Indian communicative productions can take, not just narrative forms such as story but also conversations, jokes, anecdotes, even business meetings and dissertation defenses, as I have seen in my own personal experience.[27]

My aim in using the term "oral experience" is not to reconstitute the orality/literacy divide but to collapse it. Too narrowly focused on the modality of communication, the divide fails to recognize the rich interplay of multiple media in people's lives. So, for example, when Plateau Indian students write "the end" at the end of a letter or story, they may be translating that convention from any number of previous communicative and media experiences, such as General Council meetings (with its interaction protocols, as I discuss in chapter 5); children's picture books; even classic cartoon and movie conventions, as Tannen has noted in written retellings of film narratives.[28] Or when they write in smaller letters to finish up the assignment by the end of the page, the page itself may be constraining length and therefore elaboration. Or they may be trying to conserve paper, a gesture indicative of poverty, ecological awareness, or both. And so on. Such experiences, understood within the context of the community's resources and attitudes, shape discursive practices.[29] Simply put, communities cannot be classified as either oral or literate, even on a continuum. Rather, in most communities, including those on Plateau Indian reservations, speech and written material are married in almost all communicative events; uncoupling the two modalities is the rarity.[30] My emphasis on oral experience is not on the *oral,* but on the *experience.* The givens of that experience—performance, presence, interaction—drive the premises of Plateau Indian rhetoric.

But the high affect of Plateau Indian texts does not necessarily or exclusively aim to perform presence for dramatic purposes alone. If enthusiasm constraint and lack of affect may be read as lack of conviction, as mentioned earlier, high affect conveys the opposite: sincerity, conviction, and lack of affectation. Straight-speaking, another form of high affect, largely occurs at the semantic and syntactic levels; rhetorically it may be described as straightforwardness, which may sometimes come across as blunt, even confrontational, by Euro-American standards. This bluntness might be explored by first talking about what it is not: poetic language. The absence of figurative language in Plateau Indian texts would not be so conspicuous, if not for the expectation that Indian speech, especially when spoken in Native languages and translated in English, is markedly poetic, a notion inherited from nineteenth-century romantic discourse on the noble savage.[31] Ironically it was the "poverty of Indian language," coupled with Indians' innately inferior cognitive abilities, that created the preconditions for all this poetry.[32] Indians lacked the ability to think abstractly and lacked the language to express abstractions anyway—basically, an early version of the Sapir-Whorf hypothesis upon which the theory of linguistic relativity rests (largely dismissed today by most linguists): that language makes thought possible; without words people cannot have those thoughts. Bypassing these limitations, figurative language allowed Indians "to think and express themselves by means of natural objects which [were] then used figuratively."[33] This early link between primitivism and poetic language helps explain the fetishization of translated speeches of Indian leaders in the nineteenth and twentieth centuries.

The issue of the ideological uses of this link aside (which will be examined in chapters 3 and 4), figurative language might seem to mark Indian discourse for other reasons, according to linguistic anthropologist William Leap. Generated at both the semantic and syntactic levels, and often personalized by the speaker, figurative language is inspired by "ancestral language semantic structures, idioms, and other reference conventions common to the tribal membership as a whole."[34] Leap explains how formal and informal registers affect figurative language, at least for the Lakota, who might say "'An idea is hanging outside my head'" (formal) as opposed to "'I have an idea'" (informal).[35] But when using an Indian-English language variety as code-of-choice, later speakers tend to use the "rapid, to-the-point presentations of meanings characteristically associated with that code," as in the second example above ("I have an idea").[36] This crossover might explain the relative syntactic and semantic directness of Plateau Indian English. More properly understood as a linguistic feature rather than a discursive one, and therefore outside the scope of this book, I will merely say here that the absence of figurative language marks Plateau Indian texts, both before (at least, as those texts were translated into English) but especially after Native languages were displaced by Plateau Indian English, a discourse-positive marker that might be called, simply, plainspokenness.

Humor, another form of high affect, is one more discourse-positive marker in Plateau Indian texts, used often as bluntly confrontational in formal as in informal situations and with intergroup as with intragroup settings. Like the use of highly selective detail (more on this shortly), a rhetor's use of humor individuates an argument and personalizes content—paramount attributes of effective persuasion in Plateau Indian rhetoric, as subsequent chapters in this book substantiate.

Suspended Thesis/Suspenseful Arrangement

Kaplan's fifth terrible question—What arrangement of evidence is likely to appeal (be convincing) to readers?—is grounded in the fact that *"convincingness"* itself is relative to culture, insofar as audience expectations and interpretive processes are shaped by discourse communities.[37] The kind of evidence brought to bear certainly affects an argument's convincingness, depending on the degree to which an audience finds experiential knowledge or distanced knowledge or other kinds of knowledge more convincing. So does its arrangement. The two factors are, in fact, interconnected. As practiced in Plateau Indian rhetoric, arguing-with-story is not necessarily bounded by chronological organization, at least not as a personal story referenced in persuasive texts. Arguing-with-story is very adaptive to strategies of indirectness and nonlinear organization, developing the larger point of the argument by the end of the text, the larger point ultimately stated explicitly or suggested or maybe even left unstated altogether for the audience to ponder.

The larger argument itself is not necessarily recursive, with the point stated over and over. What is recursive is the *return* to story to develop pieces of argument. Erickson notes that conversation among African American male adolescents followed a "'logic of the particular' characterized by argumentation by anecdote; rhapsodic stitching together of topoi (commonplaces); and routinized speaker/audience interaction, such as that associated with blues singing or preaching style."[38] Erickson's finding suggests that genre conventions and rhetorical premises are portable across modality and cultures. In describing Ute discursive principles that govern student writing, Leap has argued that "how the writer organizes information within the narrative and arranges it on the page is as important a text-resource for the reader as are the details of the text-content."[39] In Plateau Indian rhetoric it is a *sense* of story that structures discourse, with story's suspenseful, unfolding development, with story's unstated point. By way of arguing-with-story, other points are made or suggested, again relative to the audience at hand. The point is not only highly variable depending on the audience's construction of meaning; the point is also multiple.

Kaplan's question about arrangement is terribly controversial for other reasons, as he himself discovered when he first published his "squiggles" essay in 1966 that launched the field of contrastive rhetoric. To illustrate how organization patterns are specific to cultures, Kaplan drew lines to represent characteristic organizational patterns by culture: English, a straight vertical arrow; Semitic, a zigzag; Oriental, a spiral; Romance, a random line; and Russian, the same random line as Romance but dotted.[40] The essay was rightly controversial not only for its cultural labels and overgeneralizations about entire cultures but also because it suggests a link between cognition and culture. That link—generally referred to as cognitive styles or cognitive orientation—draws much of its explanatory power from the discourse of scientific positivism. The notion of cognition styles is grounded in Piaget's theory of cognitive development, which posits that children zero to fifteen years of age typically move through four stages as they learn to think; the last two stages from "concrete" logical operations to "abstract" operations are of particular interest here. Concrete thinkers deduce empirically from their immediate environment; abstract thinkers, from hypothetical-formal propositions. Put another way, as cognitivists in composition and proponents of the critical thinking movement have said at least since the 1980s: learners *naturally* develop from egocentric to sociocentric thinking, unless for some reason their development stalls out at the egocentric stage.

As this reading of Piaget suggests, discussion on cognitive styles quickly devolves into binaries describing not only the way people think but also how they interact, concrete versus abstract somehow corresponding to egocentric versus sociocentric behaviors. Such alignments in turn have drawn scholars from other fields to draw additional parallels, once again dichotomously and oppositionally expressed: oral versus literate; field-dependent versus field independent; right-brain dominant versus left-brain dominant. Among the fallacies of such categorization is that it splits and pits emotional sensibility against rational thought, subjectivity against objectivity, holistic against analytic thinking. These are further associated with stereotypic characterizations of whole groups of people as emotional or rational, collectivist or individualist, past-, present-, or future-oriented, which deeply encode racist, classist, and sexist attitudes.[41] Thus entire groups, not just individuals, can be said to stall out at the egocentric, concrete-thinking stage of development. The orality/literacy divide reemerges, becoming the Great Cognitive Divide (as I have often heard rhetorician Victor Villanueva call it) with its attendant stereotypes: oral cultures think concretely and holistically; literate cultures think abstractly and analytically. From there it is a short walk to the discourses of primitivism and nineteenth-century scientific racism.

Yet it is difficult to have that discussion specific to the discipline of composition studies without evoking charges of cognitive reductionism, without implying intelligence deficiency, without resorting to binaries, without using value-laden language. To characterize Plateau Indian textual arrangement as nonlinear suggests it is governed by holistic thinking rather than analytic logic, a particularly popular notion appropriated by New Ageism and reproduced by scholars, both Native and non-Native, who are really just trying to make the point that American Indian ways of knowing and being in the world are distinctive—at heart, an epistemological point, not a cognitivist one, but expressed in terms of what it is not: Eurocentric formal logic.[42] As education and literacy scholar Mike Rose has shown, in research models thinking that is field-independent may be positively identified, but field-dependence cannot; thus it can only be ascribed by default, as not-field-independent.[43] To characterize Plateau Indian arrangement as indirect and recursive might also seem like a polite way of saying Plateau Indian texts lack both cohesion and coherence. The first term, *cohesion,* is associated with surface connections; the second term, *coherence,* is the underlying cognitive operation.[44]

Thus conceived, "coherence" at a deep structural level assumes a marriage of thought and language, while "cohesion" as mere surface feature assumes their divorce.

But as Bizzell has rightly pointed out, following developmental psychologist Lev Vygotsky, the relationship between thought and language is dialectic, a relationship captured in Vygotsky's term "verbal thought."[45] When a child comes to understand that he is not just naming ideas but also developing and evaluating them, in Vygotsky's words, *"the nature of the* [child's] development itself changes, from biological to historical."[46] Thus verbal thought is not natural but conditioned by historical-cultural processes. Coherence renders a stretch of discourse unified when that arrangement holds "cultural significance for those who create or comprehend it."[47] Insofar as local cultures have different habits and different expectations for organizing discourse, certain patterns of coherence will emerge more often than others. And as just one factor among many contributing to coherence, cohesive devices might be more appropriately understood as recontextualization cues, as in the case of Plateau Indian written texts, when rhetors attempt to translate the presence, purpose, and speaker-audience relationship.[48] The perception, anticipation, and interpretation of those cues are highly contingent on local culture:

> Cohesive devices call upon a speaker's background knowledge of syntactic/semantic and sociocultural knowledge in a process of interpretation. They enable participants—hearers or speakers—to "read between the lines": to fill in elided material, to make references to preceding discourse, to interpret the relationship of incoming material to the prevailing topic or theme, in short, to follow the links in a chain. Such devices rely on conventionalized expectations about what must be made explicit and what is to be filled in, and about how this is to be signaled. Our evaluations of each other's communicative effectiveness are based on how well these expectations are fulfilled.[49]

Further, some speakers' interpretative practices, informed by their community's customary ways of thinking about the world, align more readily than others to Eurocentric formal logic, which typically braces academic discourses and school literacy tasks. Conversely, those whose practices do not align will have an added difficulty in educational settings.[50] Arrangement—and its constitutive kinfolk, coherence and cohesion—is both logical and not logical, depending not on audience or even discourse but on discursive community, whose interpretative strategies are bounded by values that make that community cohere as a community in the first place.

Situated Elaboration/Selective Detail

Finally, Kaplan's first three questions might be productively grouped together for consideration: (1) What may be discussed? (2) Who has the authority to speak/write? Or, who has the authority to write to whom under what circumstances? (3) What form(s) may the writing take? Taken together, these questions speak to issues of authority and, by implication, appropriateness. Less obviously, these issues actually hinge on matters of development and elaboration. Like arrangement, "elaboration" is another controversial descriptor of discourse because such descriptions often seem to imply judgments of cognition proficiency or deficiency; they also typically involve issues of socioeconomic status, culture, and even rurality—all of which obtain in rendering the stereotype of the laconic, when not silent, Indian. While the type also draws from nineteenth-century noble-savage and way-of-the-warrior discourses, more recent scholarship has lent its support, especially the work of sociolinguist Basil Bernstein and linguistic anthropologist Keith Basso, which has since been refuted and qualified. Because both scholars have been so influential in discussion of elaboration generally (Bernstein) and Indian silence specifically (Basso), a brief overview is in order to glean what is valuable and relevant to the discussion at hand. With additional insights from Tannen, I expound on my own characterization of volubility in Plateau Indian speech and writing as situated, not only highly dependent on situation but also on other factors, such as topic, authorization, and genre—in other words, Kaplan's first three questions.

In his studies of urban and rural schoolchildren, most notably, Bernstein advanced the notion of "elaborated code" and "restricted code," which he thought of as the regulatory principle governing elaboration, usually indexed as explicitness/implicitness and low-context/high-context dependence. He later correlated these attributes to socioeconomic class and family role systems, a correlation that he argued was predictive of relative success in school interactions and literacy tasks. Although Bernstein's work on the connections between language use, socioeconomic class, family roles, and school success have proven foundational to scholarship in the sociology of education and literacy studies, his notion of elaborated and restricted codes have proven more controversial, in part because of the infelicitous valences of the terms themselves but also because he seems to argue that working-class students are cognitively deficient.[51] In fact, his work demonstrates, at least in a latter-day rereading, that "first, their native discourse community's conventions are very different from school conventions, and, second, their lack of a variety of speech patterns makes it hard for them to see their problems in school as problems of learning to relate to new speech patterns (or an unfamiliar discourse community)."[52]

Much scholarship has supported the view that silence is a standard feature of Indian discourse, praise that can be damning, as rhetorician Cheryl Glenn has pointed out: "Indians are perceived to be fiercely silent, if not personally cold, to be solemnly dignified, if not linguistically impoverished."[53] Most influential in this regard is the work of Basso, who studied silence among Southwest Indians for forty years. In his last book he argues that silence is a major discursive feature of West Apache speech in six particular socially ambiguous situations. Testing Basso's study herself, Glenn interviewed her own Native informants, seven people from five different tribes, about using silence in those same situations; all took issue with most of Basso's findings. Although anecdotal at best, her limited refutation does align with the more rigorous research conducted by sociolinguist Susan Philips among the Warm Springs Indians (a Plateau group), whose work focuses on the role of silence in school settings.[54]

Between the poles of silence and elaboration on the volubility scale is brevity, which itself has different effects depending not so much on the situation as on culture and other factors, including gender. The variability of the "brevity effect" can be illustrated by an example from a larger study of differences in conversation style conducted by Tannen.[55] When a husband responds to a wife's entreaty to attend a party with a brief "okay," the American subjects in the study read his answer as direct, informal, and therefore sincere; Greek subjects, however, evaluated his "okay" as an indirect way of expressing his underlying unwillingness to comply to his wife's perceived preference.[56] While both groups linked a lack of enthusiasm with a lack of elaboration, they interpreted the sincerity of the husband's "okay" quite differently. Notice, too, that sociocultural knowledge shapes expectations and therefore interpretation—in this instance the expected (stereotypical) roles of husbands and wives in conversation: wives are talkative; husbands are not.[57] Thus Tannen's argument qualifies Bernstein's notions of codes: cultural groups may prefer or even require elaboration or ellipsis, depending on the message and context, the latter including who is speaking to whom about what.

That brings me back to Kaplan's first three terrible questions, which might be summed up this way: Who has a discourse community's authorization to speak, to whom, about what, and under what circumstances? In Plateau Indian rhetoric, who has permission to speak is generationally marked. Although elders have priority, all adults have equal access to the floor. Children and young adults have more constraints. They are not forbidden to participate in adult conversations or in public settings, but adults do speak first in public settings, ending their turns with "I have finished" or words to that effect. Nonadults must have at least an implicit invitation to speak, which may or may not be forthcoming, depending on the situation. Upon invitation, young people do participate in adult conversation, in family and other informal settings, often co-narrating anecdotes with adults, eventually at later ages narrating stories on their own. In school settings where students are expected to participate in class discussion, they are nonetheless culturally constrained by the high value placed on modesty, being actively taught not to stand out among their classmates. Otherwise, once adults have the floor, they may speak as long or as short and on whatever topic they wish, regardless of agenda or time or topic, as I illustrate more fully in chapter 5. Nor is anyone ever required to speak if he chooses not to.

At the Treaty Council of 1855 (the topic of chapter 3), for example, the headman Kamiakin (Yakama/Palus), who was renowned for his oratory and storytelling, famously refused to speak even though the U.S. negotiators who controlled the floor repeatedly asked and even badgered him to. Finally he did: "I have nothing to talk long about." His brevity here is not dictated by cultural-boundedness. As Leap has explained, "Silence, hedges, and distractors become features of Indian English discourse in settings that are alien to the speakers' home community and cultural traditions," particularly so when the speech event is controlled by non-Indians.[58] Leap goes on to recommend: "Change the ground rules and shift the principles of cooperation so the speech event includes (rather than excludes) the Indian English speaker's sense of effective discourse and the use of silence, hedging, and distractors should also decline."[59] I would add that, in this instance, Kamiakin's refusal to speak may not have been just a political expedience; rather, he may have been registering his contempt for the proceedings, the results of which (the reservation system) were a foregone conclusion.

On the last day of the Treaty Council, Kamiakin did speak on the record in reluctant support of the treaty, but with few, select words. Another aspect of elaboration, detail is often pegged as one determinant of length. Previous scholarship maintains that *copia* of detail is a standard feature of orality generally.[60] Besides reconstituting the oral/written divide, this generalization does not acknowledge (1) that there are different kinds of *copia* and (2) that those kinds are marked by socioeconomic class and ethnicity (3) because those markers reflect language-use socialization processes in the home. In Leap's work with Ute students retelling a story, for example, he found that they used "nonexhaustive presentation of detail" to personalize their content and take "ownership over the narrative."[61]

Leap's conclusions support my own in a study I conducted with two seventh-grade classes in a rural, reservation school. Of the forty-nine students, more than half were of Latino-Mexican descent and a third were Plateau Indian, with whites, Filipinos, and African Americans comprising the remaining minority.[62] Almost all of the students had lived in the same school district and attended the same school and experienced the same pedagogy their entire lives. The main variable was ethnicity, while a second variable was socioeconomic class. Although almost all of the students were poor, those coming from educated families were predominantly white. In producing their own fictional narratives based on a line drawing taken from a state test, the Latino students consistently reported the facts within the drawing, with little or no elaboration, whereas the white and Plateau Indian students elaborated on the drawing—but in different ways. The white students elaborated using vivifying detail, such as itemizing the contents in a picnic basket and using direct dialogue, whereas the Plateau Indian students used impressionistic detail to produce open-ended stories.[63] These differences I attribute in part to the literacy event of the bedtime story. In brief here, it is the talk and interaction with adults while reading—or while retelling Coyote stories—that socializes children to think and to use language in certain ways. Coupled with cultural permissions that allow increased opportunities for children to listen, learn, imitate, co-produce, and ultimately produce their own stories, such interactions prepare Plateau Indian children to enter their respective discourse communities, where their communicative competence will be used and evaluated and valued.

Among the communicative competence learned within home communities is not only knowing how to tell story but also when and where to tell a story about what—actually, a matter of appropriateness, a meshing of timing, genre, and topic. As Kaplan has explained, "Genres are nothing more or less than conventional solutions to recurring communication problems. Although students who are native speakers of other languages may bring with them a rich inventory of genres, there may be a mismatch between the genres in other language[s] and those in English, or the genres may serve unexpected purposes."[64]

Two examples from my experiences in two graduate seminars illustrate the cultural boundedness of topical appropriateness. As part of a presentation, a white graduate student showed visuals from the controversial Bodies exhibit, which displays skinned and plasticized cadavers for educational and aesthetic purposes. Discussion ensued about the ethics of the exhibit. The one Plateau Indian student in the seminar did not participate in the discussion, and after we took our usual break halfway through the seminar, he did not return. When next we talked privately, he confirmed that he was appalled by the discussion, unable to even comprehend the spiritual transgression of such an exhibit, a perspective that had not even come up. I asked him why he did not speak up and contribute this view. "It was a white discussion, not an Indian one," he replied. His silence protested showing photographs of dead people and talking about the cadaver display in terms of (just) ethics, aesthetics, and education—and in such a matter-of-fact, distant way. In short, the seminar had discussed the topic in ways consistent with academic ways of knowing, interacting, analyzing. His silence (and then his absence after break when we were to resume the discussion) registered disgust but something more too: fear of the spiritual consequences in our own lives for disrespecting the dead. The student chose to respond with silence (and then disappearance), but the topic itself also silenced him. Like Kamiakin, he simply had "nothing to talk long about."

Silence as a response to inappropriateness is not limited to Plateau Indians, as this second example illustrates. In introducing her presentation to a seminar on cultural rhetorics, a Plateau Indian graduate student passed around photographs of what appeared to be an ordinary cat, explaining how its tail was a clue that it had special powers. She then launched into her story, telling it very much as she would write about it years later in her dissertation, from which I now quote:

> During a seminar with Dr. Barbara Monroe, I had relayed to the class my lucrative trade with my sister: a cat with powers for a washing machine. As is my cultural naiveté, I disclosed this story unknowing how the discussion of animals with powers was completely improper in the WSU [Washington State University] classroom. My education in cat powers came from my father, who had instructed me to watch for cats with their tails formed into a ball on the end. Such a cat was born into a litter at my sister's house in July 2006, a kitten with a teeny ball curled up on the end of her tail, a sign of good luck. I wanted such a lucky cat, but did not feel right in robbing my sister of all the good luck that this cat would bring. As it turned out, my sister's washing machine broke down and in her huge household of eight people, she would suffer having to take that much laundry to the Laundromat. I bought her a washing machine and she gave me the lucky tail kitten, with the logical assumption that the cat had already brought her luck, a new washing machine.
>
> Much later after bringing the kitten home, I would see a translucent version of the cat following me around the house. At first I thought I was just seeing things, but then the boys [her children] saw it too. We noticed that as the cat slept, its ghost followed family members around the house. So there goes her "sleep ghost," running here and there. Now she has grown out of being a kitten and her sleep ghost does not run around the house in a regular manner anymore, just about once a year; however, this is something that does not happen in typical

American households, but rather within the homes of Nez Perces [a southern Plateau Indian tribe] who have the ghosts of the *weyekin* religion still in practice. Just as my father instructed me about the cats, I transmitted the information to my children, who witnessed the sleep ghost and will keep this cat in family oral history. The cat and the washing machine contain the sacred with its *weyekin* element and the secular with its washing machine—a living example of a wholly rhetoric of a Nez Perce family.[65]

The students in the seminar initially responded to the story of the Plateau Indian graduate student with silence. Someone finally broke the silence to ask if she really did think the cat had special powers, while someone else later questioned the appropriateness of the topic for a seminar discussion, much less an academic paper (and, if he had known, later a dissertation). The Plateau Indian student was completely nonplussed, never anticipating that something as central as spirituality would be deemed inappropriate in academic settings and genres. Notice that the author uses details very selectively and delays stating the point of her story until the end. The audience has to wait for it.

And waiting for it, the audience may become impatient, having no idea where the story is going. Expectations about elaboration—how a piece of discourse on a particular topic is developed and arranged using what kind of detail—deeply inform an audience's perception of appropriateness as well as, ultimately, convincingness. When those expectations are frustrated, the perception is that Plateau Indian discourse is redundant or digressive. Although Plateau Indian rhetors exercise a full range of volubility from elaborated discourse to silence, depending on the situation, more often than not, they seem to speak and write at length, rather than in brief, either about "nothing" (as adjudged by a Euro-American audience) or on a tangent that intersects with their lived experiences. Or perhaps the perception that Plateau Indian speakers take more time is simply a matter of Euro-American expectations frustrated.

At the Treaty Council of 1855, for example, both Americans and Indians complained that the other side was talking too long and in a general way, failing to reach their points in a timely, effective manner. I have often heard Native teachers and graduate students say much the same thing about academic discourse: the point gets lost in seemingly random detail. Conversely, teacher comments like "digressive" or "off-topic" or "inappropriate" are unhelpful at best and alienating at worst, reminding Native students that the world of school and college is not their world. In their rhetorical world, topic choice (scatological and sexual topics included) is largely unrestrained by place, encompassing the full range of life experiences from the sacred to the mundane, the latter often holding spiritual import. Theirs is a rhetoric that might justly be called "a wholly rhetoric."[66]

Abiding Values

Language use is not just linguistic and discursive but also epistemic and semiotic, encoding a people's epistemology. As such, it carries forward not just a rhetoric but also a worldview. It does so across multiple generations and across languages, even when the ancestral language has been lost.[67] The multiple strategies of personalization that characterize Plateau Indian rhetoric privilege the primacy of experiential knowledge. Why would a presumably collectivist culture so highly value personal experience?

Just as the concepts of "directness" and "face" take on culture-specific meaning in Chinese American rhetoric, what constitutes "personal" hinges on Plateau Indian understanding of personhood.[68] Although much has been written on Indian communalism generally, less attention has been given to the Indian concept of the individual, which is highly variable across tribal groups. To a lesser degree perhaps than the Ute or the Lakota, who prize what other American Indian studies scholars have termed "self-dependence" or "social independence," Plateau Indian culture also holds in profound respect individual intuition and initiative.[69] As a logical extension, individuals are expected to accept responsibility and pay the consequences of their own actions—but not for others. Anyone trying to exert control over another's actions or opinions only puts that responsibility, and the onus of consequences, on his own back. Unsolicited advice, however persistent, does not overstep that boundary, offered on a take-it-or-leave-it basis. The individual is still making her own decisions on her own life path.

A story often retold in one Plateau Indian tribe neatly captures this principle. A man refuses to eat and isolates himself in his room. His wife prepares him a meal that evening, but he refuses to eat or even respond to her call. The next evening, she again prepares him a meal, but again he refuses. And so on for three more nights. On the fifth night the wife finds the man dead. The story aims to show the danger of isolation from the group.[70] It also makes another point. His wife's good advice ignored, experience taught the man an undeniable truth: eat or die. Thus the independent self is also an *interdependent* self, an interrelational construct made manifest in many cultural and linguistic practices. For example, when a Plateau Indian introduces herself, she usually identifies her family connections. This practice of self-location does double duty: enabling the speaker to make connections with new people while also authenticating herself as a "real Indian" with credentials, an oblique form of self-promotion. The Native languages of the Plateau peoples reflect the importance of these identifications in their rich, expansive vocabulary for personal connections by birth and marriage. For example, the Sahaptin language typically has more than forty words for classifying relatives, including four kinds of grandparents, six kinds of siblings, six each for uncles and aunts, nephews, and nieces, as well as nine kinds of in-laws.[71] Identity is relational not only in terms of people but also in terms of the land, as discussed in chapter 1. Thus selfhood is an intimate, coterminous weave of personal autonomy, family lineage, and ancestral land.

The nineteenth-century Nez Perce headman Looking Glass's words (spoken in a Sahaptin variety and translated into English) at the Treaty Council of 1855 implicitly speak to these connections: "A long time ago the Great Spirit spoke to my children. I am from the body of my parents and I [was?] set on a good place. The Great Spirit spoke to his children the laws with track[s] on the ground strait and after that there have been tracks on my ground. And after that the big chief, the President, his ground was stept on in the same way. And for that reason I am not going to trample on his grounds, and I do not expect anyone to tramp on mine."[72] This excerpt reflects the principles of equality and nonviolent tolerance, expressly asking for respect for different paths on different grounds. The Great Spirit or "the Creator" in Sahaptin translates into English as "he who makes my path or my way." To disrupt one's trail, personalized by the Creator, is "to disrupt nature's order and abandon the ancestral wisdom embodied in the trail's course."[73] Personal experience is only personal in that it is one body's experience of the accumulated wisdom gained from intergenerationally transmitted knowledge. Insofar as a person stays on that Creator-given path, his personal experience can be trusted. To stay the course, he must act on what he knows to be true in his heart, a knowing that is ultimately intuitive. Without contradiction, self-determination in Plateau Indian culture means collective affirmation, for affirming collective wisdom for oneself serves as an example for the next generation. In other words, one does not make one's path in life so much as one discovers it, already laid out before one.

A respect for personal autonomy is the precondition of egalitarianism and pacifism, values particularly strong on the central and southern Plateau but less so on the western and eastern borders of the Plateau, because of contact with coastal tribes in the West who did value social caste and with the Plains Indians in the East who did value war.[74] These values find expression in many domains of Plateau Indian culture, only two of which I discuss here—political organization and childrearing practices. These two domains hold important implications for Plateau Indian rhetoric and education, as subsequent chapters show.

Before the Conquest, political structures reflected the belief in noncoercive persuasion. At all levels—from the family and clan to the band and tribe—power was diffused. Traditional political organization of the Plateau peoples might be described as "radically democratic."[75] Nineteenth-century American Indians are often portrayed as analogous to medieval European fiefdoms, with chiefs as lords making war on neighboring fiefdoms for economic advantage. That portrait is as ethnocentric as it is false, especially regarding the Plateau peoples. On the Plateau the main political unit was not the tribe (which was intentionally porous through the practice of exogamy aimed at cementing bonds with other tribes as trading partners) but the autonomous clan, with one or more clans occupying a village. Even within the village, especially on the southern and central Plateau, social caste was virtually unthinkable, so highly held was the principle of egalitarianism.[76] Village governance reflected these same principles. Titles were largely achieved through bravery or oratory, not necessarily ascribed by birth; they indicated respect and recognition, not governance and authority.[77] Headmen used village criers to make announcements each night to mediate messages from the top.

The same principle of diffused power applied to parenting. Traditionally parents used a "whip man" to discipline their children because they did not want to use force on them directly. In a document dated 1909, Chief Yoom-tee-bee recounts this story (and in ways true to the principles of Plateau Indian rhetoric) about how even the whip man could be used indirectly:

Maybe Injun child cry too much; maybe not mind parents. Then the father get *tahmahnawis* man [i.e., the whip man]; who puts mask on face; big basket over shoulder. He comes where crying child is. Maybe I have boy all time cry. I say: "Tahmahnawis man, you take my boy. Put him in basket. Take him away! Bye and bye you eat him."

Then my wife say:

"No! tahmahnawis man. Do not take my boy. I give you salmon to put in basket. Bye and bye you eat salmon."

Then I tell tahmahnawis man:

"All right! You no eat my boy now. Leave him! I tell you if he cry more. If he cry, you come get him bye and bye. Eat him!"

Then my wife give tahmahnawi man huckel-berries; give him dried salmon in his basket. Then he leave my boy; go 'way in the dark. My boy cry no more.[78]

Even in the twenty-first century, the tradition of the tahmahnawi man continues. In an effort to address the 45 percent dropout rate in their schools, four school districts in the early 2000s formed what they called a "Whip Man Board," a truancy board to hear students' problems about attending school.[79] When children are disciplined publicly, they were usually corrected as a group rather than individually, as they were at the Treaty Council in 1855. In that instance, an elder reprimanded at length a group of young men for not paying attention, without singling out any one person by name. Group discipline treats all alike, but it also serves to avoid personally humiliating or calling special attention to any one child.[80] In like manner, discipline can be administered from any number of people besides the parents, including relatives, elders, and teachers. Authority is thus decentralized and dispersed but also all-pervasive, while individuals of all ages are respected and afforded different face-saving mechanisms.

The relative weight of personal autonomy and collective responsibility in Plateau Indian culture generally has shifted over time under threat of cultural genocide, with collective responsibility perhaps foregrounded now. Still, the two values should be considered complementary rather than competing. For example, the vision quest was traditionally a spiritual practice that an individual experienced in a unique way and never verbally revealed to others; in life, as on quest, a person had to find his own way. But one elder tells students today what she calls a modern version of the vision quest: everyone is put on this earth with a special talent and for a special purpose; your job is to find that talent and fulfill your purpose, giving back to your family and the tribe.

Childrearing practices aim to teach children that they are individually talented and equally important. Put another way, children are not talented in all things nor do they need to be, for others in the group will fill those gaps and perform those functions. Children are taught to become self-sufficient at an early age, learning to dress and feed themselves. That same self-sufficiency, however, enables them to contribute to the family good—dressing and feeding younger siblings and cousins, for example, or offering the fruits of their first berry-picking to kin before partaking themselves. Because of cross-age care-giving practices, children and young people are often unsupervised by adults, giving the under-age another opportunity to practice self-sufficiency and group responsibility simultaneously.

An abiding respect for the individual, not just the collectivities of which that individual is a part—this is the bedrock value that deeply informs Plateau Indian argument and persuasion across many formal and official, not just informal and community, arenas. As Leap has pointed out in regard to American Indian groups that value self-independence more generally, "Expectations about appropriate language use and other rules structuring public and private discourse [are] also consistent with an egalitarian-centered community politic."[81] "Speaking straight" and speaking straight from the heart, like knowing one's path, is something only one person can do, based on his own experience in the world. Embodied arguments may take many discursive turns, reflecting individuals' rhetorical choices while still working within cultural parameters for convincingness and appropriateness. In subsequent chapters these parameters are explored, substantiated with primary material from Plateau Indian rhetors themselves—from headsmen at nineteenth-century treaty councils (chapter 3) to secondary school students in the twenty-first century (chapter 6)—speaking straight for themselves.

3

Speaking Straight in Indian Languages
1855–1870

"I am of another nation, when I speak you do not understand me. When you speak, I do not understand you," Spokan Garry asserted at the Spokane council in 1855.[1] His statement carries multivalent meaning, suggesting that the Indians and the Americans were separated by many kinds of differences—at once linguistic, political, cultural, and rhetorical. His statement also calls to mind the problem of translation on all these levels. It is the problem that the dominant party always seeks to suppress, replacing it with narratives of "mutual intelligibility," as if the subordinate party had equal footing in controlling the outcomes, not to mention the subsequent representations, of the event.[2]

As American studies scholar David Murray has explained, cultural differences do exist; the problem is how they get translated, or framed, and put to ideological use. Certainly this is the case with Indian speeches. Fetishized since the eighteenth century and well into the twentieth, surrender and protest speeches were framed to appeal to a white readership. Even though the speeches often castigated white actions, they were nonetheless read with nostalgia and a sense of dramatic irony from the vantage point of hindsight. The Indian leader's apparently natural eloquence translated as a sign of authenticity and nobility, vanquished and vanishing, riding off into the sunset, and inevitably so. All the more reason to bring civilization to the ignorant, language-poor savages left behind, who had to translate into a new world order. Indian speeches continue to be ideologically re-invested today. Chief Seattle's web-of-life speech, for example, which was actually written by a white ally as political protest and never delivered by Seattle, is most commonly framed as a statement of ecological awareness.[3] Such acts of "rhetorical imperialism," according to indigenous studies scholar Scott Lyons, can only be circumvented, at least in part, by looking to treaties and other early writings where Natives exercised a modicum of "rhetorical sovereignty."[4] Even then, the problem of translation at all levels remains.

What follows is analyses of seven Indian speeches in full, with additional speeches quoted in part, from four different Indian-American councils on the Plateau, from 1855 to 1870. These speeches were originally spoken in varieties of "Indian" (as Plateau Indians refer to their respective Native languages today, derived from multiple varieties of Sahaptin and Salish) and then translated and transcribed in English. However capable and objective the translators may have been, undoubtedly much language-encoded information was lost in translation at all linguistic levels: syntax, semantics, and pragmatics, or verbal etiquette.[5] First, *syntax* embeds all kinds of information in Indian languages, such as a speaker's confidence in his statements (as indicated in complex tense/aspectual markers) (183); degree of formality (as indicated by complex syntactic choices without parallel in English) (78); and the relative points of thematic stress as well as agency (as indicated in topicalization and left-branching syntax) (56; 77–78). Second, *semantics* encodes nuances of an Indian speaker's "conventions of reference," including euphemisms, slang, and sacred as well as secular meanings (77). This much missing information at both the syntactic and semantic levels of language undoubtedly affects the third linguistic level: *verbal etiquette*. However compromised by translation, verbal etiquette—or to recall sociolinguist Dell Hymes's term, communicative competence—nonetheless reconstitutes across generations and across languages (149).

While acknowledging that much is forever lost in translation, I would nonetheless argue that there is still much to be found. To wit: Plateau Indian speeches during the treaty period, even in English translation, bear the markings of a rhetorical *ethnie* still operative today. Focusing on rhetorical and discursive analysis, I realize, runs the risk of aesthetisizing Indian oratory; however, my aim is not to make a case for natural eloquence but to establish that the Plateau Indians do have a distinctive rhetoric, the roots of which are traceable to 1855. Although issues of translation obviate any close readings, including any explication of figurative language, broad discursive moves do stand out across dozens and dozens of Indian speeches from two archival collections heretofore never examined rhetorically. *What* the Indians are saying is equally important as *how* they are saying it, each taking a different tack in arguing the issues at hand, while still employing the same rhetoric.

Chosen on the basis of speaker representation from several tribes of the southern, northeastern, and central Plateau, the many speeches under examination here, cited either in full or as excerpts, share common discursive moves. These commonalities suggest the rhetoric they broadly enact was indeed Plateau-wide in scope. These conventions prevailed despite language differences across speakers: the southern Plateau spoke several varieties of Sahaptin, while the northern Plateau spoke several varieties of Interior Salish. Language pluralism and frequent contact may have actually predicated, rather than precluded, the development of shared communicative competence. The Plateau peoples frequently gathered on their seasonal migrations to hunt and gather food, to barter, to negotiate marriage, to celebrate feast days. A shared rhetoric would have facilitated these transactions and maintained these complex webs of intergroup relationships. As discussed in chapter 2, and as previous scholarship supports, even when the original language may be lost or unknown, its discourse patterns persist for several generations.[6] Although a full consideration of the linguistic processes that map discursive choices remains outside the scope of this book (and my own areas of expertise), my rhetorical analysis of tribal council speeches spoken in Indian, translated into English, and then transcribed nonetheless points to the foundational practices of Plateau Indian argumentation to this day.

Historical Context

Contact in the Pacific Northwest came relatively late, compared to the other side of the continent, but when it did come, the pace of change was greatly accelerated. The Lewis and Clark expedition first mapped the region in 1805, and the Hudson's Bay Company introduced the fur trade in the 1820s. The business brought economic stability to the Indians because the company adopted fair and mutually beneficial practices like fixing fur prices and ending the liquor trade. Intermarriage further strengthened white-Indian relations. Peaceful coexistence was assured because the Hudson's Bay Company did not attempt to interfere with the Indian way of life. Nor did the earliest missionaries, who set up mission outposts where Indians could come for Christian instruction if they so chose.[7]

Major conflict arrived with the first agrarian mission and colony founded by Marcus Whitman, who aimed to disabuse Indians of their ways and convert them to Christianity—and white culture. In 1847, when the Cayuse were decimated by an outbreak of measles, they retaliated against the Whitman mission. This bloody conflict was but the first sign of what would become a growing trend: with more settlers and increased contact came increased incidents of violence.[8] The Plateau Indians were severely weakened by another form of white contact: disease. Throughout the region, villages were depopulated by influenza, small-pox, measles, syphilis, and intemperance, killing inhabitants by the hundreds. Many villages along the Columbia River lost half their populations; at least one village on the Snake River had no survivors.[9] The death toll on the West Coast, awash in waves of immigrants by the 1850s, was even higher than it was inland, which was only now becoming "discovered" as gold miners presaged the settlers to follow. The impact of these epidemics cannot be overstated, as historians have often noted: "Diseases . . . weakened the Indians by decreasing their numbers, demoralizing their populations, and destroying their political, military, and economic strength."[10]

Conditions in 1855, the days of the Treaty Period, were not the same as they were in 1825, the days of the fur trade.[11] In 1853 the Territory of Oregon was split up to create the Territory of Washington, and Isaac Stevens was appointed its first governor. Charged with securing treaties from the Indians on both sides of the Cascades, both coastal and inland, Governor Stevens had to apply to the New Northwest a U.S. policy framework that had evolved over half a century of conquest on the eastern portion of the continent.[12] That policy aimed to accommodate national expansion by liquidating Indian land titles and relocating Indians to reservations, where bands and groups could be concentrated, confined, and controlled by the Bureau of Indian Affairs, backed with military presence on nearby posts.[13] The reservation was envisioned as an indoctrination camp to prepare Indians for ultimate assimilation into a white-majority society. On the reservations a nomadic hunting, fishing, and gathering economy would be transformed into a sedentary, agrarian one. Besides farming, Indians would also be taught the trades and English; they would also continue to receive Christian instruction. Both day schools and boarding schools would acculturate children to white ways, eventually eradicating Indian language and culture altogether by disrupting intergenerational transmission.[14]

Although Governor Stevens had to work within official policy, he had his own agenda. He wanted to make a bid for the railroad to come through the New Northwest and had already started surveying the territory to make that case to Congress. Stevens held three offices at once: territorial governor, chief engineer in charge of surveying a northern rail route, and territorial superintendent of Indian affairs. He saw his multiple roles not as a conflict but a convergence of interest.[15]

Before embarking on his historic treaty tour of 1855, Stevens enlisted General Joel Palmer, superintendent of Indian affairs for the Oregon Territory, to join him at Walla Walla, since some tribal lands crossed into General Palmer's area of jurisdiction. Their common goal: to clear the land to make way for settlement. Having no prior experience with treaty-making, Stevens studied the treaties with the Oto, Omaha, and Missouri and used them to draft a template for his upcoming tour. Thus the so-called Stevens Treaties incorporated both standard and nonstandard policies as compared to other treaties: ending hostilities, ceding land, establishing reservations (standard policies) but also recognizing the Indians' right to fish, gather, and hunt "at common and accustomed places" (nonstandard policies).[16] In his correspondence Steven wrote: "It never could have been the intention of Congress [as misstated in the Donation Land Act of 1850] that the Indians should be excluded from their ancient fisheries."[17] The Stevens Treaties thus included protection for "native hunting, grazing, and gathering rights on 'unenclosed land,'" a provision that ironically opened the door for Indian activism and legal action in the twentieth century and beyond.[18] It is a provision unique to the Washington tribes; by comparison, only one Oregon tribe retained such rights.[19]

The Plateau Indians knew that American encroachment was inevitable; they held out hope, however, that it would not be apocalyptic. They construed, based on news from the coastal tribes along the Puget Sound, that Governor Stevens wanted to "purchase" their land and remove them to reservations. In 1854 several Plateau tribes met to strategize how to respond to treaty overtures, according to local historian A. J. Splawn, the only Indian account to survive based on direct communications with the Yakama and their oral histories.[20] Some apparently thought if they made it clear that they would not sell their land, Governor Stevens's upcoming treaty tour would fail.[21] As evidenced in the minutes of the Walla Walla Council, others refused to accept gifts, in fear that such an exchange would constitute a purchase of their land. Others apparently figured that they might be able to influence reservation boundaries and ensure that they were at least located on ancestral land, and not on the land of rival tribes. However various their specific bargaining strategies, the Indians knew that treaties did offer them a degree of protection and that failure to come to terms could mean that they would get nothing in return for massive cessation of land.[22] Further, it must be noted that by 1855, Plateau Indian culture had already started moving toward agrarianism. Some Plateau Indians, especially headmen, owned horses and cattle; some had already started to farm and irrigate their gardens, including Kamiakin (Yakama/Palus), the headsman of the Yakama who would later lead the Plateau Indians into war. Thus, as one historian has observed, the treaty councils faced off whites and

Indians, two "parties whose capacity to draw upon a common set of assumptions about the past and future was closer than often assumed."[23]

This was the historical backdrop for Governor Stevens's treaty tour of 1855, which resulted in ten treaties with tribes on both sides of the Cascade Mountains; all were ratified by Congress in 1859. The tour set in motion the removal of Plateau tribes to reservations, a process that took more than twenty years, complicated by a series of wars and by new shifts in federal Indian policy. Under examination in this chapter are verbatim Plateau Indian speeches from four councils: Walla Walla (1855), Spokane (1855), and two other smaller councils in the Colville area (1870). The first was a treaty council; the second was called to secure the peace; and the latter two councils were summoned to take census and to canvas needs in anticipation of removal to reservations—an action declared by executive order, not negotiated by treaty. The distinction between treaty and executive order is both legal and emblematic. Legally, treaty tribes secured certain guarantees theoretically forever, whereas "executive order" tribes did not, making them more vulnerable to unilateral legislation. Emblematically, the distinction signals a paradigmatic shift in federal Indian policy during the Treaty Period, 1830–71, as reckoned by white history.

In 1830, Congress passed the Indian Removal Act, which authorized President Andrew Jackson to enter into treaties with eastern tribes to "relocate" them to reservations. The act was later generalized to all tribes and future presidents in order to accommodate western expansion. In 1871, Congress ended all treaty-making with tribes. Treaty-making implicitly takes place between independent, sovereign nations—an acknowledgment that in 1830 the fledging democratic U.S. government was willing to concede to Indian nations, but in 1871 a powerful, imperialistic U.S. government was not.[24] Although by 1855 "the fiction of negotiations between equal, consenting parties" was already breaking down, contemporary U.S. policy still dictated that the show must go on: as a nation founded on democratic principles, it was important to maintain the pretense of nation-to-nation negotiations even as American settlers, backed by the U.S. Army, made manifest its imperialist design.[25]

Walla Walla Council, 1855

The official minutes of the Walla Walla Council of 1855 are "a unique rhetorical artifact," for they transcribe verbatim the English translation of Indian speeches at what was the longest, the largest, and the most heterogeneous Indian gathering in U.S. treaty history.[26] At other councils the words of U.S. officials were commonly recorded, but Indian speeches were typically abridged, summarized, or omitted altogether. At the earlier councils with coastal tribes west of the Cascades, treaty negotiations were conducted in Chinook Jargon (not to be confused with Chinookan), a limited trade language, not the Indians' native languages, which have a much more expansive range, semantically and syntactically.[27] At the Walla Walla Council, however, several varieties of Sahaptin were employed, translated in shifts by four interpreters, at least one of whom had lived among the Indians for several years.[28] Generally the Plateau Indians came into contact with many groups who spoke different codes. Language pluralism being the norm, not the exception, the Indian speakers were well aware of the process, and the problems, of translation. At Walla Walla the Indians frequently voiced their concerns about translation at several points during the proceedings; many times they had trouble hearing what was being said. Such remarks implicitly speak to the thoroughness of the record, if not the accuracy of the translation.

Each sentence spoken by the commissioners was translated by interpreters to two Indian criers, who spoke two varieties of Sahaptin: Nez Perce and Walla Walla.[29] The criers then shouted it to about two thousand Indians sitting in a semicircle on the ground, the headmen in front.[30] The process was reversed for Indian speakers addressing the commissioners.[31] Government secretaries kept separate sets of notes, which they compared each night to produce one definitive version. This translation process, torturously slow, nonetheless lent itself well to reporting the event, giving the secretaries and other eyewitnesses ample time to record everyone's words and sometimes even gestures. Cross-references of these accounts confirms the provenance of the translated text, now preserved in a scholarly edition as *A True Copy of the Record of the Official Proceedings of the Council in the Walla Walla Valley*, the report Governor Stevens submitted to the federal superintendent of Indian affairs.

Governor Stevens did not just preside over the proceedings; he controlled them. As one historian explains: "Stevens ran the treaty sessions as if he were a judge in a court of law. Though all had the opportunity to speak, to ask questions, and to demand explanations, and though there was room for minor modifications of the treaty drafts, the end result of the council was inevitable."[32] Although the proffered treaty was templated, and the outcome of the council a foregone conclusion, as even the Indians were well aware, the official transcript of the Walla Walla Council nonetheless provides a rare glimpse of Plateau Indian oratory in the Conquest era. An analysis of the *Official Proceedings,* along with other eyewitness accounts that gloss these intercultural interactions, reveal that the Plateau Indians worked from very distinctive premises for public oratory and deliberation. An analysis of the *Official Proceedings* at Walla Walla yields the conclusion that arts of persuasion are multiple, each instance contingent on culture, history, and power.

"Speak straight," as the Indians enjoined throughout the proceedings, holds a host of meanings in Plateau Indian languages, as evident even in the recontextualized English translation. The phrase might stereotypically be understood simply as "speak truthfully." The phrase can also mean, at times, "don't speak in a roundabout way," suggesting that the Indians found the organizational pattern of the Americans' speeches unfamiliar, puzzling, or just downright suspicious—a point that I return to later in this chapter. Most commonly, "speaking straight" entails bodily presence, unmediated by another person or, at times, paper. But bodily presence alone does not ensure truthfulness. At one point Hah-hah-tsilpilp (Nez Perce) unmoors any necessary connection between presence and truthfulness: "And here where we see each other face to face we will talk straight. . . . I wonder if we shall both tell the truth to each other?"[33]

Speaking for others, especially when they are not present, always poses the problem of authorization. The Indians were constantly asking for verification that Governor Stevens's words carried weight: Was he speaking truthfully? Was he authorized to speak for the absent president of the United States? This meaning of "speaking straight" carries special import in Plateau Indian culture, given its political structure, its belief in personal autonomy, and—at bedrock—its epistemology: one knows the world through one's own personal, embodied experience. "Speaking straight" from personal experience, rather than from unknown sources, holds the most validity in Plateau Indian discourse. Although these various meanings of "speaking straight" are widely dispersed in the record at Walla Walla, the words of Stacchus (Cayuse) come closest to encapsulating them all:

> How is a chief's language? How is the Big Chief's talk? Where has their talk
> sprung from? That *they have spoken straight* on the part of all the Indians; the
> Lawyer [a Nez Perce headman] although young has spoken well for me. *Who is
> it that is going to speak straight for all of us.* Now I want the whites and the Indi-
> ans to show all their hearts. You know and we all know life while we are living,
> and I ask you my friends to *speak straight and plain* to us, as if I spoke to the
> President I say yes. *I would wish that the President was here so that we might all
> listen to him.* He would enlighten us, he would give us life, he would make
> us to live as we ought to live, we would give each other our hands to hold always.
> [Emphasis mine][34]

Not surprisingly, the discursive feature that stands out most prominently and most unequivocally is the kind of supporting evidence brought to bear in

Plateau Indian argument. The *Official Proceedings* amply demonstrates that the Indians in attendance typically argued from personal frames of reference. What may be surprising is their bluntness, given the power imbalance at Walla Walla. Their speeches were dramatic and suspenseful, achieved by verbal irony and delayed thesis, rhetorical strategies that make the point, when it comes, all the more pointed. Readings of three speeches, all quoted in full to provide complete context, illustrate some of these rhetorical commonalities, as well as some individual variation, in Plateau Indian oratory in the mid-nineteenth century.

The first is a speech by Peo-peo-mox-mox (Walla Walla), who spoke straight and with feeling, his words couched in bitter irony.[35] After General Palmer's and his own speeches over the first four days, Governor Stevens finally opened the floor on the fifth day of the treaty council, asking if the Indians would like to speak today (a Saturday) or Monday. The Nez Perce, largely Christianized, had requested that the council not meet on Sundays. Peo-peo-mox-mox answered, straight away:

> Why not speak tomorrow as well as today? We have listened to all you have to say, and we desire you should listen when any Indian speaks. It appears that Craig [the Nez Perce interpreter] knows the hearts of his people, that the whole has been prearranged in the hearts of the Indians, that he wants an answer immediately without giving them time to think, that the Indians have had nothing to say so far it would appear that we have no chief.
>
> I know the value of your speech from having experienced the same in California, having seen treaties there. We have not seen in a true light the object of your speeches, as if there was a post set between us, as if my heart cried from what you have said, as if the Almighty came down upon us here this day, as if he would say, what are you saying? Look at yourselves: your flesh is white, mine is different, mine looks poor. Our languages are different. If you would speak straight then I would think you spoke well. We have come together to speak about the earth and not of God. You were not afraid of the Devil!
>
> You see this earth that we are setting on. This country is small in all directions. Why should you fear to speak on Sunday? Should I speak to you of things that have been long ago as you have done? The whites made me do what they pleased, they told me to do this and that and I did it. They used to make our women to smoke. I suppose there they did what was right. When they told me to dance with all these nations that are here then I danced. From that time all the Indians became proud and called themselves chiefs.
>
> On another subject I have something else to say. Now how are we here as a

post? From what you have said I think you intend to win our country, or how is it to be? In one day the Americans become as numerous as the grass. This I learned in California. I know that is not right, you have spoken in a round about way. Speak straight, I have ears to hear you and here is my heart. Suppose you show me goods, shall I run up and take them? That is the way we are, we Indians, as you know us. Goods and the Earth are not equal; goods are for using on the earth. I do not know where they have given lands for goods.

We require time to think, quietly, slowly. I see Americans in all countries, it is not the country to think about, we may think about another. There is the Mission (Catholic Mission). It is right there and it is right it should be there. You have spoken in a manner partly tending to Evil. Speak plain to us. I am a poor Indian, show me charity. If there was a chief among the Nez Perses or Cayuses, if they saw evil done they would put a stop to it and all would be quiet. Such chiefs I hope Gov. Stevens and Gen'l Palmer are. I should feel very much ashamed if the Americans should do anything wrong. I had but little to say. That is all. I do not wish you to reply today. Think over what I have said.[36]

Most evident in Peo-peo-mox-mox's speech is its confrontational content delivered with high affect, ultimately arguing for postponement of the proceedings to give everyone more time to reconsider other possibilities. He opens with a direct challenge, his anger barely disguised ("Why not speak tomorrow as well as today?"). Clearly insulted, he criticizes the interpreter William Craig but is really castigating the implications of being translated. Not only is someone else speaking as if he knows another's heart, Indians are being hurried to give immediate response, as if the outcome is a foregone conclusion. But Craig is not the real target of Peo-peo-mox-mox's anger: it is Governor Stevens. Peo-peo-mox-mox's use of indirection is intentionally artful, rather than politically expedient, for he builds up to a blunt assertion just a few moments later ("you are not afraid of the Devil!"), obviously unafraid to state his views. The buildup from understated irony to a direct confrontation is dramatic and suspenseful. Too long and to ill effect, Peo-peo-mox-mox says a bit later, he has been told what to do and has done it ("The whites made me do what they pleased, they told me to do this and that and I did it. . . . When they told me to dance with all these nations that are here then I danced.").

Before drawing from his own experience, Peo-peo-mox-mox shows his deep distrust of appropriated history.[37] He openly rebukes the previous speaker, General Palmer (the superintendent of the Oregon Territory) in particular for using a five-hundred-year historical overview to back his claim that Indians and Americans cannot get along and therefore the Indians need to remove to reservations for their own safety ("Should I speak to you of things that have been long ago as you have done?"). He goes on to relate his own experience with Americans in California ("I know the value of your speech from having experienced the same in California, having seen treaties there."). Well-known to his listeners was the fact that Peo-peo-mox-mox's son Elijah had been murdered in California and his killer, an American, had never been brought to justice.[38]

Peo-peo-mox-mox continues, announcing that he is moving to another subject but actually picking up the post analogy he had introduced earlier ("On another subject I have something else to say. Now how are we here as a post?"). Once again he references his devastating personal loss in California, upbraiding his hosts for not speaking straight. He concludes this passage by appropriating a racist image of Indians as eager for gifts and then turns that image on its head by asserting that exchanging land for goods is impossible as well as unprecedented in his experience. Peo-peo-mox-mox closes with a mixed appeal. On the one hand, he seems to ask for mercy ("I am a poor Indian, show me charity"), a typical gesture toward modesty in Plateau Indian discourse, and to appeal to the Americans' better nature, reminding them of their Christianity, which they have also brought to the Indians. Counterbalancing this ostensibly submissive posture, however, is his closing reference, which can only be read as bitter sarcasm: "I should feel very much ashamed if the Americans should do anything wrong."

A second speech underscores many of these principles of persuasion, while challenging the parameters for using personal experience as support. The speaker is Tip-pee-il-lan-ah-cow-pook, or Eagle of the Light (Nez Perce), whose speech I quote in full:

Yes my friends, you see where the Sun is. He hears me. It is from beyond where the sun is that sent you here to talk.

The red people are put on this earth. A white man was sent on this earth from the Light (meaning the East). The red man was sent from the West and now the Big Chief from the Light has sent his talk here to the red people.

The President has spoken to me through you and I hear it. He likes us, he has fixed places for us to sit on and love one another. And I also like the white people as the President likes us.

On a road ready finished he has sent you here. Look at the face of the Earth; there is a road to travel on, roads up the valleys and roads on to the end of the Earth. From the time you started you found a road till this time.

You are now come to join together the white man and the red men.

And why should I hide anything? I am going now to tell you a tale. I like the President's talk. I am glad of it when I hear it here and for that reason I am going to tell you a tale.

The time the first white men ever passed through this country, although the people of this country were blind, it was their heart to be friendly to them. Although they did not know what the White people said to them they answered, yes, as if they were blind. They traveled about with the white people as if the people that said that had been lost, and those lost people said to them yes.

I have been talked to by the French and by the Americans, and one says to me to go this way, and the other says go another way, and that is the reason I am lost between them.

A long time ago they hung my brother for no offense and this I say to my brother here that he may think of it. Afterwards came Spalding and Whitman. They advised us well and taught us well, very well. It was from the same source, the Light (the East) they had pity on us and we were pitied. And Spalding sent my father to the East—the states—and he went. His body was never returned. He was sent to learn good council and friendship and many things. That is another thing to think of.

At the time, in this place here, when there was blood spilled on the ground, tho' there was blood upon the Earth we were friendly to the whites and they to us. At that time they found it out that we were friends to them. My chief, my own chief said, I will try to settle all the bad matters with the whites, and he started to look for council to straighten up matters. And there his body lies, beyond here. He has never returned.

At the time the Indians held a grand council at Fort Laramie. I was with the Flatheads and I heard there would be a council this side, next year. We were asked to go and find council, friendship, and good advice. Many of my people started and died in the country, died hunting what was right. There was a good many started there. On Green River the Small-pox killed all but one. They were going to find good council in the East. And here I am looking still for council, and to be taught what is best to be done.

And now look at my people's bodies scattered everywhere hunting for knowledge, hunting for someone to teach them to go straight.

And now I show it to you, and I want you to think of it. I am of a poor people.

A preacher came to us Mr. Spalding. He talked to us to learn, and from that he turned to be a trader, as though there was two in one, one a preacher and the other a trader. He made a farm and raised grain and bought our stock as though there was two in one: one a preacher, the other a trader.

And now from the East has spoken and I have heard it. And I do not wish another preacher to come and be both a trader and preacher in one. A piece of ground for a preacher big enough for his own use, is all that is necessary for him.

Look at that, it is the tale I had to tell you and now I am going to hunt friendship and good advice.

We will come straight here, slowly perhaps, but we will come straight.[39]

What stands out as unusual in Tip-pee-il-lan-ah-cow-pook's speech is his use of appropriated history for evidence, but notably that historical precedent only goes back two generations. He opens by agreeing with the previous speaker's assertion, granting that the red man and the white man were both put on this earth in the West and the East respectfully, and the commissioners have now come to join them together. He then says, "I am going to tell you a tale." His "tale," though, is no fictive narrative but a recounting of local history: the first contact in this part of the Pacific Northwest with the Lewis and Clark Expedition in 1805. He continues, this time placing himself in the narrative in a generic way but abruptly bringing up the execution of his brother. Just as abruptly, he moves on to recount the coming of the missionaries, Spalding and Whitman. It was Spalding who sent Tip-pee-il-lan-ah-cow-pook's father back East for talks, and "his body was never returned." The sudden insertion, without buildup, that his father never returned, alive or dead, is coupled with the ironic comment that his father learned "good counsel and friendship and many things" back East. This rhetorical tactic makes Tip-pee-il-la-ah-cow-pook's point indirectly but powerfully: the white man is not to be trusted.

He goes on to recount a second incident, using much the same rhetorical strategy and language, implicitly drawing parallels between his father's fate and his chief's ("My Chief, my own chief, said, I will try to settle all the bad matters with the whites and he started to look for counsel to straighten up matters; and there his body lies, beyond here. He has never returned."). Tip-pee-il-lan-ah-cow-pook then tells of a third incident that he can personally vouch for, having been there himself. In telling this tale, he echoes language from the other two incidents (e.g., "go and find counsel, friendship, and good advice"), closing this section of the speech with a bitterly ironic play—at least as it would read today via translation—on the word "hunting" ("Many of my people started and died in the country. Died hunting what was right. . . . And now look at my peoples' bodies scattered everywhere hunting for knowledge, hunting for someone to teach them to go straight.").

Tip-pee-il-lan-ah-cow-pook's position about the treaty approximates that of Peo-peo-mox-mox's, but less directly, asking that they proceed more slowly yet "straight." His last sentences underscore his larger argument and reiterate his opening remark and his wordplay on "hunting": "Look at that, it is the tale I had to tell you, and now I am going to hunt friendship and good advice. We will come straight here—slowly, perhaps—but we will come straight." Tip-pee-il-lan-ah-cow-pook's speech illustrates the beginnings of a discursive shift in Plateau Indian argumentation: the use of historical evidence. In this case, it is the use of relatively recent history orally transmitted secondhand or thirdhand. Conspicuously absent from Indian speeches at Walla Walla are any references to ancient oral histories or "time immemorial"—a phrase actually from the treaty that in the future becomes commonplace in Plateau Indian discourse.

Other Indian rhetors took different positions and different rhetorical tacks. For example, Lawyer (Nez Perce) argued for signing the treaty straight away. Christianized and educated by missionaries, literate in English, Lawyer took his own notes of the proceedings at Walla Walla. He was called "Lawyer" because he was well spoken, like a lawyer, according to a Nez Perce elder whom I consulted. Mountain men apparently gave him his nickname back in 1832 because of "his ability in argumentation around the campfire."[40] Aptly enough, the theme of law, if not legal discourse itself, runs through Lawyer's speech. Also evident are many features of Plateau Indian rhetoric: the recursiveness, the main point delayed until the end, the modesty ("we are a poor people"). As with Peo-peo-mox-mox and Tip-pee-il-lan-ah-cow-pook, it is hard to tell exactly where Lawyer is going with his argument; unlike them, however, he uses appropriated history to front, rather than back, his later claims—a history dating back to the Spaniards and Columbus, roughly approximating the version told by General Palmer earlier in the proceedings. Lawyer then returns to his roots, recounting what he knows from his forefathers' experience: the advent of the Lewis and Clark expedition. With the third paragraph, Lawyer explicitly pulls the two accounts together, a rhetorical move emblematic of his multiacculturation: "From the time of Columbus and from the time of Lewis and Clark we have known our friends." Only at the end of his speech does he make his case for the reservation boundaries and other specifics he wants to see in the treaty. Here is Lawyer's speech in full:

My friends, you have been speaking to me a poor people. This Earth is known as far as it extends. This earth has red people on it and it has had as far as it extends. The people are lost. They don't think whose talk has come to us poor people. On the other side of the big water there is a large country. We also know that towards the east there are a great many different kinds of people. There are red people and yellow people, and black people. And a long time ago the people that travelled this country passed on the waters. And there is that country on that other side of the big water. And here is this on this side. On the other side of the big waters they have their laws. Yes! they have their laws there. We now hear the laws they have there. And we now know they have those laws there. We also know the white people pass about in the waters as they wish to. I do not know what they find in travelling about on those waters or what they are hunting, whether it is timber, leaves, grass, or what. It was the Spaniards in that direction that first travelled about in their ships. They were the ones who first discovered this country and it was in that way they travelled to look for things. In that way they travelled when they found this country. The red people that along the shores to the big waters, those were the people, and at this place they landed to see those poor people. At that place the red man started and ran off, or a part of them did because they did not know the people who came to see them, and the rest came and met them. There is where the white people first placed their children, when they first came into the land. From this country they took back samples of rich earth, of flowers, and all such things. They also reported that there was a country on the other side, and it was peopled and these people reported they had found a country. And it was known that there was a new country found. And one of the head men said I knew there was a country there before. Columbus the discoverer said can you make an egg stand on end. Although he tried he could not do it. He did not understand how. It fell over. Then Columbus showed them all that he could make it stand and he did it. He made the egg stand. After they saw it done they could all do it.

Those children that he had placed in this country among the Red people from them the blood ran on both sides. That is when the laws came into the country to these poor people. There were a great many white people came back to that place. That is the reason the red people travelled off further, and from that they kept still travelling on further as the white people came up to them. And this man's (Delaware Jim) people are from the same people. They have come till they are here to us now. And from that country, some central part, came Lewis and Clark. And that is the way the white people travelled and came in here to my fore-fathers. Where they came into our country they named that stream Koos-koos-ki, it was then they knew us poor people. They passed through our country and knew all our country, and all our streams, and on their return my fore-fathers used them well. As well as they could.

From the time of Columbus and from the time of Lewis and Clark we have known our friends. We poor people have known you as brothers although we were a poor people, a people knowing nothing when we first saw the white chiefs Lewis and Clark. From these poor people there were some of them that started in that direction (east) and of these there is only one now living (Spokane Garry). They went to be taught. They returned after they could see a little and told us about the Great Spirit. They told us the laws for the poor people. They had seen and heard them. My chief said our old laws are poor. The new laws we are getting are good laws, are straight. He said there were three laws. The laws of the Commandments, our old laws, the laws of our forefathers, and the new laws we are getting showen to us and when the French and American traders first came to us they told us there were laws and those laws would be sent to us.

Ellis our chief spoke strait for the white people. The President has sent you here to us poor people. Yes! The President has studied this and sent you here for our good. That is the reason I said on Monday, use well my chief, we are a poor people.

The governor has said the President has sent him to take care of his children. It was you that had spoken thus my brothers (Gov. Stevens and Gen. Palmer). I want the President to see what I, a poor man, has said. I have got your talk here (pointing to his note book) and although a poor man I can look at it from time to time. I can take care of that. My brother, we have been talking a long time and are all tired.

I think on the stream just below where Mr. Craig lives, will be a good place for one mechanic, or on one of the lands you have shown me. I also think that perhaps in the country where I live may be good places for some more of them. In case there were crowded below it would be a good place where I live.

Now my friends I have spoken. Those things that have been talked of, you know. I have shown you my heart. You have said to them all you had to say. I have also given you all I had to say.

There, my friends, I have spoken. Those things that have been talked of you know. I have shown you my heart. You have said to them you have said all you have to say. I also have said also all I have to say.

You spoke of a road through my country (the reserve). It is a bad country to make roads in, but perhaps it may go through. That is the reason I think we have both talked, 'tis all our talk. Our Father Chief has said take care of one another. There is no reason that I should speak long although I have more to say. That is the reason I say take care of us well. That is all I have to say at this time my bretheren. I will have one word more to say when we are about to part.[41]

Toward the end of this speech, Lawyer refers to his taking notes of the proceedings, coupled with his desire for the president to "see" what he has said: "I want the President to see what I, a poor man, has said. I have got your talk here (pointing to his note book)." His attitude toward literacy presages the rapid uptake of literacy on the Plateau after the Treaty Period (further discussed in chapter 4), and for much the same reason: to hold the U.S. government to its word, as written down in the treaty. While Indian culture is generally imagined as oral as opposed to written, the case of Lawyer demonstrates the easy coexistence of the two modalities. Also, Lawyer's last rhetorical move turns to practicalities very abruptly: where the promised mechanic as well as others, including himself, should live on the new reservation. Lawyer's delayed thesis remains unstated but nonetheless clear: his support of the treaty and the boundaries for a Nez Perce reservation, boundaries that would later change without notice to just a fraction of the land as laid out at Walla Walla.

The outcomes of the Walla Walla Council were not just shaped by asymmetrical power relations between the United States and the Indian nations. They were also informed by tribal politics, marked by multiple internal divisions based on race (red versus white), tribalism (tribe versus tribe), and intratribal hierarchy (clan versus clan), not to mention the complication of personal motives. The *Official Proceedings* bears witness to the whole gamut of positions among the Indians, from Lawyer, who accepted the treaty and sought the best terms possible; to Tip-pee-il-lan-ah-cow-pook and Peo-peo-mox-mox, who asked for more time to deliberate; and others, like Young Chief (Cayuse), who asked for a fair price paid up front. And then there were those like Kamiakin (Yakama/Palus), the famous headman whose contemporaries described him as the most eloquent orator of his day, who sat silent for several days during public deliberations. When Kamiakin did speak publicly, he spoke briefly to say he was tired and wanted to go home; after putting his X mark on the treaty, he did just that, not to retire but to resist, evacuating his family and marshaling a confederated response to white invasion: the Plateau Indian War of 1855–58 that ignited just four months after Walla Walla.

Spokane Council, 1855

By the time Governor Stevens met with a portion of the northern Plateau tribes in December 1855, the Yakima War (also known today as the Plateau Indian War of 1855–58) had already broken out and threatened to spread across the Plateau.[42] The killing of a federal Indian agent by a young Yakama triggered the war, but it was already in the making at the Walla Walla Council back in June, where the Yakama lost 90 percent of their ancestral land and were confined to a reservation.

With the threat of a widening war on his mind, Governor Stevens had a different agenda at the Spokane Council, seeking instead guarantees that the tribes assembled—the Spokan, Colville, Okanagan, Coeur d'Alene, among others—would not join the Yakama war effort.[43] Although the ensuing "treaty council" did not in fact result in treaties at this time, Governor Stevens did succeed in securing the peace. The record of this council, including verbatim Indian speeches as they were translated in English from Interior Salish, appears in the journal of Stevens's secretary and aide, James Doty, who also had served as one of the scribes at Walla Walla. The scholarly edition of Doty's *Journal of Operations of Governor Isaac Ingalls Stevens of Washington Territory in 1855* serves as the source for this discussion. Although the provenance of the *Journal of Operations,* clearly written in Doty's hand, is well established, his contextual and editorial comment must be taken as biased as Stevens's own official reports.[44] Both Governor Stevens and Doty were well aware that their reports would be preserved and read by their superiors, and therefore they would naturally want to present themselves and their actions in the best light possible.[45]

Just as the council was to begin, news arrived that Kamiakin, the Yakama headsman, had been defeated and was in full retreat just a hundred miles away.[46] Even so, Governor Stevens rightly concluded that this was no time to talk about land cessation, focusing his opening speech instead on tamping down fears stirred up by Indian reports of the Walla Walla Council. He assured them that they would not have to sell their land or else soldiers would take it from them, as rumored after Walla Walla. Stevens went on to say that he did think it best that they sell a portion of their land and live on reservations, but they were not required to. His job, Governor Stevens maintained, was to protect them and their land; in return, he sought their assurance they would not join Kamiakin's forces (46).

The Indian response at the Spokane Council confirms the rhetorical propensity, evident at Walla Walla, to rely on personal experience for support, and if not one's own experiences, then the experiences of others that one knows and trusts. The Spokane Council, however, fleshes out that principle, highlighting the importance of oral transmission in Plateau Indian culture. Several speakers mention what they heard about the Walla Walla Council, or more specifically, about Governor Stevens's haughty manner, which they directly attribute to the cause of the war. In his speech Quin-quim-moe-so (whose tribal affiliation is not noted, the record only indicating he is "a Chief who lives at Walker & Ells old Mission") (58) says that his people had already heard his views on the events at Walla Walla, which he formed when he heard the news in the summer. Thus Quin-quim-moe-so takes care in establishing the provenance of the views he is about to re-espouse. This attention to attribution is a signature move in Plateau Indian rhetoric. Coupled with Quin-quim-moe-so's confrontational stance is his pacifist position:

> I will not hide my mind. All my people heard me this summer, when I heard, Governor, what you had said at the Walla Walla Council Ground. I thought you had done well. Though when you were through speaking, one thing you said was not right. You alone arranged the Indians land. The Indians did not speak. Then you struck the Indians to the heart. You thought they were only Indians, that is why you did it. I am not a big Chief, but I will not hide my mind. I will not talk low. I wish you to hear what I am saying.
>
> The Indians have a long time been a poor people, a long time ago they thought not of evil, the Americans are the causes of the Indians hearts being that way.
>
> That is the reason Governor, it is all your fault the Indians are at War. It is your fault because you have said that the Cayuse and Walla Wallas will be moved to the Yakima's land. They who owned the land did not speak, and yet you divided their land.
>
> And after that I heard that, for the Spokanes you would move us to the Nez Perces' land.
>
> When we received that news we all spoke—all my people, and I told them I would not move from my land. I would not travel through a country that does not belong to me.
>
> Now I am speaking out my mind. I do not feel well towards those Indians who are at war. My heart commenced to be sore. Now when the war commenced I was thinking how would the Governor arrange that? I don't hide my heart. Why do you wish to know my heart. It is well arranged. It is you Governor who should take care of me, and I am good towards you. My heart is not hard if you treat me well.
>
> This is my heart. I know not the hearts of those who are in trouble. I know only my own mind.[47]

Privileging experiential evidence, Quin-quim-moe-so refers to preconquest history only in the most general of terms (e.g., "The Indians have a long time been a poor people, a long time ago they thought not of evil, the Americans are the causes of the Indians hearts being that way."). He mentions it only to lay blame on the Americans for corrupting the Indians. More commonly, "history" is a matter of personal recollection, as Spokan Garry (Spokan) indicates in an earlier speech: "From the time of my first recollection, no blood has ever been upon the hands of my people" (48). In the following speech excerpt from the Spokane Council, Sho-homish (Sans Poile/Spokan) states explicitly that he does not know his forefathers, only his father, and possibly his grandfather, although what he knows about his grandfather may have only come secondhand from his father (the text is unclear on that point):

> *It is a long time since I was born. I do not know my forefathers.* Since I remember my Father knew nothing about war. He talked well of all the nations always, and that is what I am thinking we have to do, to do well in this world. . . .
>
> *I was yet young when the French came into my country,* when I saw them I put them in my heart and loved them. Since that my heart has always been the same.
>
> I saw you not, but now that I have seen you, the words you spoke are the same as if I had seen you then.
>
> *My Grandfather* never was an enemy to the Whites. When I saw the Governor I was glad in my heart. What I am saying Governor is only to show you my heart and then I will stop. [Emphasis mine][48]

Quin-quim-moe-so's speech keeps faith with other rhetorical trends at Walla Walla. He makes appropriate gestures toward modesty, just before immodestly reasserting one's pride (e.g., "I am not a big Chief, but I will not hide my mind. I will not talk low."). Furthermore, he castigates the governor for not allowing the Indians to draw up their own reservation lines, in effect, speaking for the Indians—an unconscionable breach of tribal and personal autonomy so highly valued in Plateau Indian culture ("You alone arranged the Indians land. The Indians did not speak."). Interestingly, Quin-quim-moe-so complicates that notion, using the communal "we" to refer to his tribe, but quickly differentiates his own position from that "we": "When we received that news we all spoke—all my people, and I told them I would not move from my land. I would not travel through a country that does not belong to me" (59). Other rhetors make the same move: they are apparently authorized to speak for the tribe, referring to "we" but then distinguishing what "I" believe or will do. Take the example of Peter John (Colville), who said: "But even if my people should take up arms against the Americans, I myself would not" (56). On the other hand, Ky-y-sells-bee (his tribe is not indicated) speaks for his tribe, as well as for himself, their views apparently in agreement: "It is not true that our hearts are Indian hearts. I know what the Governor has said to us, he wants to know our hearts,—my heart" (60).[49]

Such moves were conspicuously absent at the earlier council at Walla Walla for both political and cultural reasons. The headmen in attendance at Walla Walla were not authorized to speak for their people, since they had not consulted with them beforehand to render an official opinion on the proposed treaty. In fact, most of them begged for time to confer with their people before signing a treaty. Further, the clan—not the tribe—was the main unit of government, and choosing a "chief" over several clans that might constitute a "tribe," then as now, was fraught with political conflict. Positions of power were not ascribed through birth so often as they were achieved through oratory, military prowess, economic wealth, and the like. Governor Stevens, however, did not take these constraints into consideration, either through ignorance or arrogance, designating "chiefs" at Walla Walla to speak and sign for their tribes. This cross-cultural misunderstanding about "chiefs" in part explains why one chief (unnamed; presumably Coeur d'Alene) speaks for all the other (clan) chiefs from his tribe: he has been preauthorized to do so. This chief says:

> A long time we have not known our hearts. Now we see each other here altogether. Today our hearts shall meet. I believe we will not be bad now. *Today I will say what all the Chiefs have in their hearts.*
>
> I think the hearts of the Coeur d'Alene a little sore. Why have they such minds, is it to be enemies of the Americans? Do they think to be enemies of the Whites? I think not. [Emphasis mine][50]

The Coeur d'Alene chief goes on to reference the long memory of Indians, although in fact his historical account dates only from his own boyhood: "What you have told the Indians they will not forget. There is one thing I wish to explain. Since I was a boy, they was always, fighting here" (53). He goes on to give his own gloss on the current conflict:

> When the Chiefs stopped quarreling, the country became quiet. Why is the country in difficulty again? That comes on account of the Small Pox brought into the country, and is all the time on the Indian hearts. The reason the Indians have that on their hearts, is because the Whites brought the Small Pox into the Country. The Indians were afraid of that. They would keep thinking the Whites had brought the Small Pox into the country. The Indians were afraid of that. They would keep thinking the Whites had brought sickness into their country to kill them. That is what has hurt the hearts of the Yakimas. That is what we think has brought this difficulty between the Indians and the Whites.[51]

The chief's argument is unique among others proffered that day: fear of disease, which another wave of settlers will surely bring, is the reason for the war. This kind of originality is highly valued in Plateau Indian rhetoric, in that it offers a unique idea to the total conversation while personalizing one's own argument. The Coeur d'Alene chief then abruptly accuses the governor of talking "a little too hard" at Walla Walla, faulting not only the plan to move the Coeur d'Alenes and Spokans to Nez Perce country but also the governor's manner. The chief goes on to say that when his tribe heard about these things, they decided that they would die on their land if anyone tried to move them. But, unexpectedly, the chief gives the governor the benefit of the doubt, offering him an opportunity to correct this information directly to the Indians in attendance right now. He concludes with a statement that might read as a contradiction to his earlier veiled threat to fight the removal process, reaffirming his tribe's pacifism: "I do not think I shall be an enemy to the Whites: What I am saying is, that I cannot yet see into your hearts. I don't think we shall ever have war" (53). Thus the chief eventually answers the central question before the Spokane Council: Will the northeastern tribes support or remain neutral in the Yakima War? But his answer is equivocal (a bargaining gambit in negotiation discourse generally), and the audience has to wait for it.

Throughout the Spokane Council, speech after speech worked from the same rhetorical principles, with one notable exception: the two major speeches of Spokan Garry. Like Lawyer at Walla Walla, Garry was Americanized, but unlike Lawyer he was not an American sympathizer, although he did promote peaceful relations.[52] In 1825 the Hudson Bay's Company sent Garry and another boy, with their families' permission, to a missionary school in British Columbia, where Garry learned to speak and write both English and French. When he returned to his home after five years, Garry founded a church and a school. He was instrumental in getting a Nez Perce delegation to travel to Saint Louis in 1831 to solicit the first Protestant missionaries for the New Northwest. Garry continued to advocate for schooling (he co-authored the first Spokan primer in 1842) as well as for a separate Spokane reservation for forty years.[53] His early activism earned him the reputation of a troublemaker among many whites, some of whom sought to discredit him. According to one contemporary sub-Indian agent named William Parkhurst Winans (whose field journal figures prominently later in this chapter), Garry was "educated, but by not using what was taught him, has forgotten to read and write, but his recollections of the bad habits of Whites is better than his Knowledge of books (perhaps it is because he has so many living examples before him) which he sometimes illustrates by getting drunk. He speaks English brokenly, is cunning suspicious and disposed to see his side of the question."[54]

Even in 1855, Garry was well aware of his growing negative reputation with whites, as he noted in one of his speeches at the Spokane Council: "The Indians and French about here are always telling the Whites lies, about Garry. *Now* I will speak for myself."[55] Multiacculturation enabled him to appropriate major features of Euro-American oratory, but he used them to argue for the Indian side. Again, Garry seemed well aware of cultural differences in communication and not just language differences, as quoted at the opening of this chapter. Although he was familiar with American ways of arguing, he had by no means mastered those practices. For example, numbering the points of their arguments and refutations is something that the U.S. commissioners did regularly in their speeches at Walla Walla. Garry apparently noticed this tendency, for in his first speech at the Spokane Council he references the "things" that Governor Stevens offered the Indians: "[At Walla Walla] You spoke on nine different things during three days and I was looking on what you spoke. When you had spoken on these nine different things, then you asked the Chiefs to speak" (49). Much later in the same speech, Garry refers to this list again, this time giving some indication of what "things" he is referring to: "After you had spoken of those nine different things, as schools and farms and shops, if you had then asked the Chiefs to mark out a piece of land—a pretty large piece—to give you, it would not have struck the Indians so to the heart" (50). Counting points, or things, or days, and using that counting as an organizing principle is conspicuously absent in early Indian speeches, up until 1870.

In his second speech at the Spokane Council, Garry seems to refute Indians' frequent assertion that they are "poor"—a standard rhetorical gesture in Plateau Indian discourse that honors the self-effacing modesty so valued in Plateau Indian culture, as if to counter how such gestures might be misread by Euro-Americans as pathetic and humiliating. Both of Garry's major speeches at Spokane bear witness of multicultural knowledge of rhetorical conventions, although familiar Plateau Indian discourse patterns—and values—clearly dominate. In the first half of his second speech, Garry revisits the recurring topics of "poor" Indians and skin color—and the constructed connection between the two:

> Governor, see the difference there is between these Indians and you. See how everybody is red and you are White. *The Indians think they are not poor.* When you look at yourself, you see you are white. You see the Indian is red, what do you think? *Do you think they are poor when you look at them that way?* When you look at those Red men, you think you have more heart, more sense than those poor Indians. I think the difference between us and you Americans is in the Clothing; the blood and body are the same.
>
> Do you think because your mother was white, and theirs black that you are

higher or better? We are black, yet if we cut ourselves, the blood will be red—and so with the Whites it is the same, though their skin is white. *I do not think we are poor, because we belong to another nation.* I am of another nation, when I speak you do not understand me. When you speak, I do not understand you.

To-day, Governor, we meet together. You say you want to know my heart, and that is the reason I am talking.

Since we have been speaking, it is as if we had been talking for nothing. Now you take those Indians here for Chiefs. Do you think it? If you believe what they say, it is all right. If you take those Indians for men, treat them so now. *The Indians are proud, they are not poor.* If you talk truth to the Indians to make a peace, the Indians will do the same to you.

You see now the Indians are proud. [Emphasis mine][56]

In the second half of his speech, Garry blames the governor's haughty remarks at Walla Walla for causing the current bloody conflict, his words adding insult to previous and current injuries, including reservation boundaries and removal policies without Indian consultation. He continues:

On account of one of your remarks some of your people have already fallen on the ground.

The Indians are not satisfied with the land you gave them.

What commenced the trouble was the murder of Pee-opee-mox-a-mox's son, and Dr. Whitman, and now *they find their Reservations too small.*

If all those Indians had marked out their own Reservation, this trouble would not have happened. I am thinking always of that. No doubt your White people are thinking the same. We are down-hearted and you are.

Governor you want to know all the Indians hearts, we are going to tell the truth on each side.

You want to know the hearts of the Indians and they want to know yours. We want you to take the Indians for Indians, and not hide your mind from them. If your heart is true, show it to the Indians and all will be right. I am showing my heart that you may see it.

Now the Indians are in trouble. *If you could get their reservations made a little larger, they would be pleased—this is my mind,* but perhaps it is too late to do it.

For myself I am an Indian. If I had the business to do I could fix it by giving them a little more land.

Talking about land I am only telling you my mind.

What I was saying yesterday about not crossing the soldiers to this side of the Columbia, is my business. Those Indians have gone to war, and I don't know myself how to fix it up again. That is your business.

Since, Governor, the beginning of the world, there has been war. Why cannot you manage to keep peace? Maybe there will be no peace ever. Even if you should hang all the bad people, war would begin again, and would never stop. [Emphasis mine][57]

Evident here are the signature moves of Plateau Indian rhetoric: the organizational suspense and experiential supporting evidence (i.e., the murder of Peo-peo-mox-mox's son and the so-called Whitman Massacre, by white history's reckoning, in 1847). And like the Coeur d'Alene chief before him, Garry only indirectly answers the governor's peace overture in a subtle bargaining gambit backed with hinted threat. Garry argues that the war started because the reservation lines were drawn too small and by the Americans, not the Indians, their autonomy thus disrespected. But if the reservations were "a little larger," war might still be averted. His closing remarks, however, do not sound promising. The reference "the beginning of time" actually sounds more Euro-American and Christian than Indian, a rhetorical flourish common in appropriated historical accounts of General Palmer and Lawyer (the Nez Perce chief) at Walla Walla. This particular flourish recurs in Plateau Indian argumentative discourse hereafter.

After Garry's second speech, Governor Stevens comprehensively refuted the arguments raised by the Indians and defended both his words and his deeds at Walla Walla. Called upon specifically to respond, Garry replies: "All these things we have been speaking of had better be tied together as they are, like a bundle of sticks" (65). Exactly what Garry meant then is impossible to ascertain now, across languages, across time. But his analogy might serve modern readers as emblematic of culturally marked organizational patterns evident in 1855: Americans, building their ideas point by point, like "sticks"; the Indians, presenting their points in "bundles," arranging their ideas associatively and recursively.

Colville Councils, 1870

Fifteen years later, and on another part of the Plateau, point-by-point argumentation appears in at least one Indian speech but with a twist characteristic of Plateau Indian rhetoric. Under discussion here are the verbatim Indian speeches recorded in the field journal of a sub-Indian agent, William Parkhurst Winans, during two tribal councils on a single trip in 1870 through the northern Plateau in what is now the Colville Reservation. Winans proved to be no friend to the Indians. The Colville Reservation was established in 1872 by executive order, but within a month a second executive order was issued, and the fertile river valley was lost. The Indians were thereafter confined to the dry highlands that white settlers had found unsuitable for farming.[58] It was Winans who convinced President Ulysses S. Grant to redraw those boundaries that confined the Colville to largely inarable land.

In 1870, Winans had been dispatched by Colonel Samuel Ross, superintendent of Indian affairs, to collect census data—to include both Indians and livestock—and to take requests for religious, school, and trade instructions as well as equipment, in anticipation of the executive order requiring removal to the reservation. This kind of council agenda would normally warrant only paraphrased notes in an agent's field journal to document his progress, which he would then use in his report to the superintendent. That was not the case for these three councils, however, because the Indians themselves insisted that their words be transcribed. They apparently understood well the legal force of written records, trusting that modality more than oral transmission. Winans explained this preference in his report to Superintendent Ross upon completion of the trip: "The Indians complained to me at Council that the Supt never heard what they had formerly said to the Agents, and requested me to take down their speeches in writing and forward them to you, in compliance with their request I enclose the speeches of Qua-tal-ikun, Wilson, Moses, To-nas-kut and Wee-ah-pe kun."[59]

Winans's list is indicative rather than inclusive, with mention of at least one Indian from each of the three councils; in fact, he recorded the speeches of far more Indians than these. Most of the speeches, but not all, are written in Winans's hand. This fact suggests that the other scribes in attendance took turns writing and resting, as would be necessary for real-time minute-taking, and Winans then transcribed their notes into his journal. Furthermore, the speeches from the three councils of 1870 are robust and rich in stylistic and content differences; in contrast, the speeches in a fourth council (not discussed here) the following summer are comparatively short and stylistically similar, indicating they are summary notes rather than verbatim speeches. Thus both external and internal evidence strongly support the provenance of the record for the two 1870 councils now under discussion.

At the first council Winans opened with the same questions that he would ask at the subsequent councils. His questions were immediately reiterated and responded to by Qua-tal-i-kun (Mid-Columbia), also known as Half Sun or Chief Moses.[60] In an uncharacteristically direct move in Plateau Indian rhetoric, Qua-tal-i-kun opens with those three questions to overtly map his speech, as Americans were wont to do, but he does so in reverse order, saving the unexpected point for last, as Indians were wont to do. Like Spokan Garry, Qua-tal-i-kun had been sent by his family to a missionary school as a child, where he learned English, but he refused to use the language for the rest of his life; even though he was a polyglot, he generally spoke in a Yakama language, which was then translated into English.[61] In the speech below, Qua-tal-i-kun appropriates the white man's rhetorical tools but adapts them to keep faith with traditional ways with words, as his defiant message, sardonic tone, and delayed climax vividly illustrate:

> I am a child in Knowledge to have listened to what you have said. There *are three things you have spoken of First you want our numbers; Second, you desire to Know if we have any religious instruction or wish to have any; and Third you want to know what our wants or wishes are.—The first I understand; the second I partly understand; but the third I don't understand at all.* I don't understand why you want to know what we wish or what we desire, do you think we will accept anything from the Government? The Agent at Colville has had Potlatches and sent us word to come and get blankets, Calico and shoes, but we never have gone, or have we accepted or received anything from the Government, and we never will, we have plenty to supply our wants, we have Horses and Cattle and when we need anything we have money to buy it. Is it out of pity that the Superintendent desires to know of us so that he can help us? We need no pity, all we desire is to be let alone, we don't want the assistance of any one, we want to live just as we are, not desiring to have our mode of living changed at all, or be interfered with, our land is a grazing land, not suitable for White Men, they want farming land, therefore I don't fear them settling on it.—*As to the Second* we have no Religious Instructor we desire one, we would like to have a Protestant Clergyman sent among us, religious instruction is of more importance than all things else, we live but a day here, but our life hereafter is for ever, therefore we should have instruction for the longest life first, after that we can see to the comfort of our bodies. We have always been friendly to the Whites, even when the Spokanes and other Tribes around me were fighting the Whites I Kept my men at home, forbidding them to go near any of the War parties under pain of punishment, you see by this I've always been friendly and I always desire to be so. *As to giving the Superintendent our numbers* that is not necessary, we are already numbered, the Chief of us all God has numbered us and no man shall number us. I have spoken. [Emphasis mine][62]

Qua-tal-i-kun is careful to establish that the Indians have never accepted from the government anything of monetary value, implicitly making clear that their land has not been "purchased" nor are Indians "poor." He goes on to point out that they have always been pacifist, which ties into his last point and common appeal to Christian and Indian values, concluding that all have been numbered by "the Chief of us all": God. Qua-tal-i-kun, of course, was not the only one to use Christian discourse. According to Winans's field journal, at least one Indian, known as Swah-mous or Cultus Jim (Methow), said a short prayer in English, although he later spoke in Indian.[63] In another instance, Wilson (his tribe is not noted), whom Winans describes as "a self-constituted [Protestant] preacher" and "the only one of his tribe who wants to improve his condition" (19), says that for "placing my life in danger to save the three White Men, I desire three things—viz a Preacher, a Doctor, and a Teacher and any other assistance that the Superintendent may think will better the condition of the people around me."[64]

At the third and final council on Winans's tour in the summer of 1870, largely attended by the Okanagan, Winans delivered much the same speech as he had at the other councils, only adding the admonition that the young men should obey their chiefs and the elder men should punish those who do not. (Winans then appointed seven elders to do just that.) His specific question asking if his audience wanted teachers and preachers elicited the response quoted in full below (also excerpted in this book's introduction). Using high affect and arguing-with-story, including hypothetical direct quotations, Wee-ah-pe-kum or Kis-a-wee-likh (Okanagan) recursively addresses Winans's question by cataloging the many evil things that whites have already taught Indians. Also evident is the speaker's Christianity, the common ground upon which he makes his appeal to his white audience. Right at the end of the speech, Wee-ah-pe-kum answers the question directly, requesting religious instruction as well as farm implements. He closes with a figure that may have been drawn from either Christian or Indian religious thought. And throughout, Wee-ah-pe-kum argues from a history of the Conquest that he himself has witnessed and experienced:

> Before we saw the Whites we only Knew our Fathers and listened to them because we had no other to look up to. When the Whites came among us we could not keep our children together, they would follow the White Man's example and from them they learnt wrong. The very Indian Boys that work for the Whites are the one's that steal from them and bring us all into trouble. Those young men learn the values of money and being the White Man's adopted Children they learn to murder and rob. They don't respect their Chiefs. I am pleased to hear you say the Chiefs must be obeyed.
>
> When you see my Boy working for the Whites ask him "Did your Father send you"? if he says no, send him home; for, when he comes home at night I will say

to him "My son I am thirsty, go and get me some water to drink," and he turns around and says "You God damned Indian how much will you give me"; or if you see my daughter prostituting herself for money, ask her, "Did your Father send you to earn money in this manner?," then, take a whip and drive her home, for when she comes back, her Mother will tell her to get some wood to cook her Father's supper, she will turn around and say, "You damned old Bitch pay me for my trouble." All this they have learned from the Whites. When the Whites come to our camp the first thing they do is to steal our Wives and Daughters, and when I tell them to go away, and ask my Wife and Daughter to stay with me the Whites abuse, threaten and God damn me, and take my Daughter to prostitute her to their passions, when I follow their example and do the same to my fellow Indian, I get into trouble, I get my head broken, and punished by my Chiefs, you don't punish the White Man for the same conduct I'm guilty of, I get punished for doing what they taught me.

You tell us to stop drinking and not to get drunk; the White Man makes and gives us Whiskey and then takes our Women from us; the Indians are poor and ignorant but they don't deserve such treatment from the Whites. If they want to better our condition let them stop bringing Whiskey in our Country.

You are the only Agent that has ever assembled our people together and spoke to them for their good. You have given us good advice and tell us to adopt the habits of the Whites; when we see them drinking and get drunk we follow your advice by doing the same as they do, you must send better white men as teachers than those who live around us now, if you want to better our condition by adopting their habits. If you find any of your people running off our Wives and Daughters, take them and put them in jail. The same God made us both, and if a White man does wrong he should be punished as well as the Red Man, for God is just, he does not regard color. I dig roots and catch fish, God so willed it, If I do wrong, kill someone, and am hung for it, it is God's will. You say you are sent by the Superintendent to learn about us to help us for our good. I'm glad, I will do all things to help the condition of my people. If you say that hanging me will better the conditions of my people I will be satisfied to die. We have but one God, for all men, you and I will appear before the same judge, therefore I want religious teachers sent among us, we want all the help we can get to be wiser and better here, and prepare ourselves for that long life that is to come. We want to be more comfortable and happy and would like to be assisted with agricultural Implements, and instructed how to use them. Some are fearful about their land. I do not fear of being driven out of my land if I do right, but I do wrong I will fear.

This land is but a Camp, we stay for a night for all die, and reach their destination. I have spoken.[65]

Cross-Cultural Miscommunication

How were speeches on both sides perceived? The sardonic and defiant tone of the Indian speeches, as dramatically exemplified by Wee-ah-pe-kum's speech, apparently did break through the language barrier. Contemporary eyewitness accounts evaluated the proceedings as "stormy," "philippic," "bold and frank."[66] Both Indians and whites faulted each other for speaking in a roundabout way, as Peo-peo-mox-mox complained of Governor Stevens, who purposefully did not come to the point quickly at Walla Walla in order to ease tensions, opening with niceties and then offering a long historical overview of white-Indian relations.[67] Interestingly, white commentaries faulted the Indians' speeches for the same reason. One wrote that Indians "spoke only in a general manner."[68] Another wrote that the Indians' speeches had "too much repetition to [record] them fully, but a few extracts may show the manner in which these wearisome meetings were conducted day after day."[69] And the stereotype of the poetic, laconic Indian was certainly disrupted for General O. O. Howard, who complained twenty-two years later at another council:

> Toolhoolhoolzote, the cross-grained growler . . . had the usual long preliminary discussion about the earth being his mother, that she should not be disturbed by hoe or plough, that men should subsist on what grows of itself, etc., etc. He railed against the violence that would separate Indians from lands that were theirs by inheritance. . . .
>
> He was answered: "We do not wish to interfere with your religion, but you must talk about practicable things. Twenty times over you repeat that the earth is your mother. . . . Let us hear it no more, but come to business at once."[70]

In fact, the Indians were far less verbose by comparison. According to the *Official Proceedings* and eyewitness accounts, Governor Stevens spoke for three to four hours at a time. Clearly at odds were cross-cultural differences in what counts as appropriate, effective, convincing argument and persuasion. But at stake were more than just simple misunderstandings. Because of the white-Indian power differential, misreading Indian discourse too often typecasts Indians as mentally slow, emotionally stoic, or nobly laconic or poetic or silent. Whether overtly racist or romantic (the latter, actually, is just another form of racism), such reductions allow whites to see Indians as less than human, making it easier to take paternalistic, illegal, or violent actions against them, then as today.

Just how short a distance it is between paternalism and violence is illustrated by the fates of some of the signatories at Walla Walla. Four months after the treaty was signed, Indian Agent Bolon was killed in September 1855, by the twenty-year-old nephew of Kamiakin, and ten days later the U.S. military invaded the southern Plateau, triggering the Yakima War, also known as the Plateau Indian War of 1855–58.[71] In December 1855, under a flag of truce, Peo-peo-mox-mox was taken prisoner and then given an ultimatum to die or surrender. He surrendered. Two days later, Peo-peo-mox-mox supposedly tried to escape and then was shot at point-blank range by Oregon volunteers who encircled him. They flayed and dismembered him, cutting off his limbs and hands and tearing out his eyes; they made his skull into buttons and preserved his ears in a bottle of whiskey and sent them back to Salem as trophies.[72]

Owhi and his son Qualchin (Yakama) suffered similar fates under flags of truce: Owhi was shot in the head at point-blank range after he escaped and was recaptured; Qualchin was slowly hanged within fifteen minutes of his arrival in Colonel Wright's camp.[73] Kamiakin survived and lived out his life as an impoverished fugitive. Late in life, when Winans offered him blankets as gifts from the U.S. government, "he extended his arm to show his ragged shirt sleeves and said, 'You can see I am a poor man, but I will never accept anything from an American.'"[74] Kamiakin died in 1877. His grave was desecrated and his remains later mutilated by anthropologists.[75] Spokan Garry also died impoverished, his farm stolen by white settlers. In March 1856, Governor Stevens fired his trusty secretary, James Doty, for being drunk and derelict of duty, and in June, Doty committed suicide out of remorse for having let him down.[76] Stevens did not live to see his dream of a northern railroad route, which was later commissioned by Congress; he died in 1862 in the Civil War.[77]

But the treaties as well as the proceedings of the councils under discussion here did provide a pyrrhic victory for the Indians, only realized more than a century later. It is often said that Indian culture is past-oriented, looking backward to tradition, while Euro-American culture is future-oriented, progressively looking forward. The archival records give the lie to this cliché. If anything, it was the Indians, not the Euro-Americans, who were future-oriented, keenly aware of how their actions on these fateful days might affect future generations. Stevens, on the other hand, failed to fully realize the implications of his words, preserved in the *Official Proceedings* as well as in treaty language. "You will not be called according to the paper to move on the reservation for two or three years," Stevens assured the Indians at Walla Walla. "Then is secured to you your right to fish, to get roots and berries and to kill game."[78] In the twentieth century the Supreme

Court developed basic principles to guide the interpretation of treaties and the subsequent disputes over land, water, mineral, and wildlife. These principles assert that ambiguities must be resolved in favor of the Indians, and treaty language must be construed liberally rather than literally, and in keeping with how the Indians would have understood them at the time.[79]

The obvious modern bias in favor of the tribes aims to partially offset the disadvantages they suffered in the treaty-making process itself. According to legal rulings, because treaty terms were discussed and written in English, Indians did not know what they were signing; they were coerced to do so, implicitly threatened with force. In short, the Supreme Court has ruled that the treaty process was "fundamentally unfair" and therefore treaties must be interpreted very broadly in favor of the Indians.[80] "For example, a treaty that creates a permanent reservation for a tribe is presumed to reserve enough water to make the reservation livable. If a treaty's purpose is to change a nomadic tribe into an agrarian one, it is presumed to reserve grazing rights to the tribe even though it says nothing about grazing."[81] Even nontreaty tribes have faired well in the courts, for some of the same legal reasons. In 1994, after a forty-three-year lawsuit, the Colville Confederated Tribes were awarded a lump-sum $53 million with $15.25 million a year thereafter for damages when Lake Roosevelt, the reservoir created by the Grand Coulee Dam, flooded villages and burial grounds, destroying fourteen-hundred miles of salmon runs.[82]

Today the Plateau tribes gather on the Yakama Reservation for the Treaty Days powwow, not to commemorate what was lost in the Treaty of 1855 but to celebrate what was gained, and preserved, for future generations. Within just three generations of the nineteenth century, Plateau Indians had to survive disease, Christian missionaries, gold miners, war, removal to reservations, boarding schools, dislocated families, and language loss. But among the things not lost was an indigenous rhetoric, preserved in treaty and tribal councils. Although the Plateau Indians were ultimately defeated, both politically and militarily, their way with words nonetheless prevailed, keeping intact a discursive legacy that is still legible in reservation schools today. That lineage, from the Treaty Period to contemporary times, can be documented in primary materials from the intervening Allotment Period, the Termination Period, and the Self-Determination Periods, as subsequent chapters show.

4

Writing in English
1910–1921

n 1915 government rangers caught a band of Yakama shooting and trapping wild game animals in the prohibited area of Mount Rainier National Park. The band was led by eighty-two-year-old Chief Sluiskin, who as a boy had tended Chief Owhi's horses at the Treaty Council of Walla Walla. When the rangers informed the band they were in violation of state law, Chief Sluiskin produced three documents to show that they had been granted the right to hunt and fish. One document dated 1854—a year before the Treaty of Walla Walla—was a treaty written by Governor Stevens; two other documents, written by a judge and a former Indian agent, urged that the Indians should be left alone and not cited for any violation.[1]

The newspaper article describes the encounter this way: "'Ugh, wait,' mumbled old Chief Sluiskin, as he trotted to one of the two tepees that provides shelter for the 30 redskins—the party consisting of that number—and returned with several papers. The rangers read the documents while the old leader smilingly watched them and spoke in his native tongue to his followers."[2] A "lengthy talk" ensued, facilitated by girl interpreters, graduates of the local Indian school, who spoke English fluently. The matter unresolved, it was then referred to officials in

Washington, D.C., who eventually ruled that they were unable to sort out the tangle of legislation and treaties to determine which tribes had which concessions, and in what parts of the state.

Chief Sluiskin was not the first nor would he be the last to test the legal limits of state and federal laws and then use written documents to back claims to sovereign rights. His protest nonetheless typifies the nonviolent methods of Plateau Indian activism, with its focus on concerted, strategic legal stands, directly confronting those in power in a manner consistent with traditional ways of direct democracy. This episode calls to mind long-standing tribal values of multilingualism, literacy, and education. These values carried forward through the Allotment Period (1877–1934), the dark period of critical transitions from oral to written communications and from ancestral language to English, giving rise to Plateau Indian English. The move to literacy, of course, did not obviate oral communications; nor did it suddenly enable Indians to cross the fictive Great Cognitive Divide from concrete to abstract thinking. Largely advanced by scholarship in the 1980s, those paradigms, I hope, have been laid to rest in chapter 2. The question is not what literacy does to people's thinking, but what people think about literacy.[3] Only when a community regards writing as "fulfilling a culturally conserving role," it is more likely to be acquired and used.[4] That is precisely the case with the Plateau Indians. The traverse into literacy and English was largely accomplished by way of schooling, which the Plateau Indians embraced, viewing education not as a tool of civilization and assimilation, as white men had hoped, and but as a tool for cultural preservation and political activism.

That Chief Sluiskin putatively "smilingly watched" as the rangers read the documents suggests that he enjoyed beating the white man at his own game, using the white man's tools to dismantle the white man's house. He was keenly aware of non-Indian control of written media, as he is quoted in another newspaper article that same year: "White people are always making me stand up and talk. Why is this? I do not understand what they want. They get me tangled. Then the temis tells my talk different from my words. I do not want this. It is a lie. It is the same as stealing."[5] This second article attests to Chief Sluiskin's effort to set the record straight, as he corrects the rumor reported earlier that he guided Governor Stevens's son and another man to the summit of Mount Tacoma in 1870 (rather, he guided two unidentified white surveyors in 1855 or 1856, according to his narrative reported in this article). He distrusts the media even as he embraces it, using it for his own ends.

His distrust is well placed in another regard. The fascination with the public oratory of authentic, vanquished Indians, telling tales of long ago and far away, performs the spectacle of the noble savage. Eloquence coupled with illiteracy is associated with primitivism—but so is inarticulateness. Resting on assumptions of linguistic imperialism, accounts of Indians speaking Native languages are either ignored or characterized as gibberish and "lengthy talk," as seen in the article on the Mount Rainier protest, as if to suggest that Native languages are inadequate compared to English ("'Ugh, wait,' mumbled old Chief Sluiskin"). When ordinary Indians speak English in conversation, their words are often caricatured as baby talk, their speech full of hesitant filler words, evidence of their lack of civilization. As American studies scholar David Murray has pointed out, it would seem that what Indians say to each other privately is less authentic than what they say in public to whites.[6]

Chapters 4 and 5 address this gap, this one focusing on the ordinary writings of ordinary Indians to whites, the next focusing on the ordinary oral interactions of ordinary Indians speaking among themselves within council meetings. The writings under investigation here—all in English/Plateau Indian English—demonstrate that the discursive principles of the ancestral language base survived the crossover into English and literacy in both private and public domains. This indigenous rhetoric also crossed over into Euro-American genres, including the personal letter, petition, telegraph, letter to the editor, autobiography, lecture tour, and address to the state Supreme Court—all of which are represented in this chapter. This indigenous rhetoric also crossed modalities and media: from oral to writing to typewriting. In the following examples, all written between 1910 and 1921, Plateau Indian rhetors aimed to reassert sovereignty rights across a wide swath of issues: draft registration, liquor sales on the reservation, water rights, hunting and fishing rights, and citizenship. And all of these examples were written by Yakamas, arguably the most politically active of the Plateau Indian tribes, and for whom the most primary material has been preserved.[7]

All but one of the artifacts under examination were culled from the Lucullus V. McWhorter Papers, an archive of mainly primary materials on the Nez Perce and the Yakama, including transcribed and translated oral testimonies, photographs, book manuscripts, general council minutes, telegrams, petitions, news articles, and extensive correspondence that McWhorter amassed after he moved to the Yakama Valley in 1903 until his death in 1944. An amateur historian, author, and advocate, McWhorter worked tirelessly for Indian rights on local, state, and national levels. Recognized by the Yakama as a true brother, McWhorter was officially adopted as a tribal member in 1909.[8] Each section heading in this chapter aims to telegraph the topic, the genre, and the date of the example under examination. All but one example is quoted in full, in an effort to start recovering the rhetorical *ethnie* of the Plateau Indians more generally for posterity. Taken together, these representative pieces bear witness to the continuity of the rhetoric as well as the ideals and political lifeways of the Plateau peoples crossing into the twentieth century, and against seemingly impossible odds, given white control of media and Indian misrepresentation.

Antidraft Protest/Water Rights, Letter to the Editor, 1917

Among the many Indians that McWhorter interviewed, corresponded, and worked with over the years, including Yellow Wolf (Nez Perce) and Mourning Dove (Salishan), none figures more prominently in his papers than Louis Mann (Yakama), whose name crops up in different connections with the pieces I have chosen to examine. Mann was one of those "ordinary" Indians whose troubles were unfortunately common. But he is also ordinary in that he embraced English, literacy, and grassroots activism like so many Yakama did at the turn of the century, and he used literacy in efforts to reclaim and preserve sovereignty rights. Born in 1860, Mann started writing his own "History life of a bad Injun" in 1880, as he noted in a school composition book. His history opens with the story of his surreptitiously stepping inside a schoolroom for the first time at age twelve while waiting for his father. Unable to forget that experience, he later asked his father if he could attend school; his father agreed, provided Mann did not run away. The young Mann obeyed, despite being whipped repeatedly by the Methodist teacher who was trying to convert Mann, who was Roman Catholic. After finishing the first four primary grades, Mann apprenticed to an Indian and learned to make harnesses and later picked up carpentry. He then worked in lumberyards and steam mills until the Indian agent burned down the mills and blamed the fires on the tribe. Mann's narrative quickly turns to the crimes of a long line of Indian agents. And there his own history stops.

Written years later in 1912, the last page in the composition book is the beginning of a letter to a congressman. The opening line: "In the name of our Tribe of Yakima Indians We protest against Senate bill, 6693."[9] Mann's account is both an autobiography and a history at the same time. In telling his story, he is telling the story of his people's local, contemporary struggle, documenting the crimes of corrupt Indian agents. Early on, he embraced literacy and apprenticed himself to the white man's uses of literacy, making them his own but in service of his people, ultimately arguing in written English on multiple issues, in multiple genres. In his voluminous correspondence, Mann often gave McWhorter permission to seek publication for his letters, hoping to reach a wider, white audience for his views. As in his own "History," the crossover from personal to public was an easy one for Mann, whose letters never dwelled on strictly personal matters (e.g., his wife's serious illness or his child's death warranted only passing mention).

One example of a private letter turned public, "Indian View of Registration," is an opinion-editorial, written originally as a letter by Mann to McWhorter but later published in the *Yakima Morning Herald* in 1917, per Mann's request. The piece demonstrates how Plateau Indian rhetoric crossed languages (from ancestral language to English by way of Plateau Indian English); it also shows how the principles of this indigenous rhetoric infused non-Native genres—that is, the personal letter and the public editorial—defined by Euro-American conventions. Here is Louis Mann's letter to the editor:

INDIAN VIEW OF REGISTRATION

To the Editor—I am deeply grieved about the troubles of my people and the white man's war across the big sea, and about Indians registering for military service. The white people are not understanding us. Injuns are no cowards, and they will fight. The past tells how well they fight. But my people cannot understand why their young men are wanted to fight Germans so far from home. It is a money fight between white nations and why should the red man, who has always been put down by the whites, go fight for them? They think it is not their business and no use for them to fight where they did not start trouble. They fear it is only a scheme to get rid of the poor reds. I am telling you this so you will know the truth and maybe help by putting it in the paper so all will know why the Indian does not want to register. Listen:

We sent telegrams to the Indian commissioner. We made complaint but wanted to do right and live well. We asked for more water so we could raise more crops as government wants. We got reply that maybe we will not be sent to war, but will be left to farm and raise food for soldiers. Commissioner said it is our duty now to obey law and register as directed. You saw this telegram we got. The words of the commissioner is good for everybody to obey the laws made by a white man. Many of the Yakimas have registered. All will register if they understand. But now what is right for Injun is right for a white race. We were here first from all time. Land and water was ours. The white man has us fast and makes laws which he does not regard. I am not lying.

Mr. Commissioner has asked us to obey the law and his words are right for us as we see them, but why does he not make good the words from his own department when dealing with us? Where is the water stolen from our lands near White Swan on our own reservation? There are eight allotments over there which are mostly abandoned now for more than eight years because the department let a white man steal all the water for one allotment he bought higher upon the ditch. Fine homes are built on this allotment and fine orchards are there grown with water stolen from Injuns. Injun's land lay all idle and the fields leveled and irrigated years ago now are weeds and home of jack rabbit and coyote.

If commissioner wants Injuns to raise food for soldier army, let him tell Mr. Injun how to do this where his water has been stolen from him. Four years ago we were told that suit was brought to get this water back for us, and now we find the words empty and not true. It is good for a preacher to tell us what is right and for us to obey the law. Is the law all for one class of people and Injun only a dog to obey when called? We are ready to fight for a flag, but who has heart to fight under this condition of affairs? We do not expect to go on a warpath any more. Government said quit fighting and bury guns and arrows. We done this. We only want right way to live. One law for all in this government country. Not one ruling for a white man and one other ruling for a Injun. If we fight together, then let us be like brothers and treat all alike under the law.

Injun is wanted to raise plenty crops for soldiers and still the commissioner does not make good his word to get stolen water back for the eight allotments now gone back to wild condition. Can you blame Mr. Injun for being suspicious and afraid? We are wards and held tight and who is to make us fight like slaves for a white master? This is how my people feel and this is why they do not want to register. Then some cannot understand. They think if Germans come here they will fight them, but why go over water to shoot? For me, if I was young I would be ready to go fight. My ancestors went on warpath often and Injun is still wild. But I am too old and I have my family to provide. I must stay home and work like hell so not starve when snow comes.

I feel miserable because of this trouble. The white man acts as if he will live forever and never die. If he never died, then I would be all right for him to take everything in sight and war on weaker nations. But he will die and decay just as an Injun and then where will he go, all covered with blood and all his goods and lands left behind? Why this bitter feeling? Let us like like brothers and if German nation comes over here we will all fight him to a finish. Maybe Injun cannot understand how it all is, and maybe it is best to go over there and fight before he comes to destroy our homes and lands. If this is true and we are wanted, then we go and fight like chil-wit wap-souk, and no turning back, but let the white man make good his word to us so we can take his hand and call him a good brother. Give back our stolen water. Your kultus brother,

LOUIS MANN,
"Bad Injun of the Ahtanum"[10]

Mann seems to follow editorial conventions in opening his letter, with his title announcing, and his first line confirming, his topic: "Indian View of Registration." By the last line, however, it becomes clear that his antidraft protest is really about water rights: "Give us back our stolen water." He gets from draft protest to water rights by referencing and repurposing several discourses, including legal precedents, the way-of-the-warrior, and Christianity. And he mounts this argument using indigenous rhetorical resources, his ways with words underscoring the content of his words at every turn. Even in the first line, Mann hints how he is going to recontextualize the topic: in terms of "the troubles of my people." He rightly assumes that his readership already knows that some Yakamas are refusing to register for the draft for the World War. Complex and rich, Mann's line of argument is difficult to trace, but the points on that line are nonetheless cogently made.

One such point is the implicit contrast between the Euro-American war complex and traditional Plateau Indian pacifism. In making that point, Mann invokes the discourse of the warrior's way only to play against it. "Injuns are no cowards and they will fight," but this particular enemy (Germany) is too far from home. This war is a "money fight between white nations," not the business of Indians. Later, he offers what Indians would consider appropriate justification for going to war: if the Germans came here, Mann explains, Injuns would fight, but they don't understand why they should "go over water to shoot." Still later, he reiterates that "we are ready to fight for a flag"—"a flag" rather than "the flag," suggesting that such a motive is trivial, ironically, given that whites so often characterize Indian motives for war with other tribes as petty feuds. Mann implicitly references the Treaty of 1855, which forbade Indians to take up arms, but uses way-of-the-warrior discourse: "We do not expect to go on a warpath any more. Government said quit fighting and bury guns and arrows. We done this." He uses the term "Injun" consistently, frequently without articles or plural, echoing Tonto-speak. In both this public letter and his voluminous private correspondence with McWhorter, typically Mann signs off as "Bad Injun of the Ahtanum," celebrating his status as stereotypic "Injun" and a bad one at that. His signoff also serves to locate himself on a specific place on the reservation, the Ahtanum—a place also famously associated with Kamiakin, the iconic headsman of Yakama resistance.

Building on these points about pacifism, grounded in both traditional values and treaty terms requiring disarmament, Mann argues that Indians need to stay here and "raise more crops as the government wants," implicitly referencing the Dawes Act and U.S. Indian policy for the past quarter century but adding that these crops are needed to feed the troops. Unfortunately, Indians cannot raise crops because they have no water, and they have no water because it has been diverted. "Where is the water stolen from our lands near White Swan on our own reservation?" Mann's answer to his question is specific but can be generally applied to the larger issue of Indian water rights: eight allotments mostly abandoned for eight years because a white man stole all the water for his own one allotment, where "fine homes [were] built. . . and fine orchards [were] there grown with water stolen from Injuns"; meanwhile, "Injun's land lay all idle and the fields leveled and irrigated years ago now are weeds and home of jack rabbit and coyote."

Mann's argument references legal precedent in nuanced ways. His overarching point stated in the last sentence of the letter ("Give back our stolen water") works from a Euro-American understanding of land as fungible property, an understanding founded in individualistic capitalism rather than the inalienable ground of communalism. While water from the land can be "stolen," just as property can always be stolen, it is nonetheless "our" water, a communally held resource. Mann's argument draws from the so-called doctrine of discovery, as articulated by Chief Justice Marshall in the first cases of the Marshall Trilogy, *Johnson v. McIntosh* (1823). Established to avoid settlement conflicts and war as European powers invaded the New World, the doctrine held that discovery granted title to the land, consummated upon possession.[11] Mann's words—"We were here first from all time. Land and water was ours"—echo this principle, but this time in the mouth of the invaded. Besides using the Treaty of 1855 as legal grounds for not taking up arms, he also mentions that "we are wards and held tight" (as if on a cradleboard perhaps), describing the colonized position of Indians long established by the Marshall Court decisions. By contrast, if Indians were slaves, they would have to obey the white master, the inference being that because they are not slaves, they do not have to obey.

To support his appeal, Mann tells his story, narrating a firsthand account of the steps taken by the tribe to fight for its water rights, first registering formal complaints with the Indian commissioner via telegrams, the medium itself suggesting the urgency of the matter. To these the commissioner did make reply, saying the Indians probably would not have to go to war but register anyway because it is the law. Mann goes on to explain—tellingly, in passive voice—that the Indians were told that "suit was brought" four years ago concerning Indians' water rights, but like many unattributed rumors with no agency and therefore without accountability, those words were "empty and untrue." Answering the commissioner's reply now publicly, but drawing upon the legal force of the law of God, Mann urges that all should obey the laws, not just Indians. "It is good for a preacher to tell us what is right and for us to obey the law. Is the law all for one class of people and Injun only a dog to obey when called?" Himself a Roman Catholic, Mann in the last paragraph appeals to a common belief in the law of God and judgment after death: "The white man acts as if he will live forever and never die. If he never died, then I would be all right for him to take everything in sight. . . . But he will die and decay just as an Injun and then where will he go, all covered with blood and all his goods and lands left behind?"

Because their earlier efforts to work through the Indian commissioner had failed, Mann says earlier, he has taken to publicizing this wrong in the newspaper where it can reach a wider audience: "I am telling you this so you will know the truth and maybe help by putting it in the paper so all will know why the Indian does not want to register. Listen." In effect, Mann is "speaking straight" to the people, not unlike his ancestors at the treaty and tribal councils of 1855 through 1871, but via the written word of the newspaper, in keeping with the direct democratic ideals of Plateau Indian political organization. He is also clearly speaking for "my people." Although his letter to the editor was not officially sanctioned, his views are, as evidenced by the telegrams sent by the group, probably those of the General Council. Still, in closing, Mann differentiates his own position relative to this official view, saying: "For me, if I was young I would be ready to go fight. . . . But I am too old and I have my family to provide. I must stay home and work like hell so not starve when snow comes." Crossing over from speech to paper, especially in the genre of personal and public letters, poses no stretch for Mann, who apparently understands letter-writing as a confluence of two modalities especially suited to Plateau Indian rhetoric. As he says in another letter to a government official in 1920: "I'm talking to you in the letter . . . I am not writing a foolish talk I mean Business."[12]

Mann's argument is not an easy one to follow, especially for readers expecting point-by-point arrangement. Perhaps to clarify his message but more likely to highlight the newsworthiness as well as the novelty of his argument, the newspaper also ran a news story based on an interview with Mann, asking him to reiterate the Indian antiregistration position. Printed right beside Mann's letter, the news story effectively recontextualizes Mann's editorial, shifting its point of emphasis from water rights to the antiregistration campaign. The headline reads in all capitals "WHY INDIANS ARE NOT REGISTERING," with the subheading "Louis Mann Says Red Brother Is Adhering to Old Treaty Promises When He Agreed to Farm, Not to Fight."[13] In the article Mann is quoted as saying that Indians will not fight except in self-defense. The story then cites Superintendent Don M. Carr, who says that registration on the reservation was proceeding, although slowly, because so many could not read and write and did not understand the requirements. The story closes this way: "Mr. Carr says farming operations on the reservation are proceeding splendidly"—at best, minimalizing Mann's claim; at worst, undercutting it altogether.

Not that that deterred the Bad Injun of the Ahtanum. Newspaper editorials were but one tool for disseminating Indian views and effecting political change, as Mann was keenly aware. Ever active in tribal government, Mann interpreted, helped write, or singly authored editorials, letters, telegrams, and petitions to U.S. officials at both the state and national levels throughout his life. With various delegations he made several trips to Washington, D.C., to hand-deliver tribal missives as well as to provide a physical presence—a "real Indian"—as a representative of the Indian Rights Association (IRA) authorized to speak on behalf of Yakama interests to congressmen. These face-to-face contacts, as one IRA representative wrote to McWhorter, were highly effectively, especially in securing special concessions for the Yakama. Those concessions would have long-reaching impact decades later in the courts in reconstituting Indian sovereignty rights.

Water Rights, Telegram, Circa 1915

The telegrams that Mann refers to in his letter to the editor date back to at least 1915, probably earlier. While the telegrams themselves have been lost, the text of one is quoted in McWhorter's *Continued Crimes against the Yakimas* published in 1916, the manuscript of which is preserved in McWhorter's papers. Signed by Chief Weyallup Wayacika, who did not speak English, and Louis Mann, who frequently translated for him, this one extant telegram pushes the limits of genre and the medium, as it is stretched to accommodate Plateau Indian rhetorical practices. Even in a telegram, the authors manage to mount the argument, fleshed out with a few select details, of the Yakama's demand for redress. Here is the text:

> Hon. Cato Sells, Commissioner Indian Affairs. Ahtanum. Indians in council ask report Dorrington's water investigation last January. Every year we lose crops; tired promises without help. Irrigation now here, Indians plowing but discouraged. Some say quit, go hunt; fish, dig roots for living. You know situation, cannot expect us advance without encouragement. Carr and Hold say doing all can but no change. You bring suit for stolen water we continue farming content. Every year promised help never come. Goudy get no water four years. Some have no lease money cannot pay water rent advance. Cannot get bank money. Wire reply.
>
> (signed) Weyallup Wayacika & Mann[14]

After self-locating themselves at Ahtanum, the authors make it clear that they are speaking on behalf of others, with the permission of those others; what follows represents the consensus of the group, who asks for the report from the investigation in January. More than an urgent request for a report, however, the telegram aims to persuade officials to act in favor of the Indians' case. The Indians continue to plow their fields, despite heavy losses. If the government wants Indians to "advance" and become civilized, they need encouragement, "encouragement" suggesting both emotional (hope) and physical (water). The line "you bring suit for stolen water we continue farming content" seems to offer a deal: if you bring the suit, we will continue farming. And if they do not? The information delivered in indirect quotes ("some say quit, go hunt; fish, dig roots for living") might be read as a veiled threat, since fishing/hunting/gathering rights were already in dispute, as the government wanted (a) Indians to be farmers, not hunters/gatherers in order to civilize them and break up tribalism, so that (b) non-Indians would have free range over these resources.

The telegram gets ever more specific at the end, citing a firsthand example of one Sam Goudy, whose situation the officials were undoubtedly well aware from Goudy's own steady stream of letters registering complaint. Further, Chief Weyallup and Mann argue a larger point: even if water was not being diverted, many of them could not afford to pay for the water (at one dollar an acre) because they have not received the money owed them for leasing their land, alluding to the Indian trust funds managed by the Bureau of Indian Affairs (BIA). Besides employing Plateau Indian rhetoric, the authors also adopt the language of telegrams, omitting articles, helping verbs, prepositions, and the like, which coincidentally share some features of Plateau Indian English as well as Tonto-speak, oddly coupled with detailed elaboration uncommon in telegrams. They close with an imperative: "Wire reply." That the Indians in council chose to communicate via telegram (and expected the commissioner to as well) not only suggests the urgency of the matter; it also speaks to the Plateau Indian ideals of direct democracy and rhetorical principles: speak straight and directly to the powers-that-be.

Ban on Liquor Sales, Petitions, Circa 1910

Even earlier examples of literacy put in service of activism are two petitions lobbying for banning liquor sales on the reservation. Although the first one is undated, the second one can be placed in 1910 by a dated letter that refers to losing copies of the second petition. Both petitions are typed. Here is the text of the first petition:

The Petition of Chief Stwire G. Waters and Other Yakima Asking the White Man to Keep His Word

The Yakima and Confederated Tribes made a treaty with the White man on June 9, 1855. In that treaty the Indian asked that whiskey be kept away from them. Many times the Indian asked the White man to take their whiskey and run away. But the White man's treaty was all words. The White man talked with a forked tongue. The Indian talked from his heart—he has but one tongue. White man kept buying Indians liquor. Many Indians died because of liquor. White man gives Indians liquor now.

We now ask the White man to keep his word. We ask the White man to send whiskey outside the State. We want whiskey sent away from the State of Washington so we be safe. The bad White man brought the whiskey; let the good White man take it away. We ask the White man to keep his word and vote the liquor out.[15]

The signatures of seventy people, including several women, follow, after which is appended a typewritten note: "Signers to Ahtanum Clan, Yakima;—Anti Saloon Petition." After four more typewritten names (three of them followed by X-marks) appear the typewritten words "Louis Mann, Corresponding Secretary for Indian Councils. North Yakima, Wash. (Gen. Delivery)."

The title of the petition does not specify the issue or the clan's position on the issue, as petition titles are wont to do. Instead, it highlights the larger moral and legal principle for banning saloons: "ASKING THE WHITE MAN TO KEEP HIS WORD." The petition immediately cites the Treaty of 1855, establishing the legal grounds of the clan's argument, but the treaty is not mentioned again until the fourth sentence. Exclusive blame is assigned to the white man for selling whiskey to Indians, even when asked to stop. In fact, the first paragraph might be read as a story explaining the evolution of the situation. While the second paragraph clearly states what the clan wants, its point of emphasis is still on keeping one's word. For the Indians the matter is not just a legal one; it is also a moral one, where a person's word is his bond. A piece of paper documenting that bond backs it up, bearing witness to people's promises. The petitioners clearly see orality and literacy as complementary, not competing, modalities.

The second petition (figure 2) presents a very different kind of argument, both in terms of content and presentation. Here is the text, minus the underscores, of that petition:

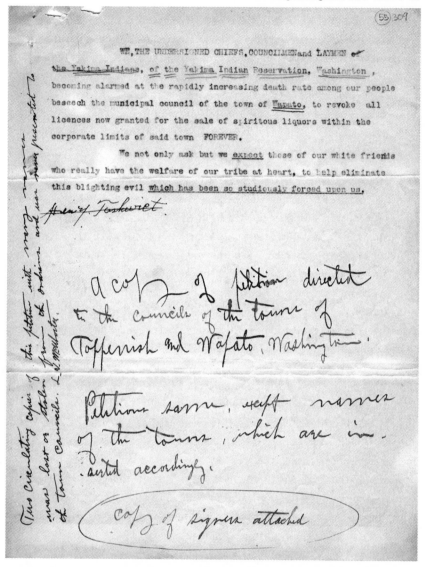

FIGURE 2. Petition to revoke liquor licenses, circa 1910. Underscores and capitalization do not necessarily suggest intonation contour. Rather, they may signify an attempt to translate ideational emphasis, speaker certainty, and the experiential factuality of speakers' statements. Ancestral languages provide multiple linguistic options for encoding this kind of information, options that are unavailable in English grammar. Compare the petition's typography to that of figure 3 in this chapter and figure 4 in chapter 6.

WE, THE UNDERSIGNED CHIEFS, COUNCILMEN AND LAYMEN of the Yakima Indians, of the Yakima Indian Reservation, Washington, becoming alarmed at the rapidly increasing death rate among our people beseech the municipal council of the town of Wapato, to revoke all licences now granted for the sale of spiritous liquors within the corporate limits of said town FOREVER.

We not only ask for we expect these of our white friends who really have the welfare of our tribe at heart, to help eliminate this blighting evil which has been so studiously forced upon us.[16]

Henry Tashwict's name is crossed out, possibly by McWhorter, but probably by someone (maybe Tashwict himself) who recognized that the signature pages were to be kept separate and then collated from all copies of the petitions. The cross-out also authenticates this copy as one that was actually circulated, not simply McWhorter's retyping, thereby establishing its provenance. As noted in McWhorter's scrawling hand on this copy, the petition is directed to the city councils of Toppenish and Wapato, with the name of the respective towns filled in. Another note, written vertically along the margin and actually signed by McWhorter, indicates that the other copies of the petition were "lost or stolen" and never presented to the councils. Four pages of signatures follow this particular circulated copy.

The petition strongly urges that the town councils revoke liquor licenses, in effect outlawing liquor sales on the reservation. The petition draws from both legal discourse (e.g., *revoke, municipal, corporate, said town*) and Christian discourse (e.g., *beseech, spiritous, blighting evil*) to make the case for the ban. It cites as supporting evidence from firsthand, albeit nonspecific, knowledge: "the rapidly increasing death rate among our people." The argument goes further, however, in appealing to the white town councils to help eliminate this problem "which has been so studiously forced upon us" (underscored in the original). It is difficult to read this last line as anything other than bitterly ironic and defiant, made ever sharper by the mock-respectful tone of "our white friends who really have the welfare of our tribe at heart" that opens the sentence.

Although the provenance of the text is clear, the 159 signatures (including 18 women's names) on the pages that follow are not so clearly authenticated. Many of the signatures are written in similar handwriting in a row, with some of them followed by X-marks. The marks themselves are similarly formed by what looks like the same hand throughout the four pages of signatures; further, petitions, treaties, and other legal documents typically included the words "his mark" or "her mark" before someone's X. There are enough diverse handwriting styles, however, to suggest that several people did in fact sign the petitions themselves.

Although it was never presented, the petition with its unorthodox process bears witness to a very early attempt (1910) to enter the legal process at a time of emergent literacy. Beyond issues of process, the petition demonstrates the principles of Plateau Indian rhetoric at work for the people. The petition opens true to the conventions of the genre, which nonetheless coincide with Plateau Indian rhetorical conventions: self-location, the group identifiers indicating consensus and authorization to speak.

The petition breaks from legal discourse in another way: its striking typographical appearance. The most obvious explanation is that Native rhetors may be using typography as performance cues. The single-, double-, and triple-underscores as well as the one word in all capitals, "FOREVER," may aim to present a dramatic intonation contour, which would be consistent with the high affect typical of Plateau Indian rhetoric. But, interestingly, Plateau Indian spoken communication in modern times is not heavily modulated. At least, that is often the perception of non-Indians, such as teachers and professors, who have often commented to me that Indians speak in a monotone with little expression or in a singsong way. As linguistic anthropologist William Leap has pointed out, that perception has to be contextualized in terms of the power differential that structures discourse in those settings where Indians speaking to non-Indians may do so in subdued tones.[17] Less obviously, Native writers may be using typography to translate linguistic options that ancestral languages syntactically encode, such as ideational emphasis and aspect, the latter registering a speaker's confidence in the experiential fact of her statements. Those options are unavailable in English grammar, at least at the level of syntax.

Another example, "Letter to the Editor, 1921" (discussed in the next section), provides clearer evidence that capitalization is not used to indicate vocal stress but ideational stress as well as speaker certainty (figure 3). Dramatic typographical markers appear repeatedly in students' writing in 2000 through 2004 (see figure 4 in chapter 6, for example). While the earlier writers of the petition and the letter of the editor were fluent in Indian, students were not. Leap has convincingly argued that ancestral language and discourse continues to animate American Indian Englishes generally, even when the ancestral language has been lost.[18] To Leap's argument, I would add that typography may also be evidence of this residual influence.

Indian Education, Letter to the Editor, 1921

The recurrence of this typography, especially after the advent of the typewriter, strongly suggests active adaption of ancestral language, grammar, and discourse

Indian of Today Writes
Grievance on Typewriter

Yakima Brave Declares Education Is the Prime Need of His Race and Writes to Newspaper About It.

Times have changed.

There used to be a day when, if Big Chief Running Antelope had a grievance, took exception for instance, to the low proof of the firewater supplied him by bootleggers, he would gather together his squaws, pack up his wigwam and set out for Washington, there to set his troubles before the Great White Father.

But not today.

Instead of making a pilgrimage and an oration, your modern Indian sits down to his trusty typewriter and pounds out a letter to the paper. And of you think that the plaint loses anything in eloquence by reason of its being put down in black and white you have another guess coming. There may be no sonorous gutturals in a typewritten page—but the writer more than makes up for their lack by liberal use of capitals. The subject of the Indian's complaint has undergone a change no less drastic than has the method in which he sends it.

Progressive Indian.

The Post-Intelligencer, for instance, has just received the following from Ben B. Olney, who signs himself "A Progressive Yakima Indian":

"The American INDIAN has started several laps behind Civilization, And I believe it the duty of this Country To give him every opportunity there is possible to give. It has taken his Land and his Birth right—AMERICAN CITIZENSHIP. Every AMERICAN CITIZEN should stop, look and listen When it comes to SAVING DOLLARS and HUMANS. AN EDUCATED APACHE INDIAN ONCE SAID KILL THE INDIAN BUT SAVE THE MAN. The American Government is spending MILLIONS of DOLLARS Annually, to look after these Indians' property and moneys. There is a Superintendent appointed to look after all INDIANS' Business so that the Indian has nothing to do but loaf. The Indian for lack of something to do, becomes Worthless to the Community. And is BRANDED such. The Superintendent absorbs all these INDIANS' Responsibilities and deprives him of what makes other RACES GOOD AMERICAN CITIZENS. Individual Responsibility is the Foundation which the INDIAN will eventually Build his AMERICANISM on. When he will have no more money for the INDIAN DEPARTMENT to look after.

"The INDIAN is peacefully sleeping in the INDIAN BUREAU CRADLE but when there is no more money to rock the cradle he will be dumped out. He will probably get up raving but will have to stay awake and go to work.

Whose Fault?

"WHOSE FAULT IS IT? I AM SURE IT ISN'T THE INDIANS'. The AMERICAN GOVERNMENT OWES US INDIANS WHAT OTHER RACES GET THAT COME To this Country—EDUCATION. Agents are too busy looking after lands and moneys for INDIANS AND overlook the vital needs, Namely, HEALTH, SPIRITUAL and MORAL WELFARE and School Education.

"We YAKIMAS are LUCKY, we have RICH soil and the most wonderful of Irrigation Systems in the United States. This Calls for Farmers and the farmer came as an opening wedge for CIVILIZATION. The farmer Called on his County for Schools, called for better roads, Called for More Irrigation. We have had all these things Come with the White man's PROGRESS to us.

"There is not sufficient taxable property to supply the demand for Schools on the RESERVATION at this time, though they are building two new Schools for the coming School term. YAKIMA COUNTY is doing this without complaining and are doing all that is possible I believe, but look at the increasing numbers of white Children coming to our Reservation.

"Our INDIAN DEPARTMENT is Lax. It's our INDIAN DEPARTMENT all over the UNITED STATES that is to blame for the condition the INDIAN is in. And The AMERICAN public is paying for it.

"HERE is Something I get from the 1920 hearings on INDIAN AFFAIRS:

"'MR. TILLMAN: 'I just want to know if we have justification for these large appropriations.'

"'SUPERINTENDENT GABE E. PARKER, OKLAHOMA: 'YES, SIR.'

"'MR. TILLMAN: 'I find on your records, MR. PARKER, of forty-four Years ago, that Congress Appropriated $4,000,000 for INDIANS, and twenty-two Years ago $8,000,000 and now they appropriate $12,000,000. Do you think the time will come when we can look for a decrease?'

"Now mind, dear reader, you are paying the bill, and the Indian gets it in the neck. Let us all bear weight with our Congressmen for EDUCATION for our INDIANS and do away with these Heavy APPROPRIATIONS. EDUCATED INDIANS ARE GOOD INDIANS.'"

FIGURE 3. Letter to the editor, 1921. The letter is framed as a mock news story, making fun of activist Indians' embrace of a new medium (typewriting) as well as their ancestral and English language use. This artifact illustrates the impact of white control of media, which can discount minority dissent, even as it allows for its expression.

conventions to contemporary times. Such adaptation, however, is too often understood in terms of developmental error attributable to language acquisition, even when Native speakers and writers are well educated, as the following artifact illustrates. In this instance, the *Seattle Post-Intelligencer* took the opportunity to make fun of typewriting Indians overusing the shift-lock key, in this racist preface to a letter to the editor. Here is the text of that preface:

> Times have changed.
>
> There used to be a day when, if Big Chief Running Antelope had a grievance, took exception for instance, to the low proof of the firewater supplied him by bootleggers, he would gather together his squaws, pack up his wigwam and set out for Washington, there to set his troubles before the Great White Father.
>
> But not today.
>
> Instead of making a pilgrimage and an oration, your modern Indian sits down to his trusty typewriter and pounds out a letter to the paper. And if you think that the plaint loses anything in eloquence by reason of its being put down in black and white you have another guess coming. There may be no sonorous gutturals in a typewritten page—but the writer more than makes up for their lack by liberal use of capitals.
>
> The subject of the Indian's complaint has undergone a change no less drastic than has the method in which he sends it.
>
> PROGRESSIVE INDIAN.
>
> The *Post-Intelligencer*, for instance, has just received the following from Ben B. Olney, who signs himself "A Progressive Yakima Indian."

This withering prefatory note to the actual letter to the editor not only belittles Indian activism (protesting "the low proof of the firewater supplied him by bootleggers" and "making a pilgrimage [to Washington] and an oration"). It also satirizes the fabled eloquence of Indian oratory, as well as the inarticulateness of Native language, suggesting that in the move from orality to literacy, "sonorous gutturals" have now been replaced by the "liberal use of capitals" in typewriting. Thus Indians' language use is ridiculed as primitive both preliteracy and postliteracy. That preface is then followed Ben Olney's letter to the editor:

> "The American INDIAN has started several laps behind Civilization. And I believe it the duty of this Country To give him every opportunity there is possible to give. It has taken his Land and his Birth right—AMERICAN CITIZENSHIP. Every AMERICAN CITIZEN should stop, look and listen. When it comes to

SAVING DOLLARS and HUMANS. AN EDUCATED APACHE INDIAN ONCE SAID KILL THE INDIAN BUT SAVE THE MAN. The American Government is spending MILLIONS of DOLLARS Annually, to look after these Indians' property and moneys. There is a Superintendent appointed to look after all INDIANS' Business so that the Indian has nothing to do but loaf. The Indian for lack of something to do, becomes Worthless to the Community. And is BRANDED such. The Superintendent absorbs all these INDIANS' Responsibilities and deprives him of what makes other RACES GOOD AMERICAN CITIZENS. Individual Responsibility is the Foundation which the INDIAN will eventually Build his AMERICANISM on. When he will have no more money for the INDIAN DEPARTMENT to look after.

"The INDIAN is peacefully sleeping in the INDIAN BUREAU CRADLE but when there is no more money to rock the cradle he will be dumped out. He will probably get up raving but will have to stay awake and go to work.

Whose Fault?

"WHOSE FAULT IS IT? I AM SURE IT ISN'T THE INDIANS'. The AMERICAN GOVERNMENT OWES US INDIANS WHAT OTHER RACES GET THAT COME To this Country—EDUCATION. Agents are too busy looking after lands and moneys for INDIANS AND overlook the vital needs, Namely, HEALTH, SPIRITUAL and MORAL WELFARE and School Education.

"We YAKIMAS are LUCKY, we have RICH soil and the most wonderful of Irrigation Systems in the United States. This Calls for Farmers and the farmer came as an opening wedge for CIVILIZATION. The farmer Called on his County for Schools, called for better roads, Called for More Irrigation. We have had all these things Come with the White man's PROGRESS to us.

"There is not sufficient taxable property to supply the demand for Schools on the RESERVATION at this time, though they are building two new Schools for the coming School term. YAKIMA COUNTY Is doing this without complaining and are doing all that is possible I believe, but look at the increasing numbers of white Children coming to our Reservation.

"Our INDIAN DEPARTMENT is Lax. It's our INDIAN DEPARTMENT all over the UNITED STATES that is to blame for the condition the INDIAN is in. And The AMERICAN public is paying for it.

"HERE is Something I get from the 1920 hearings on INDIAN AFFAIRS:

"MR. TILLMAN: 'I just want to know if we have justification for these large appropriations.'

"SUPERINTENDENT GABE E. PARKER, OKLAHOMA: 'YES, SIR.'

"MR. TILLMAN: 'I find on your records, MR. PARKER, of forty-four Years ago, that Congress Appropriated $4,000,000 for INDIANS, and twenty-two Years ago $8,000,000 and now they appropriate $12,000,000. Do you think the time will come when we can look for a decrease?'

"Now mind, dear reader, you are paying the bill, and the Indian gets it in the neck. Let us all bear weight with our Congressmen for EDUCATION for our INDIANS and do away with these Heavy APPROPRIATIONS. EDUCATED INDIANS ARE GOOD INDIANS."[19]

Ben Olney is arguing for quality Indian education, on which the editor's preface casts aspersions and effectively undercuts his point. But the author actually has a larger point to make: the Indian Department overseeing Indian affairs specifically and the U.S./Indian legal relationship with Indians defined as wards of the state generally. In making his case, Olney engages in a bit of ventriloquism, echoing arguments used against Indians before turning those arguments against government policy. Indians started "several laps" behind civilization; they loaf, but they loaf because of the current system has deprived them of individual responsibility, the cornerstone of Americanism. In a graphic analogy of Indians asleep in the (government) cradle, Olney infantilizes Indians, caricaturing their ward status; only when they are dumped from that cradle will they have to wake up and go to work. He goes on to assign blame, not to Indians, but to corrupt "Agents [who] are too busy looking after lands and moneys for INDIANS." Olney argues for quality education as just one facet of Indian welfare; he is also arguing against the entire system of managing Indian affairs, which has deprived Indians of their well-being, of which education is only a part.

Further, Olney seems to credit white progress for bringing in white farmers and with them schools, better roads, more irrigation. The two new schools, however, are not enough to serve the reservation for two reasons: lack of taxable property and increasing numbers of white children. His reasoning implicitly indicts the allotment system that impoverished Indians at the expense of white settlers. But he is quite explicit in condemning the Indian Department for lax management of Indian funds and argues that the American public is paying for that mismanagement, while "the Indian gets it in the neck." Olney closes by recontextualizing his argument in pocketbook terms in ways consistent with Plateau Indian rhetorical principles. Giving his supporting evidence before stating what point his evidence supports, Olney offers that evidence in the form of a dramatic dialogue, between Mr. Tillman and Superintendent Parker toward the end.

Addressing his "dear reader" directly, consistent with the conventions of contemporary novels as well as the principles of Plateau Indian rhetoric, Olney closes by emphasizing mutual benefits—actually, his dear white readers benefitting from both outcomes: fewer taxes and more educated Indians. The last line ("EDUCATED INDIANS ARE GOOD INDIANS") echoes the rationale advanced by Carlisle (and referred to by Olney earlier, who attributes the saying to an educated Apache, verifiable perhaps from his own knowledge): kill the Indian but save the man. Olney's argument, however, suggests that the only Indian that would be killed by Indian education is the one constructed by government policy and malfeasance. His own considerable education is on display here, along with the purpose to which he put that education: activism. That purpose was advanced by adapting a Euro-American form to Plateau Indian rhetorical principles.

Indian Citizenship, Lecture, 1921

Like Ben Olney, Nipo Strongheart was an educated Yakama who often spoke for Indian education but against BIA control of that education. Under the auspices of Chautauqua, the adult-education lecture circuit that also provided entertainment for rural America in the late nineteenth and early twentieth centuries, Strongheart delivered lectures on many other topics as well, all concerning "Indian lore and life" in every state in the Union as well as in Canada.[20] Born in 1891, he was fluent in eight Native languages. At the age of eleven, Strongheart toured with Buffalo Bill's Wild West show as a bareback rider; at the age of fourteen, he appeared in his first motion picture. In a Hollywood career that spanned four decades, Strongheart acted in eight movies and worked as a technical adviser to Cecil B. DeMille, among other Hollywood moviemakers, to ensure accurate representation of American Indians in films, one of the first to do so in the industry.[21] He maintained a steady correspondence with McWhorter and ultimately attended law school in Los Angeles. The Yakama Nation Cultural Center was built to house Strongheart's considerable library, which he bequeathed to the tribe upon his death in 1966. In his lectures he modestly downplayed his worldly experience and education, delivering instead what he had apparently learned white audiences wanted from lecture tours: Indian-ness on display.

The *Christian Science Monitor* reported on one occasion that Strongheart "fingered the red-tipped eagle feathers of his war bonnet" as he spoke.[22] His presence put on parade both the Vanishing Indian of the past as well as the "Progressive Indian" (as Olney was characterized in the introduction to his letter to the editor) of the future—both of which seemed to suit his audiences. But they also always got more than they bargained for. Here is the full text of one of Strongheart's lectures, which he delivered, reading from this typed manuscript, on July 3, 1921:

I shall explain how my people lived before the coming of your forefathers. First of all, my dear friends, allow me to speak upon the primitive life of my people. Long before the coming of your forefathers there were 1,758 different Indian tribes. Each of these different tribes and nations spoke a different language. Some used the sign language, which is universally understood, while other tribes had their individual way of speaking. The sign language is different, far different than the spoken language. Sometimes in the sign language a sign may mean one word, another sign may mean a phrase or clause, while again a sign may mean a sentence or several sentences. All of the tribes speak the sign language, yet no one knows the origin of it. We have inquired of the medicine man to reveal to us the secrets and mysteries of the sign language.

Some of the white people have the wrong impression of a medicine man. They think that a medicine man is a doctor. But he communicates with the Great Spirit for the people. The Indians know that there is one God, and we all worship Him, the same as the white people do. Many times the medicine man's first appeal is not answered. He tries again and again and usually the third appeal is answered. If the Great Spirit does not answer the medicine man is not worthy of the answer.

The Great Spirit, while communicating with the medicine man, told him to go into the forest and get a piece of strong wood and whittle and shave it down to the form of a pipe. The medicine man did this, and he painted the pipe beautifully, and he named it the "Pipe of Peace." Whenever we meet strangers we offer the pipe to smoke, and thereby we never break our friendship or peace.

We teach our children the habits and customs of our people, for we did not have schools to send them to. The white people have schools, high schools, colleges, universities, and other institutions to teach their children. The Indian women teach their daughters, and the Indian men teach their sons the ways and customs of their tribes. It was the only way they had of learning. They watched the birds and the beasts. They noticed that when two birds are flying thru the air, the male bird leads and his mate follows. This is true of animals also,—always the male leads and his mate follows, because the male wants to protect his mate from any danger that they might meet on their journey. So it is true of the Indians, too. Whenever they travel the man takes the lead for the same reason that causes the male birds and beasts to lead their mates. The Indians are like the birds in another way also.

The male bird builds his nest and then finds a mate—the Indian man prepares a home and then seeks his mate, too. Most of the white boys and men of today are more interested in the dance halls or the pool halls, and they often ask a girl to marry them before they have a home prepared for her. Many people do not realize that the birds and beasts have taught the Indian to be self-reliant.

An Indian woman teaches her daughter to defend herself from these human snakes, she teaches her the right and the wrong. The Indian girl is taught to honor and respect motherhood.

The Indian boy is taught how to be a good hunter and provider. He is taught the customary way of fighting by his father. When the boy becomes a young man, about twenty-four or twenty-five years of age he tries to earn a name for himself. The Indian people change their names very often during a lifetime. If an Indian boy is a good fighter, or if he is very brave he may have an honorable name given to him, but if he does a degrading deed an inferior name will be given him. An Indian man or woman is subject to a change of name at any time. If, perhaps, some time in the future he or she can do a brave act, their name can be changed so that it will be an honor to them.

Many people say that the Indians are a savage race, because they paint so much; but I do not know which is the wildest—the white girls (because they paint, too) or the Indians.

The primitive Indians never had war before the white people came. Each man was his own master. He was free to build his own teepee wherever he chose to put it. One man was just as capable as another. They roamed about in this vast country with no one to hinder them from doing just as they wished to do. The Indians were quite different from the white people—they did just as they wished. Too many white people just sit and wish they had this or that, or that they could do something that they probably are too lazy to do. The trouble with most of them is this: They ought to have a wish-bone where their back-bone is.

The love in the Indians heart for God is pure and without reason. The Indian and the white man worship the same God. To the Indian He is known as the Great Spirit, and to the white man He is known as Jesus Christ. Nevertheless, we are all His children, and he looks upon the Indian with the same feeling as He has towards the white man. Now my friends, why can't the white people look upon the Indians with the same feeling as God does? Are not all Christians trying to be more like him?

Whenever they call the Indians savages it makes my blood burn. A visit to the secretary, Mr. [name redacted in the typescript, possibly by McWhorter], personally, has given me permission to investigate the Indian affairs. The secretary wished to impress upon my mind that he was a graduate of Harvard, Yale, and Winston colleges. He was an intelligent man, as well as being well educated. I thought that this was a wonderful opportunity to learn something, so I asked him many questions. I said, "Do I clearly understand that you are a college and university graduate?" He assured me that he was, so then I inquired of him to tell me why Indians are called savages and white people are called civilized people. He says that the reason for calling Indians savage and the reason for calling white men civilized is this: The white men are educated, therefore civilized and peaceful, and Indians are not. If you people are civilized and peaceful why did you go to war and why did you fight? The white people have been in many wars, and yet they are represented as civilized and peaceful people. Why is it?

In the early frontier days there were many battles between the white men and the Indians. If the white men won the battle it was considered a good fight—and they were proud of it. But if the Indians won it was called a massacre.

Why do you keep us on a reservation while you give the Chinamen, Japs, and other foreigners freedom? Any alien can come to this country and be free—you do not put them on reservations. But the American Indians—the only real Americans are put on reservations and allowed to do just certain things. In the early days the Quakers were the best friends the Indians had. They always kept their word in regard to promises and treaties. The Indians suffer for the mistakes the white people made. The white people scared away the birds and beasts from our hunting grounds, so that we have had to move from place to place. Why do you impose upon us? Many people bring the unjust diseases to us and our children, sometimes causing us to die. Perhaps some day the Indian race will become extinct. The old Indians are dying away, leaving but a very few full bloods. There are more mixed bloods than full bloods, and I do not see why the Indians should be slaves.

Why do you take the aliens into this country and give them freedom? Any alien can come into this country and adopt it as his home and have more freedom than any American Indian. On election day, the American citizens and aliens—French, German, English, Russian, Italians—walk shoulder to shoulder to the polls to cast their votes. But let an Indian walk with them to vote and they will tell him, "Go back. You belong on your reservation." Now really, friends, it is a heart aching affair. America is for everybody else but the Americans, and instead of making America Americanized it is becoming more alienized. It is time to put a stop to the immigration—it is for the good of your people as well as for the Indians because the aliens make America more alienized.

The Blackfoot Indians of Montana are actually starving to death. You can go to the different places and you will see for yourself. Go to any reservation and you will see for yourself, that it is true of any of them. You find that the white people are interested in their own affairs and they do not pay any attention to the Indians. On one reservation the agent was allowed to buy the beef to supply the Indians with meat, and instead of buying beef he bought horse meat, which caused many deaths.

I know in one case where the Indians were actually robbed of their money by the man in charge. They were allowed $29.68 for their $50, Liberty Bonds. Altogether, the Indians bought $26,000,000.00 worth of Liberty Bonds during the war.

Sometimes the Indian population is over-estimated. We have 300,000 Indian men and women in the United States, but we are not allowed the privileges of the whites because we are under the supervision of the government. The Indian has opened his heart and given 18,000 young men as volunteer soldiers in your last war. 13,000 came back—the balance were left over seas. The Indians were sent as scouts to the front line of trenches and faced the dangers of shot and shell long before some of the white men did.

1,600 Indian women were Red Cross nurses. They risked the dangers of warfare as brave as the white women. Is the Indian the white man's friend or his enemy? The Indians always wish to be your friend—give us a chance and we will prove it. We ask you for the opportunity to show you that we mean it. It is an insult itself to be kept on a reservation. Is it true that a child of God can be entirely useless? If we are good enough to be nurses and soldiers of the United States army, why are we not good enough to be citizens of the United States?

The Indians had a flag long before the white man came to this country. It had red and white stripes in it with bright stars on a blue background. We could see it every evening at sunset. Our flag was made by nature. In the evening when the sun goes down, it causes the sky to turn crimson in streaks. In some places the sky remains white, thus giving it the effect of the red and white stripes. Later on, the stars come out, and there—we have the real American flag! The red and white stripes go side by side in the same flag, so why can't the red and white people stand side by side as one people with the guidance of the same God? I believe that it is time for the Indians to be released from the wards of the government. We are a united people belonging to the United States.[23]

Strongheart's speech seems to focus on "Indian lore and life," as per Chautauqua audience expectations, by drawing heavily from racist discourse, specifically primitivism, with its associations with sign language, nature, and war. His speech is actually a story that opens with prelapsarian times imagined in lore-like language and concludes with present conditions fleshed out with statistical detail. Starting with a series of origin stories, Strongheart establishes the origin of his people before the white man's arrival, implicitly the "we-were-here-first" argument that gathers its legal and moral force from the doctrine of discovery, as also seen in Louis Mann's letter to the editor, discussed earlier. The specificity of the number of tribes (1,758) stands in sharp contrast to the dreamy description of the preliterate (and nonoral) use of sign language, the universal lingua franca, in preinvasion times. Presumably only a medicine man knows the origin of sign language, Strongheart says, but that suggestion is left hanging, serving instead to explain the origin story of the peace pipe, another piece of Indian life and lore. But that story introduces the topics of war and peace as well as the binaries usually associated with them: savage, warring Indians and civilized, peaceful whites. The followup of this theme comes much later; his audience has to wait for it.

In the meantime, Strongheart sets up another theme: education. Unlike his usual position elsewhere for integrated Indian schooling, he takes a different tack here, suggesting its purely rhetorical function in this context. In contrast to the white institutions of education, Indian parents teach their children appropriate gender roles, morality, and self-reliance, lessons learned by observing nature—and lessons apparently not learned by whites, "the human snakes" against whom Indian women must defend themselves. Strongheart inserts comment on naming customs, always provisionally based on actions, actions that may run the gamut from brave to degrading. Speaking of degradation, he reconnects his earlier point about savagery and war, by associating war paint with makeup: "Many people say that the Indians are a savage race, because they paint so much; but I do not know which is the wildest—the white girls (because they paint, too) or the Indians."

Returning to the origins story of Indian life before invasion, Strongheart stresses Indians' freedom, all doing what they wished, before delivering his next barb: "The Indians were quite different from the white people—they did just as they wished. Too many white people just sit and wish they had this or that, or that they could do something that they probably are too lazy to do. The trouble with most of them is this: They ought to have a wish-bone where their back-bone is." His lecture takes yet another unexpected (this time religious) turn, when he points out the common belief in God, who recognizes all as his children, Indians included. Why can't whites recognize Indians as such too? Strongheart then bluntly asserts that "whenever they call Indians savages it makes my blood burn." Only now does he return to the savage/civilized binary introduced earlier, pointing out that whites are far more warlike than Indians. He makes that return by way of personal narrative, complete with hypothetical dialogue, weaving in the earlier theme of the inadequacies of the white man's education in his characterization of the government official. Strongheart identifies this official by name (although it was redacted in the paper copy, probably by McWhorter)—speaking straight and naming names, true to the Plateau Indian rhetorical tradition.

It is only at this juncture that Strongheart approaches the main point of his lecture: citizenship. His apparent anti-immigrant argument aims to show the contrast in the freedom, rights, and treatment afforded non-American immigrants versus the original Americans, Indians. He backs this claim with several examples, some from his own experience (the starvation of the Blackfoot and the case of the undervalued Liberty Bonds), some from dubious numerical information—this latter form of evidence perhaps holding more weight with his audience. He reminds that audience of Indian patriotism in the World War, as if to reassure his audience that Indians are also patriotic, even though they are pacifist by tradition. Finally, at the end of the penultimate paragraph, Strongheart states his main point: "If we are good enough to be nurses and soldiers of the United States army, why are we not good enough to be citizens of the United States?" He closes with an analogy, a characteristic of Christian discourse that appears increasingly in Plateau Indian rhetoric as Indians learned English. Recalling his earlier theme of nature-as-teacher, the closing analogy of the "real American flag" works to naturalize the idea of Indian citizenship, and with it, equality. Fighting for this "real flag" and what it represents stands in contradistinction to simply fighting for "a flag," as Louis Mann suggested in his letter cited earlier, more of a white man's motive for fighting than an Indian's.

Consistent with Plateau Indian naming customs based on actions, Strongheart deserved his name. Even when his Chautauqua employers threatened to fire him if he did not stop naming names and politicizing his lectures, he continued to do so, undaunted, for more than nine years. Advocating for Indian issues and delivering stinging rebukes of a corrupt system, he remained strong-hearted, rhetorically counting coup on the white man's wrongs against the Indian.

Fishing Rights, State Supreme Court Brief, 1921

A descendant of a signatory of the Treaty of 1855 helped defend one of the rights guaranteed by that treaty, the right to fish "in common and accustomed places" and, in this particular case, in accustomed manner: spear-fishing for salmon at the falls at Prosser, Washington. Addressing the state Supreme Court in 1921 in his own accustomed manner, Chief Meninick delivered this speech (quoted in full below), which "characterized him as a leader and orator."[24]

White men and red men all are brothers. The Mighty Spirit made all his children. To the white man he gave cattle, sheep and grain for food. To the red man he gave game, fish and roots and berries. He placed the Indians here on the bosom of the Earth, our mother. We are the native children of these plains and forests; we did not come from foreign lands. We had no cattle, sheep, or grain. For us the Great Spirit created the wild game in the woods and the fish in the streams and this has been our food from generation to generation since the beginning.

Our people were here before the white men came and even before the missionaries came. We are the real Americans. This country was our home and these were [multiple strike-throughs—indecipherable] and now our rights.

After the white men came, they wanted to divide our lands and they were troubling our people, so the Government sent Gov. Stevens to Walla Walla to make a treaty with the redmen.

Governor Stevens asked that the Indians go on Reservations and let the white men take the other lands to farm and raise cattle and sheep. The Indians did not like to give up any lands because they wanted to hunt and fish and go and come as they wished. They feared that if they gave up any land to the white people it would intefere with their fishing and hunting; but Stevens promised them that there would never be trouble about these things. But now I and my Indians have been arrested for fishing and I am here to answer.

Let us go back in our memories to the time when the Treaty was made in Walla Walla. Let us call back the Spirits of the dead. From their graves I summon Governor Stevens and the other white men who represented your government. I also call on the spirit of my father who was the chief Meninick, who signed that treaty and the other chiefs. Chief Judge, let you represent the spirit of Governor Stevens and I will represent the spirit of my father, Meninick and I will speak the words he told me often. When the chiefs at that council did not want to sign the treaty, Stevens asked them why and the chiefs said: If give your possession of the lands we will lose our rights to fish in the streams, but Stevens said No. The whites wanted only to farm and would never intefere with the redmen fishing at their old fishing places. But my father said "When we are dead then who will witness to what you promise. Then Gov. Stevens said "I will write it down in the treaty that you and your people have right to take fish at these old fishing places, and I will pledge the Americans to keep this promise as long as the sun shines and as long as the river runs. Then Those were his words, and my people believed in him and signed the treaty. Now I can in the witnesses that Gov. Stevens himself appointed. For the shite topped mountain still stands, the sun still melts its snow into the rivers that still carry its fresh waters to the sea that invite salmon to come to our old fishing places Top-tut where we were arrested for fishing. Goo is one of those old fishing places where the Indians were fishing when Gov Stevens gave the solen promise which our people accepted as the pledge of the government. We say that when your officers punish us for taking fish at the places reserved, you violate your treaty and your promise and while you may punish us you have the power, yet before God, where justice is more than that of men, we are innocent of having done wrong.[25]

Appropriate to the occasion, Chief Meninick appeals on legal grounds deriving from the Treaty of 1855, but he does so in ways characteristic of Plateau Indian rhetoric. His opening draws from both Christian discourse and the ideological complex of racism, as he makes the point that the Mighty Spirit made both white and red men but endowed them differently, giving the white man cattle, sheep, and grain but the red man game, fish, roots, and berries. His origins story does not stop there, though. The chief argues from the doctrine of discovery, the same doctrine used to legitimize European imperialism, co-opted later by the invaded, as Mann and Olney did in their writing cited earlier. But the chief extends that argument, tapping into the anti-immigration sentiment of the times: we were here first and we were always here, unlike everyone else, who are all immigrants by definition.

Chief Meninick then shifts to the heart of his argument, as he presents supporting evidence in a kind of narrative. He asks the court to reenact a crucial scene in the negotiations at Walla Walla, which becomes ever more dramatic when he asks that all present summon the dead back to speak. Asking the court to "go back in our memories to the time when the Treaty was made in Walla Walla," he designates the chief justice as the representative of "the spirit of Governor Stevens" while he, Chief Meninick, represents his own father, speaking "the [same] words he told me often." Interestingly, the governor's putative phrase about keeping his promise "as long as the sun shines and as long as the river runs" does not appear in the official record but does in Governor Stevens's secretary James Doty's own journal. Doty's inclusion suggests that Chief Meninick's dialogue is not totally fictitious. As such, this is a powerful example of the credibility of intergenerational oral transmission.

After dramatizing this scene by taking on both sides of the dialogue, Chief Meninick calls in "the witnesses that Gov. Stevens himself appointed": the mountain that still stands, the sun that "still melts its snow into the rivers that that still carry its fresh waters to the sea that invite salmon to come to our old fishing places Top-tut where we were arrested for fishing."[26] He arrives at his point at last, after having already offered powerful support for it, stating his thesis in the very last sentence: "We say that when your officers punish us for taking fish at the places reserved, you violate your treaty and your promise and while you may punish us you have the power, yet before God, where justice is more than that of men, we are innocent of having done wrong." While the chief's argument is still a legal one, he does not convey it in just legal terms, but also in moral and spiritual ones, and he does so using a high-affect, dramatic reenactment.

Late Harvest

These early Yakama activists embraced literacy and English, understanding the value of these tools to conserve Indian societies. Their efforts were not wasted, although most did not live to see them come to fruition. Today, liquor sales are banned on most reservations. In 1924, President Calvin Coolidge signed the Indian Citizenship Act, which did not really give Indians any new rights. As detailed by subsequent law and court decisions, American Indians were citizens only as individuals and then only if they lived off-reservation; those living on reservations must still live as colonial subjects "under federal Indian law without the constitutional guarantees of U.S. citizenship," such as legal protection against sexual discrimination.[27] Voting rights in state and national elections were later passed on a state-by-state basis and ultimately by civil rights legislation in the 1960s.[28]

After decades of protesting the low standards in Indian schools and advocating for tribal control, several pieces of legislation passed in the 1970s opened up real possibilities for Native education, before tribal sovereignty was undercut once again by No Child Left Behind in 2001 (the topic of chapter 7). In the 1921 fishing rights case argued by Chief Meninick, the state court ruled in favor of the Indians, but its immediate impact was limited to just spear-fishing, not to all fishing rights, and not to hunting at all; in 1927 the U.S. Supreme Court ruled that hunting in usual and customary places—that is, off-reservation—was subject to "the police power of the state."[29] It did, however, set legal precedent. In a suit later filed by the federal government on behalf of tribes in Washington, Judge George Boldt in 1974 decided in the Indians' favor, after consulting the official minutes of treaty negotiations to determine the intent, as well as the Indians' understanding, of Governor Stevens's promise to the Indians at the time. The so-called Boldt Decision not only guaranteed Indians' right to harvest and to share in the catch of non-Indians. It also encouraged and emboldened Indian activism across the country for decades to come.

5   **Deliberating Publicly**
1955–1956

A t the General Council meeting of the Yakama Nation on January 13, 1956, council officer Burdette Kent opened proceedings with a summary behind the "squabbling" that had dominated the assembly's meetings since the previous July:

> We are here today because the progress we have made has been struck a blow. The Democracy we believed in turned into dictatorship. In the past it was a common foe. Now we fight amongst our own people. They are harder to fight. They strike from within. They split our issues. We do not give sufficient thought. The struggle now will be the longest and hardest. This grab for power brought by Indian breeds [off-reservation enrollees from Tacoma, on the west side of the state] will not end. It will be brought up again and again. As it is won should fix it so we never be attacked from that angle again.
>
> It seems the present administration [the federal commissioner from the Bureau of Indian Affairs] has chosen sides they wish to succeed. Those believe in termination. *They are happy to see us squabbling among ourselves.* It is up to everyone to think best and act accordingly. [Emphasis mine][1]

Unlike previous chapters that have focused on intergroup communications, this one examines intragroup deliberations of one tribe group on the Plateau (the Confederated Tribes of the Yakama Nation) as it seemingly squabbles about one seemingly inconsequential matter: whether or not to postpone an election. Kent's remarks succinctly capture the power dynamics behind not just this particular controversy but many others, both before and since in Indian Country: internal conflict exacerbated by federal intervention. While Kent characterized the threat from within as squabbling, the threat from without represented nothing less than an assault on tribal sovereignty. Ironically, the outside danger that threatened to pull the tribe apart served rhetorically to rally it back together.

Also characteristic was the historic divide between the General Council (the general assembly of all enrolled tribal members) and the Tribal Council (a panel of selected officers that manages the tribe's daily affairs and serves as liaison between the tribe and the federal government). The former follows the traditional Plateau Indian governance model of direct democracy; the latter, the American governance model of representative democracy. Because of the Tribal Council's enormous and far-reaching power, its historical relationship with the Bureau of Indian Affairs (BIA), its structural differences with the General Council, and the inherent distrust of representative government generally, Tribal Council elections are often fraught with contention. One such election was at the center of this particular controversy.

Originally slated for the July 1955 General Council meeting, the Tribal Council election was postponed for lack of quorum and rescheduled for November 28. Quorum was easily met at the November 28 meeting, but the election was once again postponed when the meeting was recessed for two funerals and rescheduled for December 5–7, with the Tribal Council election reslated for December 6. But at least one person, E. J. Wilton, representing off-reservation enrollees from Tacoma, wanted it rescheduled for thirty days hence; meeting again so soon would present a hardship for those coming from the coast over the Cascade Mountains. The Tacoma group had already complained back in July to the commissioner of Indian affairs in Washington, D.C., about that first postponement, and they renewed those complaints after the November postponement. In response, the commissioner sent word to the General Council to reschedule the Tribal Council elections for April, rather than December, to give all enrollees, including the Tacoma group, more advanced notice; better weather and road conditions in April would also likely improve attendance. He also wanted the General Council to put in writing the customs regarding elections of tribal officers.

If the General Council did not comply in all these regards, the commissioner threatened to waive tribal customs and conduct an election using secret and absentee ballots instead of public voting by a show of hands, as was tradition. Even though the General Council did comply with the directive to write down customary procedures and requirements for meetings and Tribal Council elections, after much heated discussion, the General Council defied the commissioner's other demand and elected their Tribal Council on December 6, as planned, rather than postpone it until April. The commissioner then called for federal hearings to investigate complaints of election irregularities. The General Council reconvened on January 13, 1956, to discuss possible recourses and decided to send a committee to Washington, D.C., to present their case in person. Federal hearings took place on February 14 and 16, 1956, at three different locations on the reservation. No official action was taken after the hearings. But writing down customary procedures had the effect of giving those traditional practices legal status, officially sanctioned by both the tribe and the BIA. Thus the political *ethnie* of the Yakama Nation was validated, modernized, and carried forward for future generations.

The primary material under investigation in this chapter offers snapshots of five General Council meetings conducted first *by* the General Council and then the three federal hearings *about* the General Council's procedures in 1955–56 at the height of the termination movement. Evident in this analysis is the impact of colonial surveillance on the internal workings of the tribe. As State Senator Ganders said when introduced as a guest at the December 5 meeting: "[I am here] watching you in the way you conduct your affairs." At issue in these meetings is, on the face of it, procedural. But at stake is nothing less than sovereignty—a connection not lost on Kiutus Jim, vice chair of the General Council, who immediately brought up at that same meeting the Treaty of 1855 and Indian veterans' service in war: "I believe at this time the people, the visitors, can see how we conduct our meeting. I am going to say a few words to show what our people know, what they learned in the Treaty and what they learned while serving at war. Under oath, sworn, they fought for justice, democracy, liberty, freedom." Using words instead of bearing arms (or "lyrical artillery" in the words of the student rapper in chapter 1)—this is the new warrior's way, veteran Kiutus Jim implicitly argues, the way to fight colonial intrusion into Native political processes. In demanding a change in both election and meeting procedures, the federal government was tampering with ancient ways of local governance—in effect, threatening to shift the tribal model from a direct democracy with public, oral/visible voting conducted multiple times to a representative democracy with secret, written voting conducted one time. Such a shift would have been seismic, for it would throw off balance the core value at the heart of Plateau Indian culture: speaking straight and speaking up for one's self, while also harmonizing multiple viewpoints for the collective good.

This chapter, after establishing the provenance of the archival material under examination, fleshes out the historical context that provides important background for appreciating the issues surrounding this particular crisis: the historical divides between the BIA and the tribes, between off- and on-reservation tribal members, and between Tribal Council and General Council. As mentioned earlier, these two political bodies operate from different forms of governance, the American model of representative democracy and the Plateau Indian model of direct democracy; further, with those differences come different interactional protocols. After describing the customary procedures and protocols that govern General Council meetings, which contrast sharply with those of the federal hearings, I discuss three features of Plateau Indian interactional discourse evident in the primary material: continuity of discourse, affordances for confrontation, and mechanisms for building consensus. In closing, I instantiate how the political *ethnie* of the Yakama Nation has been modernized since 1956 while still keeping faith with traditional values. This chapter sheds light on the expectations and experiences of persuasive discourse that students bring to the classroom, the topic of chapter 6.

The primary material consists of archival notes of eight meetings conducted on the Yakama reservation over a seven-month period in 1955 and 1956:

- Five meetings conducted by the General Council of the Confederated Tribes of the Yakama Nation on November 28, 1955; December 5, 1955; December 6, 1955; December 7, 1955; January 13, 1956.
- Three federally conducted hearings, investigating these General Council meetings, held at three locations on the reservation, two on February 14, 1956, at Satus and White Swan, and one on February 16, 1956, at Toppenish.

These notes were taken and then typed by Click Relander, sculptor, journalist, author, amateur historian, and white ally. Relander's life work focused primarily on the Wanapum Indians of Priest Rapids, but he also became deeply involved with the Yakama after he moved to central Washington in 1945. Like Lucullus Virgil McWhorter before him, Relander amassed a prodigious collection of papers, now housed in the Yakima Valley Libraries.[2] The primary materials for this chapter come from that collection.

For enrolled members only, General Council meetings are usually closed to outsiders, except by invitation; so are the official minutes of these meetings. Although the 1955–56 meetings were conducted in English, many of the speeches were spoken in Indian first and then translated into English, a long-standing custom of a multilingual society adjusted to modern circumstance: the rising dominance of English.[3] This lag time presumably allowed Relander to capture many speeches *verbatim*, as suggested by redundant sentences, false starts, and the like, in his typescripts. He also had the habit of noting when he was not quoting, indicating missed or intentionally left out portions of sentences or speeches with ellipses and "etc.," or duly noting that he stopped taking notes or that he was just summarizing (e.g., when the commissioner's telegrams were read, he labeled his summary statement, "Gist:"). While he took care to record many details, such as exact time and exact head counts as they were announced throughout meetings, he enclosed in parentheses other information and editorial comment: audience reactions; speaker's relatives; people's appearance and speech delivery; room layout; weather and road conditions. That Relander took such care with his notes reflects his own writerly bent as both an author and journalist. That he chose to take notes on these particular meetings suggests that he understood their potential historical import.

Although these are one observer's notes and not official minutes, they are detailed enough to offer up fresh insights into intragroup interaction, argumentation, and public deliberation. And while the material is limited to one tribe, my analysis holds true for other Plateau tribes and in different kinds of meetings to this day, as I have observed and experienced in Plateau Indian conferences, business and faculty meetings, workshops, job talks, college classrooms, and personal interactions; this corroborating, experiential evidence initially inspired this chapter and helped shape my analysis, although I do not cite from this experience. Instead, the written materials I have selected amply substantiates how and why the Plateau Indian political process is distinctive, marked in part by traditional interactional protocols but also by colonial conditions that breed factionalism. Despite internal and external conflict, ancient protocols prevail, and consensus is eventually reached, even though that consensus-building process may take months, years, or even decades.

Colonial Context

It would be difficult to overstate the catastrophic and corrosive impact of colonialism on Indian Country. The controversy detailed in the material at hand provides just one instance, offering a closer look at how colonial policies systematically eroded tribal sovereignty, not just from above but from within. As American studies scholar Eric Cheyfitz has pointed out, assimilation was the overarching goal of federal Indian policy for 150 years, as embodied in three major pieces of legislation: the General Allotment Act (1887); the Indian Reorganization Act (1934); and the House Concurrent Resolution 108 calling for termination of tribal status altogether (1953). Together, these aimed to break up Indian Country, exerting pressure from above and fomenting factionalism from within, thereby enacting a kind of divide-and-conquer strategy typical of a colonial agenda.[4] The abiding consequences of these acts, two of which have since been annulled, still adversely affect reservation politics, as my analysis of the meetings show.

The first piece of legislation was the General Allotment Act (1887), commonly called the Dawes Act, and subsequent legislation (most important, the Burke Act of 1906). In effect, these acts separated Indians from their land and isolated them from each other. Collectively, this legislation called for allotting 40–160 acres to each individual adult enrolled member; any land not allotted could be sold by the government.[5] After being held in trust for at least five years, either the allottee or the federal government would hold title; most often, the latter was the case. At that point the land became taxable by the state, and Indian owners could lose their land for nonpayment of taxes. They could also lose it for nonuse, a determination that could be made if an Indian owner even left the premises for travel or work elsewhere. More commonly, the land went unused because Indians were simply unaccustomed and ill-equipped to farm small tracts individually, the federal government failing to live up to its treaty obligations to prepare them for this shift. Or allottees could sell their allotments. Originally the least desirable land, reservations became more desirable with increased settlement and improved agricultural methods, which in turn increased the pressure on the BIA to get Indians to sell any allotted land that could be farmed, logged, or grazed. The land of any allottee who did not sell was automatically, upon the allottee's death, inherited by all of his family. Over time, multiple owners were less likely to live on the land and, to keep it from being confiscated for nonuse, more likely to lease to non-Indian farmers and ranchers, many of them large-scale operations.[6]

This was the legal legacy that created the so-called "checkerboard reservation," a patchwork of tracts owned by Indians and non-Indians, the latter eventually predominating.[7] Underdevelopment of reservation lands accelerated this shift, as Indians left the reservation to find employment opportunities and as non-Indian towns sprung up near reservations to service these remote areas, another deterrent to Indian-owned businesses on-reservation.[8] This diaspora created yet another division within, between those Indians living on-reservation and those living off-reservation. When tribes started collecting settlement funds for treaty violations and had to decide how to allocate these funds, the split between on- and off-reservation tribal members came into political play—the latter more likely to vote for per capita distribution, while the former typically voted for reservation investment.[9] The sum result of these policies: During the allotment era from 1887–1934, Indians lost ninety million acres of communal land, a net loss of 65 percent, further impoverishing and fracturing Indian communities.[10]

The second piece of legislation took a different tack, while still moving toward assimilation in effect if not by intention, this time by undermining traditional political institutions.[11] The Indian Reorganization Act (IRA) of 1934 officially annulled the Dawes Act and ushered in the era of so-called self-determination. Under its provisions, reservation populations would govern themselves as they saw fit. They could choose to adopt IRA-sponsored constitutions or not, but they still had to have some executive body to transact business with local, state, and federal agencies, including most importantly the BIA, which controlled federal resources and Indian lands. Minimally, tribes had to institute tribal councils, a form of representative government, as opposed to direct democracy run by informal consensus, the traditional model of government that most tribes were accustomed to.[12] At least by contrast, Indians saw representative government as more vulnerable to corruption and nepotism and its processes, less transparent. As a representative form of governance, tribal councils were also adjudged as guilty-by-association with the BIA, undoubtedly the largest, the most byzantine, and the most corrupt bureaucracy of all federal agencies. The most famous example of its malfeasance is its mismanagement of the Indian trust fund, which defrauded the tribes of at least forty-seven billion dollars since 1887 in lost royalties for oil, gas, and other leases on Indian land.[13]

A third major push toward assimilation more blatantly attacked tribal sovereignty: termination, first introduced in 1953 with House Concurrent Resolution 108. Like the allotment and the self-government bills before it, Resolution 108 was "couched . . . in the classic liberal language of individualism," its stated intention to free Indians from federal control and to allow them to be subject to state laws, like all other American citizens.[14] Upon termination, property could be distributed among individual tribal members or the tribe could incorporate, but the tribe could no longer govern itself or receive federal services. In addition, tribal and federal jurisdictions in legal areas such as criminal law were transferred to the state. The bills met with pan-tribal resistance, most notably the National Congress of American Indians (an organization mentioned many times in the primary material), resulting ultimately in the Nixon administration officially abandoning termination as federal policy in 1970.[15] Between 1954 and 1966 a hundred tribes were officially terminated and about 3.2 percent of trust land was lost, mostly in California and Oregon. More ominously, the Supreme Court upheld the legality of termination and Congress's unilateral power to deconstruct Indian Country at any time. Even though no tribe has been terminated since 1966, termination is still seen as a constant threat, "the ultimate weapon of Congress and the ultimate fear of tribes."[16]

General Council Procedures and Protocols

Ever vigilant and suspicious of the Tribal Council, the General Council serves as the people's "watchdog."[17] What follows is a description of the procedural rules governing the General Council meetings of the Yakama Nation in 1955 and 1956, as they still do today with few exceptions, as both primary and secondary sources as well as my own anecdotal experience at other kinds of meetings corroborate.

As witness George Lucei testified at the Satus federal hearing in 1956, it was not uncommon back in the old days for bands of two hundred to three hundred or even five hundred to six hundred to be elected to govern. In modern times that political tradition is embodied in the General Council. The General Council is the assembly of the people, its meetings open to all enrolled members, but to others only upon invitation. It convenes at regular intervals throughout the year to discuss and decide tribal matters by public vote, either by a show of hands or by standing up. The meeting is held in the longhouse, the customary spiritual and political center of the reservation. Women are seated along the south side and men along the north. The longhouse typically has a kitchen; supper is provided to attendees each evening.

Thirty days' notice of an upcoming meeting is released via various outlets—radio, television, newspapers, posters, but most important, by word-of-mouth—along with an agenda identifying main topics to be discussed, which aims to "expedite meetings instead of wasting time in prolonged discussion."[18] Start time is stated and generally adhered to, but end time is not. Agendas may be rearranged or set aside, and meetings may be canceled for any number of reasons but most commonly for funerals. Meetings typically begin with a prayer or worship song, sung seven times, followed by status reports from attorneys, among others. The annual session runs for three days and often into the night; special sessions are called, as needed, to complete unfinished business or focus on a particular issue. Because the meeting is conducted in both Indian and English, fluency in both languages used to be a requirement for office up until 1956. Officers also had to be full-blood and generally between the ages of thirty-five and sixty-five, although these requirements have also been relaxed since 1956. Personal movement is not restricted. People may come and go and return as they please. Official "counters" regularly announce latest headcounts, as quorum for voting purposes must be maintained.

These procedures support culturally marked interactional protocols, including implicit rules for paying attention, gaining the floor, and taking turns. The chair of the General Council generally presides and recognizes people who want to speak, but anyone may take the floor between speakers without being recognized by the chair. As Walter Cloud, a General Council officer, modestly declared at the December 5, 1955, meeting, "I understand an element from outside want to introduce new procedure. I want to hear. I am not your leader. You are the leader and must decide."[19] Although audience members may interject comment in earnest or in jest, they may not otherwise wrest the floor completely from a speaker. Listeners pay attention but in ways unrecognizable by Euro-American standards. The audience members may be conversing among themselves, tending to children, passing around babies, knitting, beading, and so on. Even though they generally look or align their bodies toward speakers, their interjections and laughter, among other listening cues, indicate their attention to the discussion at hand.

Turn-taking protocols reflect a similar regard for personal autonomy so central to Plateau Indian values. Multiple meetings, with no specified end-time, give all adults opportunity to speak. Without any official time limits as in Euro-American public meetings, speakers tend to speak at length, holding the floor for roughly the same amount of time as others, not only respecting others' turns but also avoiding the appearance of showing off. Content-choice is not necessarily agenda-driven nor is turn-taking determined topically, even when specific people are asked specific questions. For example, a person may raise three issues, but those issues may seem to be dropped in subsequent speakers' turns, only to reappear in someone's or some two persons' speeches hours—or even weeks—later.[20] Such distant sequencing (as opposed to temporal and topical sequencing, as is common in Euro-American conversational protocol) helps mitigate conflict. The implicit rules governing interaction allow speakers—not the chair or the topic or the listeners—to decide when to speak, if and when they are ready. And they usually signal that they are finished by overtly saying words to that effect: "That is all I have to say."

Taken together, these protocols reflect the central political value of Plateau Indian culture: radical egalitarianism grounded in utmost respect for personal autonomy, for speakers and listeners alike. Speaking for, or acting on behalf of, another person without permission presumes a power over that person. At the same time, everyone is expected to stand up for her own views. Individual votes during General Council are publicly cast by raising hands or by standing; private voting, like anonymous criticism and rumor-mongering, runs counter to Plateau Indian ideals. Besides voting for or against a motion on the floor, tribal members may also cast "nonvotes," indicating they are undecided or at least disinclined to show their preference perhaps in light of the local politics involved on a given issue. Thus decisiveness for its own sake is not highly regarded, whereas deliberation, both public and private, is.

The abiding belief in the inalienable right of speaking straight for one's self and standing up publicly for one's views, but not for others without their permission, is the bedrock objection to representative democracy. At the January 13, 1956, General Council meeting, as the assembly was trying to decide who to send to the federal hearings to represent various constituencies, attendee Lawrence Goudy argued against limiting representation in any way, pointing out just how many constituencies there are within this one community:

> Shouldn't have a limitation on it. Look upon yourselves, churches, Betterment League, Wigwam Club, cattlemen, Satus, Toppenish, White Swan, Wapato Long House; Rock Creek; youth groups, Shaker church and even further than that we should have witnesses such as the chamber of Commerce, Yakima Newspaper and other organizations. This is important. There should be no limitation. I would like to make a motion the whole tribal council goes. They know what is going on on the reservation, and several veterans go with our older people. I ask an amendment, no limitation.[21]

At the federal hearing in Toppenish in February 1956, attendee Louis Sohappy raised the same issue, saying that speaking Indian without translation more directly represents his own constituency, who does not speak English:

> Satus Long House representative. Now speaking to my people without interpreter. Had one, he wanted more just before and can't pay him. I represent a hard people. They want their wishes represented here, can't [cross out] non-speaking English people. The Indian has a different way of speaking, yesterday, today and future. You white men different. . . . Treaty of 1855 we reserved all rights exclusively. We still have that, hunting fishing etc. But funny, we cannot pick our own statesmen.[22]

Multiple, sometimes divergent, viewpoints not only attests to the diversity within Native communities; they are actually the precondition for building consensus and restoring communal harmony.

The protocols of the federal hearings held in February 1956 stand in contrast. Like the General Council meetings, the hearings were also conducted in the longhouse, but the presiding chair regulated turns, recognizing a witness who then sat in the center of the space. Testimony was limited to ten minutes. An agenda was adhered to and strictly organized into opposite viewpoints: first, those who supported the General Council's handling of the election; then those who did not. Not everyone was supposed to speak or even attend, just "representatives" of various constituencies. Reflected in these protocols are the principles of representative democracy. The two meeting types differ procedurally in these ways: the representative governance model of the federal hearings (1) structures the agenda into arguments for and against, whereas the General Council meetings do not; (2) uses secret and absentee ballot, whereas the General Council practices public voting by a show of hands or by standing; and (3) only ballots once, whereas the General Council may ballot multiple times on one issue, a practice that encourages changing one's mind. Key mechanisms embedded in the General Council protocols, following traditional rules of order, I argue, promote airing dissent as a critical part of the process of building consensus.[23]

As discussed in chapter 2, every language also has its own principles of cooperative, conversational, interactional discourse—principles that define the boundaries of what is allowable, appropriate, and effective communication within a given speech community, including interactional protocols that govern content choices, turn-taking and floor-taking, inferencing strategies, listening cues, physical movement, and so on.[24] Interestingly, these protocols directly derive from those of the ancestral language, even among speakers who now speak only English.[25] As the following analysis of the archival material shows, the interactional protocols governing public deliberation among the Yakama (and most Plateau tribes, as I have observed) encourage the expression of multiple perspectives on a focused topic, foster confrontation, and build consensus. Working in tandem, these protocols usually manage to balance out the traditional ideals of personal autonomy and collective good, finding verbal expression in ways consistent with the same indigenous rhetoric evident in previous chapters. Three features of Plateau Indian interaction discourse stand out in the archival material: continuity, affordances for confrontation, and mechanisms for consensus-building.

Continuity of Discourse

Plateau Indian principles of interaction do allow that speakers may speak off-topic and even off-agenda, a principle that explains, according to previous scholarship, the discontinuity of interactional discourse, both in terms of content-choice and direction of the discussion.[26] I argue, however, that Plateau interactional discourse does have direction and focus, but in ways that still encourage multiple and divergent viewpoints. At the federal hearing in Toppenish in February 16, 1956, one attendee, Ambrose Smartlowit, does not trust any representation: he comes forward and represents himself, his testimony centered on his own direct experience of the issues at hand. I quote his turn at the floor in full:

> Representing self. Yes. Wilton wanted a 30-day recess etf. some say nothing at the time when meeting is order but when through and voted on they got a howl coming.
>
> On July 15 I was present at White Swan Long House and 9:30 when I came in people going in and out, don't know what but some were uneasy. Some people in West C were there in full but can you help it when you haven't got a quorum. Been attending since 1924, but turnout Nov. 28, as big as I have ever seen. Post mortem, that's when Wilton should be postpon for 30 days meeting went on Dec. 5, 6, 7, like line was busy, wires Wilton and Commissioner
>
> This (election) was the Yakimas own thinking, not the tribal attorney we feel we have our own government. Election—I don't see anything wrong everyone got . . . even mixed blood My own opinion, Wilton campaign I can't see live another part get into office These people here, the mixed bloods get the same choice on everything, the same privilege get loans, hunt in hills anytime, in fact invite white people in. I am saying this. I ain't been coaxed by no one. I talk my own here myself. Once way down while working for Navajos I see Yakima election ad there. Can't see why can't know of election here I see ad in Oregon, Pendleton, may be crazy looking at everything like Comic books.
>
> Wheeler Howard act [the Indian Reorganization Act of 1934] . . . vote I was interpreter. I was the interpreter and I was a secret ballot but didn't see anything secret about it.
>
> I was for the Wheeler Howard, yet. There were places to mark the ballot, yes, no. The people I interpreted for I could have shown them [strike out] wrong place to mark because they wanted to vote the other way, but I didn't want it that bad. This is no baloney.
>
> On July 15 I saw no fists flying.[27]

Smartlowit's remarks may seem disjointed, especially when compared to those of other speakers, but he nonetheless manages to register his position on several parts of the argument at hand: (a) there wasn't a quorum at the July meeting for no special reason; (2) mixed bloods (i.e., the off-reservation Tacoma group) get the same rights and privileges; (3) the meetings are widely advertised in multiple venues, even as far away as Arizona; (4) secret balloting can easily lead to corruption; (5) no one verbalized objection to the postponement in July at the time ("I saw no fists flying"). The expressed time and turn limitations of the federal hearings probably increased the probability that Smartlowit's remarks would be less coherent, not more, under pressure to get all his thoughts into the record in one turn. Arguably, with more time and more turns, as in General Council meetings, speakers' contributions may be more, not less, focused on the topic at hand. It may not seem so to outsiders, in part because the insiders know the context and have discussed the agenda item with others long before the meeting, since the agenda is always posted and announced in many venues well in advance.[28]

But I want to suggest an additional possibility: that each speaker is intentionally presenting a different angle for consideration, with all angles taken as a whole, offering a rich range of possible positions on the issue at hand, not just for/against, and remarkably with minimal overlap. In fact, the implicit challenge for speakers seems to be to individualize their arguments by introducing novel lines of thoughts, a feature of American Indian rhetoric more generally that previous scholarship has identified. Read collectively, their arguments show the divisive impact of colonial policies on a checkerboard reservation created by Indian/non-Indian ownership. To wit: the distrust between the General Council and the Tribal Council; the contempt for off-reservation Indians; and the fear of taxation, allotment confiscation, and—most of all—termination. For example, the December 5, 1955, General Council meeting opened with the issue of whether or not to comply with the commissioner's directive to postpone the Tribal Council Election until April. Consecutive speakers gave, in essence, the following arguments. Notice that their content-choices took different tacks, with all but one (Wilson Charley) nonetheless arguing against postponement with one person undeclared (George Umtuch, the presiding chair), not counting the white attorney, who did not have a vote:

- Walter Underwood pointed out that the tribe needed to get ready now, before Congress reconvened in January;
- Alex Saluskin first castigated the commissioner for his dictatorial methods before bringing up the threatened secret ballot, which he saw as a step toward termination, concluding that the tribe should go above the commissioner's head and directly to Congress;
- Otis Shilow said that Wilton, not the Tribal Council, was to blame for creating this crisis and argues for a "show down" with the commissioner;
- Al Goudy first quoted from three different letters that at other times autho-

rized the tribe to ensure that the majority prevailed and then moved that the meeting agenda proceed as planned, with the Tribal Council election held the next day;

- George Umtuch, the presiding officer, said that the Tribal Council should not be blamed for the commissioner's demand and asked the attorney to explain the situation in full;
- the attorney vindicated the Tribal Council and fully apprised attendees of the context and possible consequences of not complying with the commissioner's request;
- Walter Underwood wanted to hear from the Tacoma group (the off-reservation enrollees who complained to the commissioner of election irregularities);
- Walter Cloud argued that people were too busy in the fields in April, when the commissioner wanted the election, to attend meetings;
- Kiutus Jim blamed the Tacoma group for this crisis;
- the attorney once again talked, this time for "30–31 minutes" (Relander's notes did not detail what he said, just the length of his talk);
- Otis Shilow, reiterating Kiutus Jim's demand, called out the Tacoma group to speak up;
- Wilson Charley (a Tribal Council member backed by the Tacoma group) then spoke up, first talking about termination as a communist plot before vindicating his own actions at the July 5 meeting, concluding that quorum was not met that day because people kept going in and out, insinuating that their actions were intentionally obstructionist.

In all, nine people spoke, two spoke twice, and three repeated the demand for the Tacoma group to stand up and speak; the rest offered unique contributions—both in gist and in creative opening moves and lines of thought—to the argument against postponing the election.

Plateau Indian interactional discourse may be perceived as disjointed and off-topic by outsiders for another reason: the suspenseful arrangement and suspended thesis typical of the indigenous rhetoric. Speaking extemporaneously, rather than from a prepared speech, and speaking first in Indian, as some people did, must also be factored in. Take, for example, these remarks made at the December 5, 1955, General Council meeting by Otis Shilow, who spoke often and usually in Indian before he translated his words himself into English (although Relander does not note that Otis did so in this particular instance):

I think we are confused with a very difficult problem. I am going to speak on the subject. Some have made statements that the Tribal Council has been detaining certain projects.

Now you heard the man [Wilton] send a telegram and his request to the commissioner. He did not specify why he wanted so long, did not specify any particular reasons.

And friends you know you have a home and have to take what opportunities you can find to support your home. And they specify that roads are bad but I understand that traffic that is going to the coast [to Tacoma] is going all the time. I am not opposing the request to our Commissioner. It seems he wants this General Council to postpone the meeting on the request of this Wilton. I think the Commissioner is asking this General Council to postpone the election on the request of Mr. Wilton. When I was one of the three delegates sent to Washington this same man sent to all different congressmen and officers a request we desire to be terminated. I've never seen him speak to us in General Council expressing his views. In what way will we benefit.

Now a week ago we had . . . attendance, due to fact it was postponed and I never anticipated we would be postponing our meeting again.

My friends, I am greatly disgusted with the way this turns out. I think we should come to what the white man calls a show down. That concludes my talk. I will ask to speak again later. [Ellipsis in the original][29]

Notice that Shilow does not just suspend stating his position; he actually contradicts it, by first disingenuously assuring everyone that he is not opposing the commissioner's request, but in the end, urging a "show down" by defying that request and proceeding with the December 6 election. Shilow's talk is a very highly situated text, his artful inferences not lost on the local audience. Thus when he talks of the importance of supporting one's home, he is implying that in April people need to be in their fields, in order to keep their allotments in use, or risk losing them for nonuse; he may also be insinuating that the audience still have homes to support, unlike the Tacoma group, who sold their allotments and moved away. When he brings up the topic of traffic to the coast, he is suggesting that road conditions in winter are not so bad that the Tacoma group cannot get over the Cascades mountain pass—another reason cited by the commissioner for postponing until April. And when he mentions attendance at the previous November meeting, which then had to be postponed, he is reminding everyone why it had to be postponed without saying so: the deaths and immediate funerals of two tribesmen. Also true to Plateau Indian rhetoric, Shilow offers his own personal experience as evidence in accusing Wilton of lobbying for termination in Washington, D.C.—the most damning accusation of all.

Affordances for Confrontation

The total effect of all these rhetorical strategies of indirection in Shilow's talk is actually quite direct indeed, even confrontational—a descriptor of Plateau Indian interactional discourse generally. In a pacifist culture that nonetheless values speaking straight, confrontation is not only tolerated; it is actually expected. It is the warrior's way, but using words instead of fists, a way that ultimately serves to build consensus and preserve peace, and interactional protocols support that belief. Everyone can speak multiple times and at any time, which means a speaker may take the floor from a recognized speaker or an audience member may interject a correction, a question, a joke. While no one is required to speak, consistent failure to so do is considered cowardly, especially when one is called out or does not agree. Thus turn-taking protocols, and the cultural permissions on which they are grounded, offer affordances for confrontation, allowing for immediate, on-topic response, as seen in the earlier cited sequence where Wilson Charley was called out three times and eventually took the floor.

The primary material details many moments of confrontation apparently well within the limits of cultural permissions to disagree openly. At the January 13, 1956, General Council meeting, for example, attendee Dick Walker wanted both "breeds" (mixed bloods) and "longhairs" (full bloods) represented at the federal hearings, but because breeds outnumbered longhairs, he proposed a group comprised of half breeds, half longhairs.[30] In immediate response to Walker, Kiutus Jim argued to "forget discrimination" and blood quantum and instead fight as a unified group for their right to elect their own leaders.[31] In another instance, at the December 7, 1955, General Council meeting, from the audience, Frank Sohappy poked fun at the white attorney's speech, "talking in back—said attorney talked with three tongues."[32] Instances of finger-pointing abound in these unofficial minutes, with different speakers variously blaming the commissioner, the Tribal Council, Umtuch (General Council chair), the Tacoma group, and Wilton (leader of the Tacoma group) for the crisis at hand. Naming names for any offense is not off-limits. At the December 6, 1955, General Council meeting, Lawrence Goudy accused the Yakima Indian Association of Washington of wanting termination, taxation, and the forfeiture of federal assistance; he named Wilton, Charles Varner, David Varner, and Wilson Charley as the lead people trying to take over the Tribal Council. At the December 7, 1955, General Council meeting, he accused Joe Meninick of money irregularities at a conference, to which Joe immediately responded that he was not even present at that conference, which a tape recording of that meeting would verify. The matter was then dropped.

The federal hearings in February 1956 drew out other charges of misdeeds, especially from the women, but the very different protocols (one witness, one turn, ten-minute time limit) disallow both lengthy and immediate response. Potential conflicts are avoided, and personal attacks left unanswered in the official forum, but neither are they necessarily resolved. Confrontation is obviously also the female warrior's way with words. At the federal hearing at Satus on February 14, 1956, Minne Whitefoot charged Superintendent LeCrone with neglect of duty for not ordering the election to proceed at the original July meeting and protested that Garry was allowed to speak for half an hour—Garry, a member of the National Congress of American Indians, "a Communist front organization."[33] Two days later at the Toppenish hearing, Alice Wynocks testified that she went outside at the July meeting and overheard someone say that she was going to send a telegram to the BIA in complaint of election procedures; she was quite certain that it was Minnie Whitefoot's voice she overheard. At the same hearing Mrs. Rosie Jack entered her statement: "A woman said yesterday I was trying to beat her up. Which I did not. I did not. Bunch of us ladies wanting to find out about who the man was with her, the white man. She said he was my people. I said no can't be. Said get out. Said no. She said I was trying to beat her up. She's been doing this to this reservation for some time now."[34]

Yet the protocols of the federal hearing also encourage opposing viewpoints from those who felt too intimidated at the General Council meetings to speak up. Ruby Parks entered her testimony at the Satus hearing, confessing that she was among those who complained to the commissioner:

> I'm one of those people asking for an investigation. Go way back. We have this measure, enrollment act, never knew it was passed until saw paper and picture of President Truman signing it. Two meetings at Wapato, 1 meeting called quite a group involved, long, run around, 15 hours, we stuck it out and everything done to keep it from being amended, finally voted and voted to repeal or amend it and put in hands of attorney for the t.c. [Tribal Council] at that time and went home. Went on with work. Few weeks later came to me another meeting has been called and people had agreed to keep the act.
>
> After 10 years of this and haven't got anywhere finally decided to try it through the Department. I'm not ashamed of what I have done. I don't believe any good served from keeping a person from his rightful inheritance.
>
> I have no affiliation with any group. I have been accused of being Tacoma

group. I have been on the Yakima reservation 46 years. and I don't wish to be . . .

Described as a show meeting [referring to the election] I'd never been to such a large meeting before and one that was so thoroughly advertised.[35]

The presiding officer then asked Parks if she felt members needed to be notified of future meetings in a different way. Her answer broadened that question to the issue of public voting. "Yes," she said, "I think a different method of voting. I didn't vote Dec. 6. It was a choice don't know what to do and didn't figure on this Umtuch resolution [to write down customary procedures governing meeting notification and Tribal Council elections], increases tribal council power, needs study. Statement prepared submitted."[36]

Mechanisms for Consensus-Building

That Ruby Parks spoke up at the federal hearing but not at the General Council meeting suggests the power of social pressure in achieving compliance, if not always consensus. In fact, the high tolerance for confrontation might be seen as one mechanism of control. Multiple viewpoints can be aired, and objections may be registered on the spot, a turn-taking protocol that may ignite conflict but may also resolve it, as was the case with the disagreement between Lawrence Goudy and Joe Meninick, mentioned earlier. But it may intimidate speakers, even those in the majority, like Alice Wyenoke. At the December 5, 1955, General Council meeting, when she brought up mixed bloods (referring to the Tacoma group), her talk was disrupted by someone in the audience shouting, "What is she attacking me for, I didn't say anything"—after which the chair explained the blood quantum rules that did indeed recognize those with one-fourth heritage as enrolled members. Wyenoke continued but only briefly, saying that she was probably wrong but only wanted to make the point that "we decide these questions or they decide them for us."[37] Wyenoke's indirection here is not gender-marked. At least two males use the exact same tack in their speeches, professing confusion and putatively asking for clarification before making their own contribution to the consensus—a rhetorical strategy that generally serves to mitigate conflict.

The relative silence of women in General Council, compared to the verbose and volatile participation of the men, points not to gender inequality but to gender complementarity in Plateau Indian culture generally. In traditional culture before 1855, men and women equally exercised power in all spheres of Plateau life but in different ways, including the political sphere. Both genders had equal authority to participate in assembly, where both had autonomy to speak and vote, without spouses having to coincide their opinions or votes.[38] At the 1955–56 General Council meetings, for example, women sat together as a bloc on the south side of the longhouse and registered their political impact largely through voting but also by interjecting comment and an occasional speech, but only speaking briefly. Although only a few women spoke before the General Council and none was nominated for Tribal Council, the assembly did elect them to standing committees, they voted, and they testified at the federal hearings, unafraid of confrontation and personal attacks—all instances of political participation consistent with traditional ways.

The fact that only a few women spoke in General Council meetings but several spoke up at the federal hearings suggests that the protocols governing testimony at the federal hearings did offer a more conducive environment for airing dissent, free from interruption—but not from public notice and possible repercussions later. Although dissenters may have been intimidated by the tyranny of the majority evident in the General Council meetings, the main targets of that tyranny did speak up, E. J. Wilton and Wilson Charley, but notably in reconciliatory ways. Named repeatedly as the culprit who snitched to the commissioner, E. J. Wilton apparently was not in attendance at the December General Council meetings; he did speak, however, at the January 13 meeting but on a neutral, safe topic. Wilson Charley, who was repeatedly called out and whose name appeared on the circular advertising the slate endorsed by the Tacoma group, did bravely speak up at the December 5, 1955, General Council meeting. His speech might be read as a study in diplomatic indirection appropriate to an intimidated minority position, but its suspended thesis and suspenseful arrangement also hold true to Plateau Indian rhetorical tradition. I quote his turn in full:

> You can't change an Indian's way of life. Congress can't do that. The only way is when the universe comes to an end. I am glad that everyone is receiving a voice. That's wonderful. I am glad.
>
> The chairman of the General Council recalls there is a portion on the agenda, the treaty and Bill 108 (208)? Said the secretary must study treaty and report back to Congress. We asked the Tribal Council and asked why not. . . . [ellipsis in the original] Termination or emancipation of the treaty is a Communistic move. The U.S. government cannot terminate the treaty. When the adult Indian speaks of the treaty he goes back to the Universe (the beginning of man). In 1947 we set procedure. I was one of the seven whose terms expired in July so I couldn't go on. In that first procedure is set forth the terms and my term shall expire July 12th (referring to last July 12th). That is not in the writing but it is what we intended. A wonderful man in Congress talked to the superintendent and came back and

said you'll have to go back and transact business. I said I don't think I could go against the wishes. He examined the part and the next day came back and said you are right. But business has to be done and the Council went on . . . passed 24 to 16 against. the chairman declared the meeting open after got people out of every card and stick game. Set another 30 days. Sat in long house from 1 o'clock in the afternoon until 11 o'clock at night before we had a quorum, July meeting, the people began to march in but the meeting was closed (if anyone marched in after the meeting was closed they were not seen) [editorial comment in the original]. Asked third week in October. We wanted an election. Sure I was working could have left my job etc. And there are many other things like I talked about with M. G. When U.S. established the Constitution there were many lives lost. Under the same principal our treaty was based because we shed blood to make the treaty that is why we cannot do away with the treaty.

I see by the paper it says the superintendent says the Tribal Council has worked diligently for the people.

I don't want white man's progress. It leads to war, to destruction. In the old country they have grown old and are migrating to the U.S. I don't like to see that kind of progress.

I like to see my people keep their land in trust. If you set aside a reservation I want to keep it. We should never have allotted any of our land. If we had all our tribal land, all leased, we would each get a prorate. The white man found Indian had outsmarted him and has been using every trick and means to make allotments and the General Council passed, no more land sales.

If I had land along river I would rather keep it. It is more valuable than sacred life. It is a garden that produces everything for me. The white man has destroyed his garden that was left here on earth and now he wants to come in and take the reservation.

Progress. I don't want the man to come to me and say, here, now you have a million. Now you are a white man.[39]

Wilson Charley artfully defended his position as an opposition candidate, ironically, by distancing himself from the very things the Tacoma group were so bitterly faulted for: selling allotments, undermining the Treaty of 1855, and sidling up to the white man. In that last regard, Charley said that he actually stood up to the white man on behalf of his people, arguing that he could not go against their wishes. Still, he registered the unpopular point, buried in his talk, that quorum was not met at the July meeting because the meeting was closed, inferring that would be an illegal procedure justifying the commissioner's intervention.

Like affordances for confrontation, the practice of public voting, as opposed to secret balloting, exerts a centripetal force on arriving at consensus. Everyone can see how everyone stands on an issue, literally when a person stands up or when she raises her hand for or against a motion. Coupled with the high tolerance for confrontation is the high tolerance for changing one's mind—and one's vote; otherwise, consensus would never be achieved. In the Plateau Indian political tradition, the point of arguing is to persuade others to do just that: change their minds and change their votes. A public vote may be retaken any number of times, upon anyone's demand, until a supermajority is achieved. As witness Hazel Miller testified at the 1956 federal hearing in Satus, a vote of postponement was taken three times, and only once did it come out against. The voting process is bounded by presence but not by time; if consensus is not reached in one meeting, the discussion will continue and the vote retaken another day or at another General Council session later in the year.

This distinction is not lost on the commissioner—or the tribe. At the December 5, 1955, General Council meeting, Alex Saluskin dramatized the commissioner's words of reprimand, using fictionalized dialogue true to the Plateau Indian rhetorical tradition: "When the decision is made by your group that is final. No one argues." Saluskin continues to mock the commissioner's words: "I will call a secretarial [secret] ballot, do away with your customs, everything you love." That threat Saluskin labels "dictatorial."[40] And it is, at least by Plateau Indian standards, for secret and absentee balloting cuts off argument and renders the process opaque—and thus more vulnerable to corruption, especially in a multilingual community with low alphabetic literacy rates who would need assistance in marking written ballots. Those in the minority, however, experience public voting as being "dictated to," as another witness, Marguerite Vivette, testified at the 1956 federal hearing at Toppenish, explaining that "people glare at you if you raise your hand." This "freeze out system of voting," she said, which entails "all night long sessions" and "children neglected" who are kept up late and then cannot attend school the next day, "is not the old way, causing dissension and being told how to speak."[41] Interestingly, Saluskin and Vivette each find the other's preferred method of voting dictatorial—that is, impinging on one's personal autonomy. Also tolerated is the nonvote, an option some may exercise but for different reasons: either they have not decided or they were intimidated by the tyranny of the majority, as was the case for Ruby Parks. This option of indecision is clearly exercised in some student writing, as seen in chapter 6.

Humor also plays an important role in releasing these tensions and bringing people together, although usually at someone's expense—in effect, serving a policing function. As cited earlier, Wilson Charley blunts the blow of his unpopular point using humor: "[T]he chairman declared the meeting open after got people out of every card and stick game." At the December 6 meeting, as the General Council proceeded to elect their new Tribal Council against the commissioner's directive, the presiding chair pointed out that Wilson Charley could be nominated for the position he vacated in July—a comment that met with "some laughter, some confusion," Relander notes.[42] Some apparently got the joke (that the unpopular Charley would never be reelected in this climate); others did not. At the January 13 meeting, when the General Council was deciding who to send to Washington, D.C., to represent their case in person, Maggie Syyou says jokingly: "That one who dictated [the commissioner] . . . I go to Washington myself and knock him in the head. My boy overseas now uniform. When he comes home we both go there and fight and kill him or get killed etc."[43] Her words triggered jocular laughter from the audience.

Overt calls for harmony, and the timing of these calls, before reopening discussion or before a vote, is another rhetorical strategy in the consensus-building process, urging the community to come together and make common cause, reminding them that factionalism only serves their common enemy. In his opening remarks at the January 13, 1956, meeting—an excerpt of which I quoted at the beginning of this chapter—Burdette Kent closed with this call for harmony:

> Please do not class all people in one class and call that class bad. It is not well to call each other names and run each other down. Ask ourselves, who is it it will hurt. If it will hurt no one and do some good, let us adopt it.
>
> I ask General Council and all future General Councils to act not only with their heads but also with our hearts.[44]

Modernizing the Political *Ethnie*

Kent characterized the arguments among them as "squabbling," but in his mouth the word works in a different way: the very real differences among them are mere quibbles among family, compared to the assaults on tribal sovereignty instigated by outsiders. In the face of those assaults, all must unite. While Kent opened the January meeting with this call, others often reminded the assembly of this common bond throughout the unofficial minutes, as Thomas Yallup did at the close of the November 28 meeting: "Let's leave in harmony." The General Council of 1955 did harmonize on one issue. Named after the preceding chair that day, the Umtuch Resolution was approved at the December 6 meeting and officially approved by Congress in 1956, the first time ever the tribe had written down its customary election procedures, meeting protocols, and respective roles of the Tribal Council and the General Council. This action was not a capitulation to the commissioner's demand but a consensus of the supermajority. The process of writing down these procedures led to a few changes: (1) General Council officers had to be at least twenty-five years of age and had to have lived continuously on the reservation for at least five years, with no Native language requirement mentioned; and (2) no business would be conducted after 10:30 p.m.[45] The former changes reflect the majority will to restrict the influence of the off-reservation group; the latter change demonstrates that Marguerite Vivette's minority opinion expressed in the federal hearings about late nights and children was apparently heard and incorporated.

Those rules have been challenged throughout the years. A recent reform movement in 2006 protested General Council procedures on several grounds: low participation rate (about 2 percent); the difficulty of physically attending in order to vote, especially since the tribe has doubled its size since 1956; the "use of intimidation to influence voting" and unqualified people being elected.[46] To address these problems, reformers wanted to vote using secret and absentee balloting and require specific qualifications for candidates that included expertise in business or law, among other reforms. Such reforms have often been discussed through the years, but the Umtuch Resolution still stands, as written and passed in 1955–56.

In 2006 the Tribal Council selected Lavina Washines as its chair, making her the first woman ever to lead the tribe. Not all were happy with her promotion, saying she was "too aggressive when it comes to making changes," many questioning "whether a woman should hold a post traditionally held by men, but now many believe she is everything the nearly 10,000-member tribe needs in a leader."[47] As a member of the Rock Creek band on the Columbia River, Washines grew up speaking Indian, gathering roots and berries—and hunting, fishing, and drumming; in her band the latter activities were not reserved for males only. "Women fished, men helped gather (foods)," she said in a 2007 newspaper article. "That's what we were taught by our elders: equality."[48] The primary challenge facing the tribe, said Washines, was preserving tribal sovereignty while balancing "tribal traditions and modern business practices."[49] That kind of expertise is needed to manage the tribe's many business operations.

In the same meeting when the Umtuch Resolution was passed, the General Council also resurrected and voted on a motion that had been tabled since 1951 disallowing anyone from serving on both the General Council and the Tribal Council at the same time. Because the presiding chair of the General Council,

George Umtuch, had just been elected to the Tribal Council, he had to choose between the two. When Alex Saluskin closed the meeting, he thanked Umtuch for choosing to stay on as presiding chair of General Council, and said, "You have changed one of your traditions tonight because you thought it a better way." As these actions attest, the tribe clearly recognized the inevitability, as well as the desirability, of change that nonetheless conserved the values that deeply informed its political traditions. And the tribe did so by way of a contentious consensus process, striking a delicate balance between personal autonomy and collective harmony, by allowing people to act *on* their own accord while persuading them to act *in* accord with others.

At the Treaty Council at Walla Walla in 1855, U.S. military scribes were not the only ones transcribing the proceedings. Several literate Indians, who had been taught by Presbyterian missionaries how to read and write in English, and in some cases, in their own languages, also took notes.[1] This fact is mentioned twice in the official record itself, as well as in eyewitness diaries and in Gustav Sohon's artistic renditions, most notably of Timothy and Lawyer (Nez Perce).[2] All Indian notes have been lost, presumably burned at these authors' deaths along with their personal belongings, as was Plateau custom.[3]

Although the Indians' notes did not survive, the fact of their note-taking nonetheless documents the early embrace of literacy by the Plateau Indians, which was a logical extension of their long-standing regard for multilingualism and education. Traditionally children were often sent to live with another tribe to learn that tribe's language and customs, so that as an adult, he would be able to serve as translator between tribes, a practice that promoted interdependent goals of trade relations and peace. That Indians were taking notes at Walla Walla speaks to a fundamental faith in writing, their notes serving not only to track the Americans' promises but also to accurately report them back home. Their notes might help them justify their actions since most did not have prior authorization to act on behalf of their respective tribes. On yet another level, the very image of a writing Indian collapses the ersatz divide between orality and literacy, demonstrating the complementary and complex relationship between those modes of communication, rather than setting them in the usual binary opposition, undergirded by the implicitly hierarchical equation: oral = primitive / literate = civilized. Those Indians writing at Walla Walla were not any more assimilated or less authentic for doing so. Rather, they were adopting and adapting new tools to preserve their culture while moving it into modernity.

Under investigation in this chapter is the writing of Plateau Indian students, authored seven generations after the Treaty Council at Walla Walla in 1855. Like their forebears, they too (to recall the words of the student's rap poem examined in chapter 1) "can't stop representin this / reinventin Indian world." Adapting the rhetoric of their forebears while keeping faith with the values that that rhetoric embodies, these students write in modern genres about modern topics: Frankenstein, credibility of newspapers, teen pregnancy, statutory rape, the space shuttle disaster, an OutKast performance, the murders of Tupac and Notorious B.I.G., Big Foot, marijuana legalization, Emmitt Till, 9/11, *Nightmare on Elm Street,* Iraqi suicide bombers, Saddam Hussein, NASA, loss of Internet connectivity, Clear Channel and media consolidation, school-grounds improvements, open campus, and George W. Bush's chances for reelection. Like their forebears, these students employ multiple strategies of personalization. They rely heavily on personal experience to support their views, their own or others—most often someone they know personally and for whom they hold respect, like a parent, a friend, an elder—and take particular care with attributing the source of their information.

These discourse-positive markers speak to the primacy of experience-based knowledge at the heart of Plateau Indian rhetoric. And like their forebears, these students have strong positions on certain topics; when they don't, they suspend judgment, weighing multiple perspectives, a process that sometimes leads to reversing their original positions. They favor high-affect techniques to support their arguments—most notably, hypothetical dialogue and ideational emphasis, the latter variously achieved in writing with underlines, creative capitalization, and exclamation points. Humor and verbal irony are used not to entertain so much as to persuade. While certain pedagogies seem to have affected traditional features like thesis placement and arrangement, students often overtly question those pedagogies or send them up; more often, however, students' own discursive preferences simply override them. That students do so, I argue in this chapter and throughout the book, strongly suggests that their own communicative competence, as it has evolved and been transmitted over generations and in other domains of reservation life outside school, are very much alive as these students manage the complex negotiations between an indigenous rhetoric and school essayist literacy.

In short, Plateau Indian student writing in 2000 through 2004 offers a glimpse of the process of modernizing the rhetorical *ethnie,* keeping apace of the times while remaining true to traditional values. In so doing, students disrupt the colonist discourses of the Vanishing Indian, the stoic Indian, the silent Indian, the oral Indian, implicitly proclaiming their right to modernity as well as their right to rhetorical sovereignty. And they do so with the stroke of a pen, pencil, or—increasingly—keyboard. Before launching into this examination, however, I will first situate these student productions within the context of the standards and testing movements at the beginning of both of the twentieth and twenty-first centuries, of which the No Child Left Behind Act was a part. I will then briefly describe the community and school contexts, the former shaped by reservation demographics, the latter caught in the historical struggle between federal and tribal control of Native education. Finally I will outline the research project that occasioned the student writing archive from which I selected several pieces of writing for analysis. That analysis constitutes the heart of this chapter.

Historical Context

The late twentieth century had much in common with the early twentieth century, including standards and testing movements ignited by presumed educational crises. As American Indian education scholars K. Tsianina Lomawaima and Teresa L. McCarty rightly suggest, such crises are manufactured to justify extreme measures that ideologically serve to contain and control diversity. The facts behind the two twentieth-century movements are real enough, both emanating from similar social, economic, and demographic contexts. As in the first three decades of the twentieth century, the last three decades also experienced a new wave of immigration occasioned when national-origin quotas were abolished in 1965. But unlike the earlier wave, when white immigrants originated largely from western and eastern Europe, immigrants of color are now coming from Latin America, Southeast Asia, and the Caribbean. Speaking more than 150 languages, people of color now make up 28 percent of the nation's population; they are projected to make up 47 percent by 2050. These are the numbers that are configuring the new educational crisis. In the five hundred largest school districts, 52 percent are ethnic minority students; in the one hundred largest, 61 percent are minority students from low-income families.[4]

With standards must also come standardized testing, with its deeply racialized roots. In the earlier standards movement "the widespread xenophobia [of] non-English speaking immigrants" was pseudo-scientifically propped up by racial intelligence testing, which was used to justify such draconian solutions as sterilization of the so-called feeble-minded, who were mainly people living in poverty.[5] Cleaning out the gene pool would shorten the welfare rolls, or so this bio-logic went. In Indian Country blood quantum was correlated with IQ scores to provide the so-called scientific evidence for what everyone already knew: that whites were biologically more intelligent than Indians. Although such testing practices have long been discredited, recurring generalizations on brain-hemisphere preferences and learning styles based on ethnicity draw from the same ideological complex.[6]

The current standards movement differs from the first not so much in kind as it does in degree: in the sheer number of tests, in the exceptionally high-stakes nature of these tests, and in the amount of corporate influence and profit in designing, administering, and scoring these tests. The law that unleashed this testing madness was the No Child Left Behind Act (NCLB), passed in 2001, precisely when the student writing archive under examination in this chapter was written and collected. NCLB's stated goal—to help "low achieving children in our Nation's highest-poverty schools, limited English proficient children, migratory children, children with disabilities, Indian children, neglected or delinquent children, and young children in need of reading assistance"—implicitly excluded schools serving primarily white students and affluent areas.[7] NCLB required that student knowledge be measured and achievement data disaggregated by race and ethnicity, social class, and English-language proficiency as if diversity were the barrier to school achievement—not resource inequities or cultural bias. In these targeted schools, per-pupil expenditures ran one-third to one-half that of schools serving white students, before factoring in reservation schools, which doubled these per-pupil differences if included. Reservation schools are notoriously underfunded, and from 1998 to 2003 many Indian programs were not funded at all. Nevertheless, NCLB stipulated that both students and schools had to make adequate yearly progress (AYP); if they did not, schools lost federal funding and could be taken over by for-profit school management corporations. Other high-stakes consequences included students not being allowed to graduate, teachers teaching to the test, a narrowing of curriculum (focused solely on reading, writing, and math—the three areas tested), and reductionist, back-to-basics pedagogies—none of which white students in affluent schools were subjected to.[8]

The consequences in reservation schools were even more profound. In effect an English-only law, NCLB flatly contradicted the Native American Language Act

(NALA) of 1990, which reversed well over a century of federal Indian language policy. The act aimed to "preserve, protect, and promote the rights and freedom of Native Americans to use, practice, and develop Native American languages" and to use it for instruction in the classroom.[9] That NALA went unfunded until 1992, and then only meagerly, should suggest its status as symbolic gesture, with no small flourish of irony, given that federal policy was responsible for the near-eradication of Indian languages in the first place. Although language preservation itself was necessarily limited by the irrevocable losses already sustained, bilingual education slipped its strictly linguistic borders, becoming increasingly thought of as bicultural education, rightly and inevitably so, as appropriated storylines and translations were resituated within tribe-specific knowledge systems. Initially unfunded, bilingual/bicultural education thus became the spearhead of sweeping reforms from the 1960s through the 1990s. The push for self-education coincided with legal battles in other areas, such as fishing and water rights, all centralized around the issue of tribal sovereignty. It was President Richard Nixon who in 1970 lay to rest the termination movement, promising "self-determination without termination"—a promise that followed several widely publicized reports of BIA mismanagement of tribal trust funds, among other federal policy failures in Indian Country.[10] Within the contexts of these reports, Native activism, and the larger civil rights movement, the American public was more receptive and Congress more responsive to the call for opening up educational and economic opportunities for Indians.

Several pieces of legislation aimed to do just that. In 1964 the Civil Rights Act guarded against racial discrimination, and the Economic Opportunity Act funded Head Start, Upward Bound, Volunteers in Service to America (VISTA), and Indian Community Action Programs. In 1965 the Elementary and Secondary Education Act (ESEA) provided Title I funding for English reading programs, which were used to resource Native literacy efforts. In 1968 the Bilingual Education Act called for using students' native language when learning English, a Title VII amendment to ESEA. In 1972 the Indian Education Act, a Title IV amendment to ESEA, authorized funding for bilingual/bicultural curriculum development, teacher training, and parent participation. In 1975 the Indian Self-Determination and Education Assistance Act, among other provisions, authorized tribes to contract with the BIA to operate their own schools. In 1978 the Tribally Controlled College or University Assistance Act did the same at the community-college level. These laws did bear fruit: by the end of the 1970s there were thirty-four Indian community-controlled schools.[11] By 2013 there were 126 of a total of 183 schools on 64 reservations in 23 states under the oversight of the Bureau of Indian Education.[12]

The gains of the reform movement, however, did not put to rest the issue of tribal versus federal control of indigenous education. In 1988 the federal funding model changed. Previously, schools had to wait for funds until after the school year began; now they could seek grants before school started, a forward-funding model. The catch: they had to comply with federal or regional standards, not standards generated by tribes or local school boards.[13] As an unfunded mandate, NCLB further impoverished the poorest of poor school systems. And because the tests had to align with state or national (Eurocentric) standards, not a given tribe's, NCLB circumscribed the hard-earned gains of the last half of the twentieth century, invalidating the integrity of tribe-specific knowledge systems in one act. In short, the law trampled tribal sovereignty, reasserting federal colonist control once again. The power struggle continues. Native educators continue to reassert the principle that tribal sovereignty encompasses not only the rights of self-governance and self-determination but also the right of self-education—including, as I argue in this chapter, the right to speak and write and interact in ways consistent with tribal-specific knowledge systems. "The Indian problem" in education, then, is not only a cultural question; at heart it is also a deeply political one.[14] This so-called problem is discussed further in chapter 7.

Local Contexts

The student writing selected for analysis in this chapter came from two reservation schools—one public, one tribal—predominately drawing students from three small towns on or near a large reservation in the region. These three towns I will call Rondo, Rosewood, and Dakota (pseudonyms). Unlike rural areas in other parts of the country, however, this area is distinctly multiracial, its diversity reflecting local history and economics. The Dawes Act of 1887 opened up the reservation to non-Indian settlement, turning it into a checkerboard reservation only partially Native-owned. The tribe is slowly buying up parcels as they come up for sale in an effort to reclaim these lands. Although most of the settlers in the late nineteenth century were white, more recently immigrants from Mexico and, to a much lesser extent, the Philippines have made the region their home. The lure of agricultural jobs drew them to the region, and low wages have kept them there.

Although all three towns sit in the migration stream in this agricultural region, their respective populations have not fluctuated much over the past decade, with each town retaining its own characteristic racial/ethnic makeup. According to the 2010 U.S. Census, Rondo has a population of approximately five thousand, 84 percent of whom are Latino of Mexican descent, with 17 percent white, 7 percent Plateau Indian, and 1 percent Asian. Approximately 28 percent of the population is foreign-born. While 47 percent have at least a high school diploma, only 4 percent hold at least a bachelor's degree and are most probably employed by the local school district. Much more geographically isolated than Rondo, Rosewood is much smaller, with a population of about eight hundred, over six hundred of whom are Plateau Indian, one hundred are Latino of Mexican descent, and twenty-two of mixed race. Dakota is the largest of the three towns, with a population of approximately nine thousand, with 83 percent Latino of Mexican descent, 4 percent white, and 8 percent Plateau Indian. What the three towns most have in common is poverty: in all three towns the median household income is in the thirty-thousand-dollar range, with 42 percent living below the poverty line in Rondo, 36 percent in Rosewood, and 30 percent in Dakota. While three racial/ethnic groups predominate in each town, it is the ratio of Plateau Indian to Latino that defines the public face of the school that each town serves, as well as the gang loyalties both within that school and with the other schools. Indian versus Latino versus other Latinos, Rosewood versus Rondo versus Dakota—they play to the discourse of the warrior's way and the mystique of machismo. As a direct consequence, local schools often go into lockdown on threat of drive-by shootings by armed gangs, those threats sometimes backed with actions.[15]

Two of the schools participated in the research project that inspired and grounded this book: an archive of secondary student writing collected over the five-year period 2000–2004 called the Writing Across Cultures project.[16] As I mentioned in the introduction, the project came as a direct response to a comment that I had often heard from English teachers working in multiethnic classrooms with Indian minorities as well as Indian-only schools: There is something special about Indian student writing, they always insisted, but were hard-pressed to explain exactly what. The archive amassed—approximately three thousand pieces in all—actually draws from five different middle schools and high schools throughout the state of Washington, located in a range of rural, small-town, and small-city settings, each serving a different cultural and socioeconomic class demographic: (1) mainly poor, white students; (2) mainly white students from a very wide socioeconomic range; (3) largely Latino of Mexican-descent; (4) approximately one-third Plateau Indian and two-thirds Latino of Mexican-descent; and (5) one hundred percent Plateau Indian.

What the schools all had in common, in various percentages, was students living in poverty. In addition to research publication, the collection could also be used for training English teachers at my home institution. As such, it has proven instructive material indeed, as preservice teachers explore differences in pedagogies not just locally across classrooms but systemically, across schools, as they discuss differences in assignments, teacher response style, and assessment criteria and methods. This particular chapter, however, brackets off issues of curricula as well as pedagogies, narrowing the focus to the cultural distinctiveness of writing—about 940 pieces of writing in all—authored by Plateau Indian students living on or near the reservation most of their lives. My analysis zooms in on only two reservation schools—one public, one tribal—but mainly the student writing from one tribal school.

A kind of "last chance" academy, this particular tribal school in the early 2000s used the Learning Record to assess its students' work, although this assessment did not exempt them from state-mandated tests. As a portfolio system, the Learning Record does not prescribe what kinds of evidence students must produce to chart their progress, as defined by a rubric based largely on critical thinking skills (which are not, of course, culturally neutral).[17] In the Learning Records released to me by the school, the student-selected evidence ran the gamut from lab reports to drawings, with summaries of newspaper articles and literature predominating. Almost all of these were very short summaries of reading assignments (sometimes including reading in other subjects, such as chemistry) or short-answer responses to a list of questions or, occasionally, narratives (both personal and fictionalized). Only about two hundred had an argumentative or persuasive edge to them, meaning anything from a full-blown academic argument to a journal entry expressing the student's opinion, no matter how ambivalently expressed. For the journal-writing assignment, the most common assignment of all, students generally read newspaper articles and then wrote summaries, with only a minority of them responding with personal insights, support, or refutations, but those few generally did so on a regular basis. The journal-writing assignment typically yielded a single paragraph. Time was clearly a factor in these short productions, tailored to be finished within one fifty-five-minute class period, in part because of the high absentee rate from day to day (largely due to family obligations, such as attending funeral ceremonies that typically last several days). Finding, reading, and then writing about a newspaper article or sometimes a set of generic topics, like "education" or "goals," could easily take an entire class period.

Even given these limited pedagogical and curricular parameters, many students—although certainly not all students—(re)produced discourse that bore certain resemblances to that of their ancestors, while bearing witness to the forces of change. In spite of more than a century of colonial education, and in part because of Indian education activism that has worked to reclaim the sovereign right of self-education, key discourse-positive markers of Plateau Indian distinctive ways with words recur persistently in the Writing Across Culture archive: personal experience as supporting evidence, the use of high-affect techniques to re-create that experience, and suspended thesis/suspenseful arrangement. Throughout, situated elaboration is evidenced in the relative brevity of each paper with the highly selective use of detail that amplifies the writer's point.

Experiential Knowledge as Supporting Evidence

No matter what the assignment, students typically supported their theses with experience-based knowledge, although not necessarily their own. One student writer identifies what she sees as the central problem in the novel *Frankenstein:* "Frankenstein started with his knowledge and love of science, but his lack of life experience would ruin his experiment."[18] She continues: "[The doctor] did not have the heart to see past the appearance of his creation and teach it how to function among society. There was nobody to teach him how to use his mind and his power." The student's explanation speaks to the value of lived experience and the intergenerational transmission thereof. For this reason elders—meaning generally anyone heading a household, regardless of age—are held in such respect: their age and life experiences lend them special credibility. Elders' lived experiences are important for they both maintain and modernize tribal values, a process that ensures cultural cohesiveness and continuity as well as group identity.

Despite the authority and respect accorded to elders, firsthand experience is one's ultimate teacher. In a journal response one student writes with typically understated humor: "Newspaper really give out good information but are they always right. I don't know but I would love to find out. Because when I look at the wheather its always different from what it is in the newspaper."[19] The writer's own experience would seem to invalidate the weather reports in the newspaper, but he withholds judgment on other kinds of information in the newspaper, even though others have said the information cannot be trusted, preferring to find out firsthand how newspapers arrive at their information: "Other people feel of newspaper as 'take it with a grain of salt.' But if I ever find out a way to get a job with a newspaper I would be glad, Because I would learn a lot about journaling/ and reporting." The primacy of firsthand experience thus shows up consistently as a theme, either as a major or minor point in students' writing. More commonly, it shows up as supporting evidence for argument. In the following excerpt, the writer argues-with-story in opening this argument against teen pregnancy, as my added emphasis aims to highlight:

There's a lot of teen mothers who are left alone, with no partner. Why are teens becoming single parents? *I know from experience how it is or how it's going to be, I'm going to be a single teen parent.*

Teens become pregnant and than there partner leaves them, for many reasons or excuses, *for example, my boyfriend told his mom "I don't even know if that's my kid," And then he left me for another girl who already has a baby and a boyfriend.* Many guys use that excuse, you hear it everywhere, on t.v., talk shows, your friends. A lot of the guys are immature. And don't want to take responsibility for their actions. *It's almost been a month since my boyfriend broke up with me and now he's saying "I still love you." And he says he's going to take my baby away. How can he take my baby away when he drinks?* [Emphasis mine]

In the absence of firsthand experience, secondhand is the next best support, as long as the person is known, especially a friend, as in the following excerpt from a paper arguing for a redefining of statutory rape. "My friend got charged with statutory rape after he had a baby with a girl whose parents thought he was too old for her," one writer compellingly opens her paper. She continues, strongly stating her own position at the end, and doing so in the most specific of terms:

The thing of it was the parents never said anything until the baby was here so they were able to take the baby away by saying the mother was not responsible enough to take care of here. I think they would have done just fine without their parents because they chose to have a baby together and they obviously felt they were ready by bringing the child into this world. *I feel statutory rape should not be charged in a situation where the partners are over 16 and less than 3 years apart in age.* So in this case, he should not have been charged. [Emphasis mine]

This same paper demonstrates that young adults sometimes question received wisdom. Contrary to popular stereotypes, they have cultural permission to do so, for their own lived experiences are important too, as the writer of the statutory rape paper goes on to argue: "Parents also believe that their teens are not emotionally ready. If their parents don't allow them to have emotions such as loving emotions, or sexual emotions they will never really be able to tell what emotion is what. I think they should experience these kinds of emotions so they will be ready for the real world as they get older and be prepared for pain, hurt, and guilt."

In other instances, however, student writers call on the authority of their parents, citing their parents' opinions for supporting evidence, as in this journal piece responding to the news article on the space shuttle disaster: "My parents think they were cooked before they crashed down in Texas. Because the temperatures got to be what!? 35,000 degrees inside of the ship. I maybe wrong about that but don't know." Unlike the previous writer who felt that partners over sixteen and fewer than three years apart in age should not be charged with statutory rape, numerical specificity here ("35,000 degrees") is overstated for comic effect. At the same time, the writer admits that he does not know himself and therefore cannot attest to the accuracy of the information. He goes on: "Now they're searching inch by inch looking for space shuttle part plus body parts of the remaining seven Astronauts. NASA orderly told people not to pick up any parts because some maybe toxic. Do they listen? NO!" While the morbid fascination about body parts might be found in any teen's journal entry, the sarcasm and rhetorical question-answer, simulating dialogue ("Do they listen? NO!"), are common features in the writing of Plateau Indian students—just as they were at Walla Walla in 1855.

Frequently students preemptively apologize for their lack of experience-based knowledge but then go on to state their views in compelling and vivid ways. In the following example, notice the opening apology ("I did not see the performance but . . ."), the high affect (as evidenced by the exclamatory punctuation), and the use of nonrhetorical questions in both of these journal entries written by two different students, in response to a news article on an OutKast performance. The first writer objects to the performance in part because the group remixed a sacred Dine song and in part because they dressed like Natives but inauthentically so:

> Writer #1: *I did not see the performance but* I know the Dine Nation needs the apology the most for Outkast using one of their sacred songs for hip-hop music. That is really disrespectful and a representative should have asked permission to use the song. *How did they get the music of the Dine Nation in the first place?* Pretty much everything they said about the feathers and stuff is how I feel. It is all true and *why did they choose to dress like us Natives?* But they made their regalia look stupid. *Real Natives don't dress like that.* If they didn't like the look then they should not have changed it! When NonNatives see fake stuff like this on t.v. they really think that is how we are! I still get asked by Non-Natives if we still live in teepees and I take it as a joke or if I get asked too much I get angry. The only thing that bothers me is not everyone is apologizing that is responsible for this action. [Emphasis mine]

While the first writer faults Outkast for misrepresenting Native identity, the second writer faults white-controlled media for perpetrating that disrespect:

> Writer #2: Many natives were offended because the words they used are sacred and they did not get permission to use them in their song.

I did not see the performance but understand the anger. I think the group Out-kast used our identity as a show. This might have thought to be good but they forgot about having respect for the Indian people. I also believe the White people allows this to happen thinking it was good for their ratings even when they had known it was racist.

The Indian people are being robbed over in many ways, but to let it happen at an awards ceremony and on national t.v. is very disrespectful. [Emphasis mine]

But students consistently reserve judgment when only rumors or unspecified people can be cited. Information without attribution is generally suspect. "People say that Tupac and Notorious Big hate each other," one student writes. "Rumors say, Tupac murdered B.I.G. Years later Notorious or people that hate Tupac killed him. I don't know that's what the rumors say. I don't know what caused him to be so violant. I sometimes wonder what happen to him in the past." This last comment demonstrates the writer's empathy as well as a belief in the power of personal experience to shape people's lives. Another writer responding to an article on Big Foot duly notes that she finds the motives of researchers suspect: "[They just want] to get rich or famous." She points out that she herself does not have firsthand knowledge but nonetheless wonders, What if eyewitnesses have conspired to not share their knowledge? "I have never seen Bigfoot myself. but I have heard that if you do see Bigfoot you do not tell on him of where he is at. I don't have to much to write about Bigfoot because he is a mystery and don't really know if he exists." Notice that the writer feels incapable of writing at length because she has not had the experience of a Big Foot sighting. Her reasoning is valid enough: one needs a certain level of knowledge about a subject in order to write about it. What is culturally distinctive, though, is the prerequisite personal experience in order to be able to write about a topic at all.

High Affect and Selective Detail

The tendency to personalize and put one's self into the situation may be a feature of oral culture generally, but such a generalization fails to account for variations in doing so and in what rhetorical situations.[20] In these students' papers, as in their forebears' words, personalization manifests as performance cues, such as direct quotes, nonrhetorical questions, and emotive punctuation (i.e., exclamation marks, all caps to indicate emphasis, and so on). Dramatization solicits interpersonal involvement with the audience, allowing them to experience this situation too, creating the effect of "you are there" through artful narration. These personalized inserts sound storylike, the full import of which is left to the audience to ponder.

Another discourse-positive marker, selective use of detail, recurs throughout student productions. "Another reason for not legalizing weed is it's not too healthy. It kills off brain cells that are very hard to regain. It takes 7 months to regain one brain cell. It also effects your memory and eye vision. It ruins your lungs and also causes cancer or asthma." The writer goes on to point out that "some people with asthma can't even talk without coughing or using their inhaler." Such details do vivify, but they do so as metonymies, not as the elaborated, descriptive discourse that the adage "show, don't tell" aims to produce. Furthermore, the student inserts numerical detail ("It takes 7 months to regain one brain cell."), so specific as to be convincing, even though the number is fictitious. Finally, the example illustrates the use of understatement ("it's not too healthy"), among other forms of humor.

In the following example, the writer takes these same vivifying strategies a step further to respond to an article on Emmitt Till. Like the previous writer, this one makes dramatic use of selective detail and nonrhetorical questions, but he goes on to put himself in the mother's shoes (an interesting example of cross-gendering, a practice generally tolerated in Plateau life as a matter of personal autonomy)—so much so that her words become indistinguishable from the writer's. Remarkably, instead of simply describing Emmitt Till as depicted in the photograph, the writer actually enacts looking at the photograph himself, in effect inhabiting the mother's body:

> I think it was wrong for them to do to this boy. He probably didn't even commit any sin yet and he died. Also where was the family in all this. No one tried to stop this. If they took one of my family members I'd go after them for sure. They shot him and beat. His tongue was choked out. They chopped his nose in several places. His mother asked the undertaker not to do anything to him. She asked him not to fix his body so that the world could see what they did to him. I would be the same way. *Don't touch him let the world know so Americans can see what it is really like. see this boy's picture. He look's happy as the day he was born. I see a smile on his face.* This was only beginning for all black Americans. It got worse. [Emphasis mine]

Interestingly, Chief Meninick also uses this exact same strategy in his speech before the state Supreme Court in 1921, when he calls on the court to join him in dramatically reenacting a crucial scene at Walla Walla as ghosts, as discussed in chapter 4.

For another assignment students were asked to write about how technology played a role in the terrorist attacks of 9/11. The following paragraph, taken from a larger paper, reads like a private conversation between the writer and the teacher. The writer dramatizes with a hypothetical quotation, with considerable sarcasm, the plight of the people in the World Trade Center. She goes on to argue pointedly that she cannot take a position on the issue because she did not have this experience and cannot speak for others, objecting almost on epistemological grounds: How could she know with absolute certainty if she did not have this experience directly?

> The 9.11.01 was very sad for other people. To me don't know what I feel about that day when the airplanes crashed. Way back in history people couldn't rely on technology. People rode horses, carts. *Don't know what are you telling me to type here. You need to be more clear on what you want me to write about. You saying if it wasn't for the technology the Twin Towers would be still standing right now. And the people that are working in Towers would also still be alive.* Like if the towers were a little stronger and the planes just crashed into them people inside the building would be like saying, "Oh my goodness the plane has trouble controlling I hope the people in the flight is alright." I don't know. Something like that can't read other peoples minds you know I'm not a psychic can't predict the future. [Emphasis mine]

At least one other student protests that writing a paper for persuasive purposes is an absurd request, not because she does not have an opinion but because the medium is wrong. On the standard check sheet for the paper from the Learning Record, to the question "Did you persuade your audience?" the writer responds, "We didn't speak!" For this student at least, persuasion is an oral art, not a written one, an oral argument requiring interpersonal interaction in real time.

Like their forebears in the 1800s and 1900s, students may show a strong disinclination to speak for others, but they are not similarly disinclined to quote them, dramatizing with dialogue, real or imagined. On a paper on the movie *Nightmare on Elm Street,* the student writes, "Spencer doesn't want to be like [his father] never! . . . Like what Jason M. [a pseudonym] tells me, 'Its your life you live it your way.'" Students also quote themselves, as in this journal entry where the writer imagines addressing the Iraqi suicide bombers: "I just got one [thing] to say, 'Wake up and look around. There's a whole different world out there. Not many things can't go your ways. If you can't face it or deal with what do you do? you just attack. Then become hero's at your home state. But there's a price for wanted and will pay for homicides.'" This writer closes with this remark, reminiscent of the turn-ending protocol evident in the treaty negotiations of 1855: "Don't know what else to say so guess I'm finished." And like the writer of the paper on the role of technology in 9/11 cited earlier, students do not hesitate to make up dialogue to dramatize their points. In a paper on the positive and negative effects of marijuana, the writer states: "Now you're probablly thinking 'why don't they just make a pill that is associated with marijuana?' They do make a pill it's a synthetic THC."

The rich variety of humor in Plateau Indian oratory and writing—from understatement to overstatement, from sarcasm to scatological references—might be seen as another form of high affect that involves an audience, requiring more interpretative work from them. In another journal entry a student sarcastically criticizes the U.S. congressman from his district who "described United Nations inspections in Iraq as ponderously slow and part of a 'clever job' by Saddam to fracture the U.N. and isolate the United States. Yeah yeah yeah it's like that man. Clever job's by Saddam I don't think so." In another entry the same student bitingly critiques race relations as reflected in NASA decisions and a local newspaper op-ed piece, contrasting these reflections against his own experiences on his home reservation, which tell him otherwise:

> This native this indian is going into outer space. Which is kind dumb I think I mean think man he a half breed he don't even look indian. Maybe that why they picked him. because he looks more white than indian. I bet he didn't know untill now then made it a big thing. Also A Spanish guy is going up geezs man [name of local newspaper] said. It's like putting a German and a Jew together. That's Bullshxx. Natives and spanish people have been getting along for years. On the Rez we have half breed Spanish Native. (I call them indian tacos) and he's got to take all that stuff with him arrow heads pottery fluts sweet grass all kindas of natives stuff which he's not part of well I said and written what I've done on this paper.

Notice that the writer partakes of the discourse of authenticity, questioning the identity of this Indian on grounds of phenotype, while he also makes fun of the practice of using Native artifacts to authenticate identity. Also notable is the explicit sign-off typical of oral discourse, signifying that his turn is over and he is relinquishing the floor.

Humor is not only used in Plateau Indian student discourse to involve readers. It is also used as a form of persuasion in and of itself, often without aid of abstract facts favored in academic discourse. One student points explicitly to this culture-marked distinction in his reflective piece: "I personally believe the Persuasion [in my paper] is very effective. Not because I was very convincing as in terms of facts or examples, but indeed my piece was colorful in the sense it was

humorous. . . . I was pleased with myself when I heard my teacher response because I accomplished what I intended, to get a laugh." Thus personalization and
dramatization are used as persuasive techniques, not unlike the way the writer's
forebears sought to argue their points.

The writer's remarks in this reflective piece preface the following piece in his
Learning Record portfolio: a letter written to federal judge Royce Lamberth. The
judge was presiding over a class-action lawsuit, *Cobell v. Norton,* filed by the Native American Rights Fund against the U.S. Department of Interior and the BIA
for mismanagement of Indian trust funds, swindling Indians of billions of dollars since 1887 in royalties for oil, gas, grazing, and other leases on Indian land.[21]
Holding Interior secretaries Gail Norton and Bruce Babbitt in contempt for not
turning over records, Judge Lamberth eventually shut down Interior's new computer system because security breaches had further compromised access to trust
funds, making continued malfeasance even easier, not harder. The shutdown
lasted several months.[22] Unfortunately, because BIA schools' computer systems
were tied with the Department of Interior, those schools also lost connectivity.
One teacher had his classes write a letter protesting the shutdown and then sent
the letters on to the judge. This is one of those letters:

To Judge Lamberth:

First off I applaud your courage. I can not fathom the absurdity you overcame to
draw your conclusion and ultimately make your ruling. My hat is off to the individual who has the testosterone to cut the legs off a school and then turn around
an shrug it off. Honestly depriving a school of about one-hundred dedicated students of the primary tool of research and communication? The person to posess
that nerve must be doped up, drying, or something.

I just figured that it would be imperative to inform you that you have success-
fully shipped a school back to the stone-age. You sire have haulted our learning
process. You crippled our curriculum wich is based on the net and until further
notice our learning growth is stunted.

I understand how you feel that resources could be in steak [at stake] and is
quite a vulnerable point. However I do not whole heartedly agree that students
are culprits, I mean they're our future.

Finally I wish you would reconsider retracting the internet shutdown. If we
don't get that internet back the whole situation could escelate and things will
really hit the fan. Sincerely, [student's full name redacted]

True to his traditional rhetorical roots, the student uses sarcasm combined with a delayed thesis to deliver his punch. He achieves his ironic and dryly humorous tone by mixing legalistic discourse, largely absent at Walla Walla but common today in Plateau Indian government and business, with traditional plainspokenness, often expressed in vivid detail ("My hat is off to the individual who has the testosterone to cut the legs off a school and then turn around an shrug it off"). The letter demonstrates the informing influence on early language socialization in the home; both of this writer's parents had graduate degrees. Teachers at the school told me that his knowledge base, as well as his written and oral expression, was atypical of their other students. Obviously, the discourse level in his home was much different from that of a working-class home, as his vocabulary alone would suggest. This sample illustrates that any one person's home literacies are themselves a rich mix of personal, family, mainstream, and traditional influences as well as (appropriately enough, given the point of the letter) the growing influence of Internet rhetoric, with its informal diction, its humor, and its strongly stated positions—all are available for remixing in any given situation. Unfortunately, the letter also demonstrates the efficacy of colonialist divide-and-conquer strategies, for Judge Lamberth, an ally whose ruling aimed to advance and support the suit, became the target of the student's outrage.

This student's rough drafts throughout his portfolio may suggest another influence at work on his distinctive linguistic expression: that of an ancestral language base. In another letter, he protests increasing media consolidation that gives fewer networks more influence on what people "read, watch, and hear" before he zeroes in on Clear Channel and conservative dominance of the airways by the likes of Rush Limbaugh and Paul Harvey. The student concludes with his thesis.

Figure 4 shows just the first of three pages of the letter, with different typographical markers—arrows, capitalization, double-underlining, circled text—that arguably do not indicate voiced emphasis (such as all caps for shouting). Rather, they appear to mark ideational emphasis and degree of speaker confidence, which are accomplished with syntactical structure in many ancestral languages, an option without parallel in English, as linguistic anthropologist William Leap has shown. The student writer's feel for informal/formal shifts in diction, in this letter as well as in the letter to Judge Lamberth, may also derive from ancestral language influence, which persists in subsequent generations even after the ancestral language itself has been lost.[23]

Further, in the cover sheet to this letter in this student's Learning Record, he explains: "This pursuasion letter is the product of personal frustration with current events. Although this work wasn't assigned to me for a grade I completed it with my own sense of ambition. The final draft was a selection from two pos-

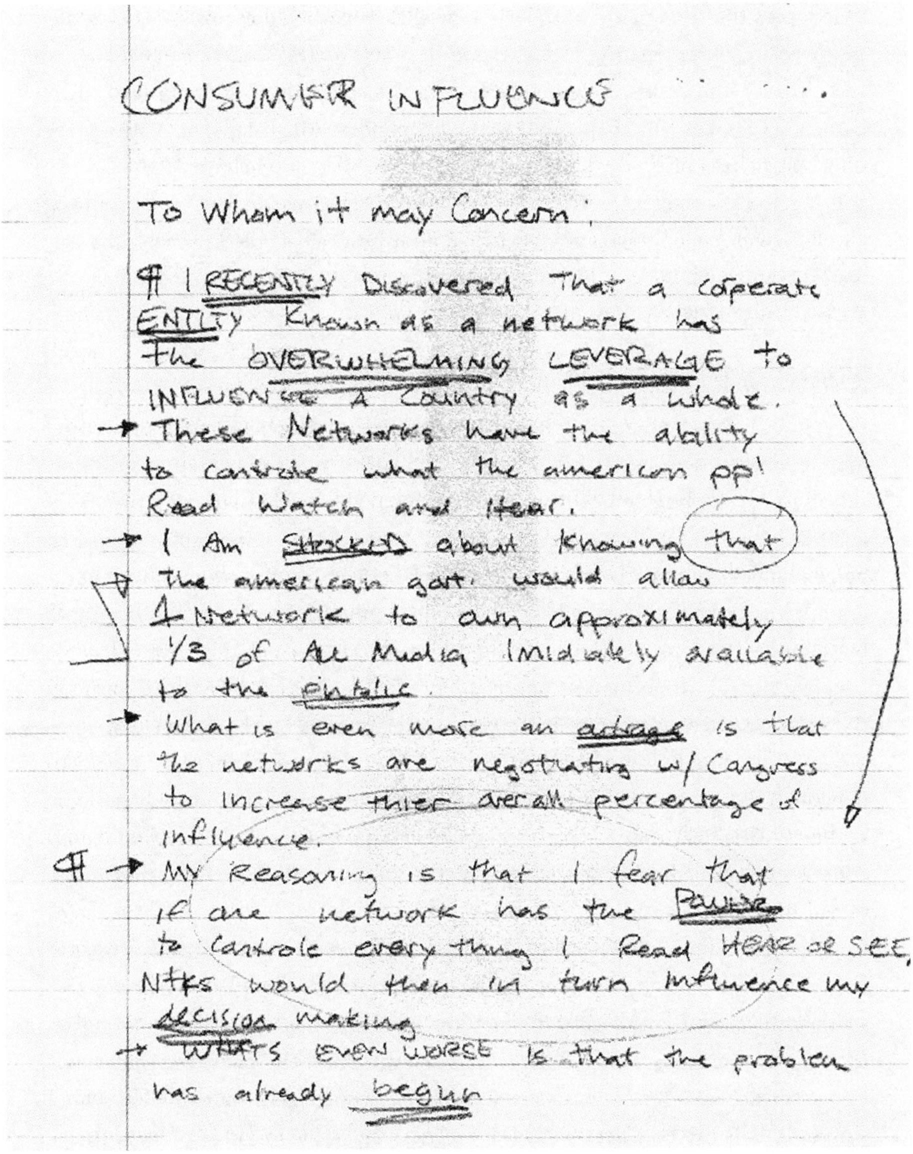

CONSUMER INFLUENCE

To Whom it may Concern:

¶ I RECENTLY Discovered That a corperate ENTITY Known as a network has the OVERWHELMING LEVERAGE to INFLUENSE A Country as a whole. These Networks have the ability to controle what the american pp! Read Watch and Hear. I Am SHOCKED about Knowing that the american govt. would allow 1 Network to own approximately 1/3 of All Media Imidiately available to the public. What is even more an outrage is that the networks are negotiating w/ Congress to increase thier overall percentage of influence.

¶ My Reasoning is that I fear that if one network has the POWER to controle every thing I Read HEAR or SEE, Ntks would then in turn influence my decision making. WHATS EVEN WORSE is that the problem has already begun.

FIGURE 4. Student's letter protesting conservative, corporate control of the media. Compare the dramatic markings of the student's letter with the typography of the letters in figures 2 and 3 in chapter 4. Unlike the other two writers, however, the student does not speak his ancestral language. That this kind of dramatic typography recurs in multiple artifacts for several generations strongly suggests that ancestral language and discourse are still active, even among English-only speakers.

sible topics that I came up with." How he came up with these possible topics is captured in the prewriting web exercise in figure 5. The student's penchant for verbal irony and satire is clear even here, as he sends up "Big Shots" and "BIA Dudes." He pokes fun at the pedagogy of this prewriting mapping, with "space filler" branching off in three different categories ("persuasive letter," "the issue?," and "network influence, political power"). In using sarcasm, and in envisioning all of his writing as persuasive letters, all addressed to people in power, the student is clearly working within the rhetorical, activist tradition of his forebears of the early twentieth century.

Suspended Thesis/Suspenseful Arrangement

While the student letter-writer adapted pedagogical tools like the prewriting map to suit his own needs, his sense of what constitutes appropriate communication remained largely informed by traditional rhetorical markers. Other prewriting tools meet with mixed success. The Jane Schaffer paragraph is a case in point. A heuristic used in middle schools across the country, the Schaffer paragraph aims to help young writers shape and develop a five-sentence paragraph. First comes the topic sentence, stating the main idea or position, followed by a concrete detail, which may be an example, fact, or other kind of support. Then comes two sentences of commentary, which elaborates on the fact presented as the concrete detail. The commentary may take the form of analysis, reasons, or insights. The concluding sentence wraps up the paragraph and restates the topic sentence. This five-sentence pattern can be expanded to include additional concrete details and commentary, as long as the same one-to-two ratio between the two is maintained.[24]

Strictly speaking, the method does not allow first-person point-of-view, nor is it really designed to produce academic arguments, complete with counterarguments and refutation. But the method is highly adaptable to more, or fewer, restrictions. Some teachers require a certain number of sentences, and sometimes even a certain number of words per sentence. The one teacher at the tribal school who used this method adapted it less restrictively, allowing her students to use personal experience to support their claims and giving them wide berth on their facts, even if they were fictitious statistics. Although the Schaffer paragraph generally affected students' thesis-placement, it did not always. And while it generally helped students develop their thoughts, they did so without following the guidelines but by following their own sense of communicative competence, weaving their personal experience in and out to support their arguments. The excerpts

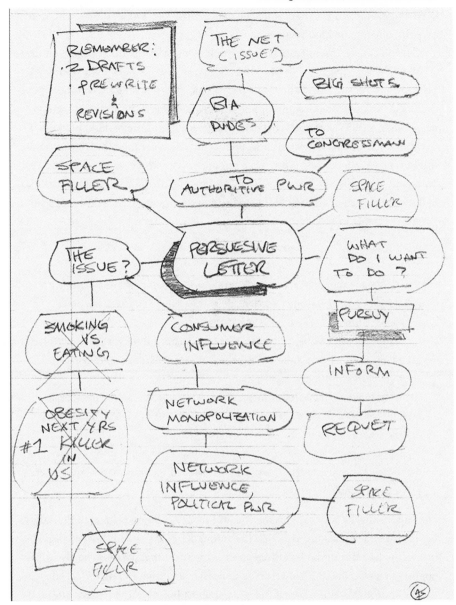

FIGURE 5. Prewriting exercise. Brainstorming before writing his letter reproduced in figure 4, the student writer is working well within the same activist and rhetorical traditions as his forebears, personalizing his words with high-affect sarcasm and bluntness and favoring the genre of a personal letter, unabashedly directed to the "Big Shots" and "BIA Dudes."

cited earlier on teen pregnancy, marijuana legalization, and statutory rape were all written using the Jane Schaffer heuristic.

Conspicuously absent from these, as well as most of the other papers in the archive, are opposing viewpoints, which I submit is consistent with traditional principles of persuasion. When students do include opposing viewpoints, they usually do so only when required. The results often show the strain of trying to negotiate this Eurocentric practice with their own culturally marked preference. In the following paper collected at the public school (rather than the tribal school) this seventh-grade author offers both supporting evidence as well as counter-arguments but without prejudice. The assignment called for students to write a letter to the principal arguing for or against improvements to the school grounds. I quote the paper in full:

Dear: Principal

Yes, I say there should be more stuff outside to improve the school. disability people don't have any thing to do outside, just sit there and watch the other people have fun.

My supporting evidence is that there should be more tree's for all students that get hot on summer days and need to sit in some shade. However student's may spray paint them with gangster sign's.

My even more supporting evidence is that we need a swimming pool for the oven hot summer days. However student may think it's funny and take a tinkle or log in there.

My even even more supporting evidence is that there should be sports for diabilities. However students may just kick them off the court or whatever where playing on. [Emphasis mine]

The paper ends without conclusion, the arguments-counterarguments left hanging in suspended tension. Although the author states his pro-improvement position in the first line and offers three points to support that position, he also gives opposing viewpoints (the "however" sentences) equal time. The rhetorical effect is that he appreciates both sides of the issue, not just his own. The student attempts to differentiate and distinguish his evidence with "supporting," "even more supporting," and "even even more supporting evidence"; the comic effect may have been intended, if his scatological reference (common in Indian humor) to a "tinkle or log" is any indication. Interestingly, this is the only student who overtly marked his supporting evidence for his pro-improvement position and his "however" counterarguments—apparently a practice he learned at another school.

Sometimes student writers state their theses strongly in the opening but then soften their positions by the end of their papers. In the following example from the tribal school—again, for the class where the Schafer paragraph was used, which requires front-loading the thesis—the high school writer states her position adamantly in the first paragraph: "[school name redacted] ought to have an open campus." She opens the second paragraph with her main reason: "so we can get some good food at lunch time." Here is the second paragraph quoted in full:

> We ought to have an open campus so we can eat some good food at lunch
> time. For example McDonalds is only a few blocks away and so is that Chinese
> restraunt [name of the restaurant redacted]. On some days the students are
> stressed out from school work so at lunch time they want some real food. And on
> other days we will have a craving for a hamburger and we can just walk to Mc-
> Donalds and get one. Plus the students can take care of their personal business. If
> a student had a headache and since the school doesn't give out asprin they can go
> to the store at lunch time on buy some. We deserve to have McDonald's because
> we get tired of school lunches.

Although she mentions another reason for having an open campus—so "students can take care of their personal business"—and another restaurant other than McDonald's, it becomes clear that going to McDonald's for lunch is what this writer is really advocating. In the third paragraph she goes on to present opposing viewpoints, responding in turn to each one, point by point, thereby ostensibly strengthening her argument, at least according to the school essayist model. In the first sentence she directly quotes what the school staff would say; by the last two sentences, however, the hypothetical statements of those holding the counterargument become indistinguishable from her own voice, reminiscent of the ventriloquism in the Emmitt Till piece cited earlier and Chief Meninick's statement to the state Supreme Court in chapter 4.

> The school staff would say, there is no use for an open campus because the school
> provides the lunch and its free. But sometimes the students want some good food
> but we can't have it since the school is a closed campus. If the school doesn't want
> an open campus the school store should make hamburgers McDonald style. And
> just because some of the students are trouble makers doesn't mean they can ruin
> it for the others. *Well just don't eat then, the school pays for it and the students act
> like its free and waste it. It is a privalage to come here and you should appreciate
> what the school does for you.* [Emphasis mine]

It is in the fourth paragraph that the writer brings both sides of the argument in tension, given both equal time. She moves from one side to the other, without transition, a jarring effect for most readers, who must discern that the sentences starting with "the students" to the end of the paragraph are those of the opposing viewpoint.

> If we had an open campus the students can take care of personal business. They can make phone calls, buy some magazines, and to talk to people, and other personal things they need to take care of. They can call their parents, talk to friends on the phone, or go buy stuff on their spare time. *The students would be irresponsible and would be late all the time and smoke and get high. The students would be late repeatedly and they would skip. They would take off and get into trouble and go get in fights. So an open campus might not be a good idea.* [Emphasis mine]

The writer maintains this tension between the two sides in her conclusion, recognizing that each side has but a partial view of the issue: "So maybe the open campus idea is not a good idea to the school staff, but the students would enjoy it. They can go and take care of personal business and do talk to friends and enjoy some McDonalds." The writer does hold her position, largely by placing it second—and last—in the reader's mind, but she softens it at the same time, as if allowing that others' views are valid too.

Many readers might see this essay as indecisive and therefore unconvincing— in a word, "wishy-washy," as preservice English teachers in my methods class have said of this essay (among others) written by Plateau Indian students. According to the conventions of academic argument as it is typically taught in reductionist terms in school and first-year composition in college, to be convincing, an accomplished writer holds firm to his thesis, considers counterarguments, which generally only really serve as strawmen to prop up his own position. Interestingly, neither the assignment nor the Jane Schaffer paragraph method asks students to include counterarguments. And in fact, no one else in the class did. Obviously, the writer arguing for an open campus brought to the assignment other pedagogical experiences with academic argument from other schools. That she does so but compromises her own stated position might be variously explained. It might be reasoned that a writer more schooled in academic writing would have already considered both sides in her head or in class brainstorming sessions or prewriting exercises, the final draft representing the logical end point of a process otherwise invisible to readers. By this logic, the writer of the open-campus paper has simply turned in an underprocessed paper, as is often the case with inexperienced or undermotivated students.

A more important consideration, however, is the role of culture in defining what is, and is not, appropriate ways for young people to argue. The student may be uncomfortable in taking an unwavering position to avoid immodestly asserting herself among others in class.[25] Her wavering position may also be a way of expressing degree of confidence or a way of reporting rumor, for which her ancestral language offers many linguistic options unavailable in English.[26] Childrearing practices may also be coming into play in her indecision—specifically those that govern when, where, and to whom young people are to speak. Tribal youth are taught that they are to listen, observe, and learn from elders or other adults in authority, such as teachers, speaking only when asked to in public settings. Their usual conversation partners are their peers and children, in whose company they spend most of their time, often caring for younger children in their extended families while the adults work outside the home. These practices are largely marked by socioeconomic class, following the working-class model of childrearing that sociologist Annette Lereau has termed "the accomplishment of natural development" as opposed to middle-class childrearing practices that follow a model of "concerted development"—one where children's time is heavily scheduled with events and activities, supervised by adults, who are considered equal conversational partners.[27] Plateau Indian childrearing practices are distinguished in another regard. For the home provides a safe rehearsal time and place where children are encouraged to practice retelling stories they have heard adults tell, their performances both guided and critiqued by the family as they perfect their skills. In public settings, however, they are to speak by invitation only and, even then, they are not going to be asked to argue a position.

Thus students may struggle with the conventions of academic argument simply because they have had little experience expressing their views and have not been prompted to practice expressing those views. By far, the most common assignment at the tribal school asks students to summarize news articles they have read. Only a relative few student writers include their personal views in these summaries. In some instances in the student writing archive, a teacher might write on the paper, "And your opinion?," and the student will then add his own view, but in a private journal, written for the teacher only. At least one teacher did ask students to respond with their views on several generalized topics, such as government, culture, equality, justice, community, jobs, future, economy, and education—and got strong position statements in response, like this one: "Education is good because to many young people are droping out and our economy is dropin more and more we need people graduating and then the natives and black cry around about being poor do something people. I for one is going to graduate my family aren't poor and stupid like these 'Bastards' on the street."

Furthermore, in keeping with the value of individual modesty, personal assertiveness equates to placing oneself above others. This value is so strong that, teachers tell me, students resist displaying their work on bulletin boards and will do so only if their names are removed. Even then, whose work is placed higher or lower on the board, relative to others, occasions much deliberation. In other words, students have no trouble stating their position, if they are asked to, if they are given a choice of topics, if their views are conveyed privately to the teacher, rather than put on public display among their peers, and if counterarguments do not have to be weighed in point by point.

It must also be remembered that Plateau culture maintains a high tolerance for *not* taking a position. This respect for the nonvote (as discussed in chapter 5) may be understood as a respect for personal autonomy and personal experience, to which each person must remain true. In one journal entry, responding to an article on George W. Bush's chances for getting reelected, one student writes:

> If I was to choose I think I'd choose no. At first I wasn't really sure, but then he showed the public he doesn't like us Native Americans. I didn't see anything about this until some one told me about it. Honestly if I was to vote for president and didn't know which one to vote for I'll probably just not vote at all. Unless someone can convince me to vote for the same candidate they are. Here on the Reservation the Indians didn't want President Bush. I hear them say the President is not even being [?] President.

This is not really indecision. It is a kind of decision-suspension, at least until someone can convince her to vote one way or another. And it is a position—a third position usually excluded as an option in for-or-against arguments—and one that is negatively valued in Euro-American culture as "wishy-washy."

Rather than read the open-campus paper as simply a flawed or underprocessed or modest attempt at academic argument, then, this student's work might be read as a complex negotiation between tradition and essayist literacy, where an indigenous rhetoric reasserts itself within pedagogies designed from Euro-American premises of argumentation that also fit Euro-American values. Writing from a cultural framework where both strong and undecided positions are allowable but speaking for others is not, the open-campus writer may be engaging in a deliberation aimed at finding either her own position or consensual, common ground. Working from the discourses of argument she has experienced on the reservation, including those in General Council meetings, as well as pedagogies from another school, the writer brings multiple rhetorical resources to bear as she attempts to accommodate the demands of academic argument introduced at school and tested for by the state. Her attempt may be less successful by state standards than some of her peers who have had more practice with academic writing or whose parents have been educated or have worked in a white system before moving to the reservation, among many other possible variables in a young adult's language use socialization in the home and reservation life. In any case, her open-campus paper lays bare the complex process of rhetorical negotiations, to greater or lesser degree, that all Plateau Indians face in school and college.

At stake is not just a test score or even a college degree. Writing academic arguments constitutes nothing less than an identity crisis for many Plateau students, not unlike that experienced by other Native groups. Intercultural communications scholars Ronald Scollon and Suzanne Wong Scollon have found that for Athabaskans, essay writing is seen as a major personal display, which would be appropriate for a person in dominance in a particular setting, which in school would be the teacher, not the student. Essay writing assumes a generalized, unknown audience, which decontextualizes the writer/reader relationship outside a specific social network; in such situations Athabaskans prefer not to communicate at all. The dilemma for Athabaskans in school is when the situation is contextualized, their writing is compatible with their values but not with the standards of essayist prose; when the situation is decontextualized, they prefer not to write. As literacy scholar James Gee has summed up: "What is compatible to do and be an Athabaskan is in large mutually exclusive with what is required to do and be a writer of school-based essayist prose. This doesn't mean that Athabaskans cannot do both (remember, we are all multiple), it simply means that they may face very real conflicts in terms of values and identity."[28]

Cross-Cultural Comparison

Rhetorical indigeneity is even more clearly marked, by way of contrast, in multicultural classrooms than in a tribal school where all students are Native. I offer one case in point. Another reservation school, this one a public school, also participated in the Writing Across Cultures project. For one assignment two classes of forty-three seventh-graders wrote persuasive papers on the school-improvement topic mentioned earlier. Of those forty-three students, five were Euro-American, ten were Plateau Indians, twenty-five were Latino/Mexican descent, and three were Filipino. Because most, if not all, had lived in this same community and had attended the same schools all their lives, these two classes were, in effect, their own control group, one where the major variable was home culture, which would include language use socialization.[29] A very brief look focusing on just the writing produced by the Indian and white students shows a sharp contrast in their respective rhetorics in at least two regards.

First, on an assignment that certainly did not lend itself well to humor, four students nonetheless ventured a humorous tone, and all of those students were Plateau Indian. The droll humor in the following examples, accomplished largely by using selective details, personalize their arguments, as Leap found was the case among Ute children in their plot summaries.[30] One tried to convince the principal that "most of all we need a track for people with disabilities to race around on wheelchairs. If we could get a wieght lifting room, for people who don't get out much. So all that fat will be turned into musele." Another listed his suggestions of improving first the cafeteria and then the school grounds: "Two: we should increase the food category, not everybody likes soy burgers. Three: we should plant more vegitation around the school, people send their children to nice schools, not getto ones."

More commonly, five of the ten Plateau Indian students cited personal experience or personal preferences as reasons behind their suggested improvements. In the following paper, the student takes a wry, understated tone in this paragraph: "It's not fun when you trip [on cracks in the basketball courts] because of one of them and there just plain ugly. Another thing is the basketball hoops aren't all together pretty either. They are not very stable, people can walk right up and shake them." He goes on to mention parenthetically his own experience turning an ankle on the track filled with holes: "The last thing is the track we use in P.E. it is very lumpy in some of the places. During run-day or some other running event during P.E. you can twist an ankle. (I have many times)." His personal experience of the track may have come up in the class brainstorming session because this reason turns up in the three papers written by white students—but notably in objectified form.

In the following example, the Euro-American student takes a very legal tone, his letter starting like a last will and testimony: "I, John Smith [a pseudonym], am writing this letter to you to tell you some things that I want you to look at and consider as a possability." The writer goes on to suggest that the track needs to be all grass or all dirt but minimally "something flat." As support, he cites the possibility of a sprained ankle, generalizing the example that the Plateau Indian student personalized: "When someone were to try to run on the grass they might just possibly twist, sprane, or break their ankle, because the track is NOT flat so then it becomes unsafe." Another white student writes, "Everyone won'ts to have better track and field. One reason is because people twist their ankles. On the track because it's so holy."

Another paper written by a white student provides more conclusive evidence that the writer consciously chose not to include personal experience, opting instead to use generalized experience outside her own. In her first draft she writes: "Next, I think we should spray the weeds around the perimeter because it look really bad. I noticed that, when we were running our Perimeter in P.E." In her second draft, however, she omits this supporting sentence altogether. Still, she very masterfully weaves in what "others say" as support for her suggested school improvements: "I have heard some soccor players say that our soccor field embarrasses them when we have visiting teams come" and "Some students have brought up the fact that we don't have a good variety of sports areas. I have heard some students say that we should have a tennis quart. Others have suggested a better track." The truth of exactly how many made these statements aside, the argument seems stronger because more people agreed on this or that point, not just the author—but stronger only in discourse communities and classrooms dominated by the conventions of school essayist literacy.

Mixed-Blood Literacies

Teachers at the tribal school have told me that getting students to write is "like pulling teeth." While the same might be said of other students at other schools, it seems to carry special import in reservation schools. The indigenous rhetoric at work in the archival materials from 1855 to 1956, as discussed in previous chapters, is *not,* in fact, evident in *most* students' writing at the tribal school. But when traditional influences do occur, they do so dramatically, as my selected examples show. This variability does not disprove my thesis; rather, it supports the view that Plateau Indian rhetorical practices, like identity, are multiple, relative to individual experience and family education, among other factors. Arguably, tradition does shape what counts as communicative competence for all students, perhaps in ways invisible in the written texts collected in the Writing Across Cultures project but visible in varying degrees and in other contexts, such as oral interactions between individuals or within groups, as sociolinguist Susan Philips has shown.[31] Other nontraditional discursive practices also manifest in the work of individual students, their work thereby modernizing the rhetorical *ethnie.* Taken together, these student examples illustrate how individuals draw on tradition-based cultural repertories as well as personal rhetorical resources to forge multiple identities in the school context.

That these students draw on multiple discourses to express and re-present themselves holds important implications for composition instruction at all levels for all students, in reservation schools and in school and college classrooms that draw on multiple demographics. Most Indians of the twenty-first century already practice what indigenous studies scholar Scott Lyons calls "mixedblood literacies of negotiations."[32] What they need now is the "spaces [in educational institutions] to practice them."[33] I argue in chapter 7 that those spaces are already there, awaiting educators to take advantage of them.

7

**Reassessing the
Achievement Gap**

"**W**ould it not be good if you wanted to talk with my brother, or if you wanted to talk with our Great Chief? If you knew how to write and wanted to
talk you could send it to him on paper and he would know your heart. Would it
not be good then to have schools among you?"[1] Thus argued General Joel Palmer,
superintendent of Indian Affairs for the Oregon Territory, at the Treaty Council
at Walla Walla in 1855.

General Palmer did not have to convince the Plateau Indians of the virtues of
literacy and schooling. Like multilingualism, education had always been much
prized in Plateau Indian lifeways, as a means of cultural transmission but also
a mechanism for revitalizing change. In the early and mid-1800s, parents often
voluntarily sent a child to boarding school back East or to mission schools to
learn English and American ways; Lawyer (Nez Perce), Spokan Garry (Spokan),
and Chief Moses (Mid-Columbia) are prime examples of this common practice.
Literacy in English was not just a tool for assimilating into white society, as General Palmer assumed, but also a tool for conserving Native sovereignty, opening
up a pathway for Indian activism later in the nineteenth century. Whether in-
formally transmitted or formally taught in institutions (a Euro-American distinction, not a Native one), education modernized the *ethnie,* keeping the culture

vibrant for future generations. Their divergent goals for education—assimilation and cultural genocide versus preservation and revitalization—ultimately raised the larger question, Who would control Native education, the federal government or local tribes?

Also evident in General Palmer's remarks is his assumption of Euro-American cultural normativity—and, by implication, superiority. Although the Plateau Indians traditionally valued language pluralism, they were about to be subjected to federal English-only policy for the next 170 years. While the Plateau Indians sought to better the lives of the next generation through higher education, their educational opportunities were largely limited to an elementary education, "elementary" in terms of grade level and a curriculum focused on domestic and manual labor training. And although Plateau Indians believed that each child learned at her own pace, taught and tested by life experience, federal and state policies would mandate that all students would be taught so-called objective knowledge and measured by standardized tests, leaving behind children of color and children living in poverty.[2] And thus was born the so-called achievement gap, yet another permutation of "the Indian problem."

This chapter examines that gap qualitatively but also critically from the standpoints of discourses of Indian-ness. I then turn to the long-standing conversation among educators about how to address the gap. Most agree that the keys to Native achievement are cultural relevance and a positive Native identity. But I question what is culturally relevant today, for which Native identity, and within what educational context: Native-run schools and colleges, public schools on or near reservations, white-dominant schools, and white-dominant universities. I add my own contribution to this conversation in very practical terms, offering examples of curriculum and approaches that honor the rhetorical sovereignty of Native students at all levels.

Constructing the Achievement Gap

In general terms "the achievement gap" refers to the disparity in academic achievement between African American, American Indian/Alaska Native (AI/AN), and Latino/a students and their white and Asian-American peers as well as between students from low-income families and those from middle- and upper-income families.[3] The gap is documented by various measures: test scores, high school graduation rates, and college entry and completion rates.[4] AI/AN test scores are among the lowest in Washington state, even when scores are disaggregated for race and income. Specifically, on state writing tests from academic years 2007–8 to 2011–12, in all testing grades 4, 7, and 10, low-income AI/AN students scored the lowest of all other low-income groups (including white, Asian, Black/African American, Hispanic/Latino, and Pacific Islanders). In all groups not identified as low income, AI/AN students scored the lowest.[5] Furthermore, the scores of AI/AN students *not* from low-income homes nonetheless

- were comparable to the scores of *low-income* whites and Pacific Islanders in grade 4, from 2009 to 2012 (21);
- were only slightly better than the scores of *low-income* whites in grade 7, from 2008 to 2012 (23); but
- dropped *below* those of *low-income* whites in grade 10, from 2010 to 2012 (26).

Statewide, Native students are more likely to drop out and to do so in earlier grades, with the lowest on-time high school graduation rate of all groups.[6] The rate was 55 percent in 2007–8.[7] Not surprisingly, the gap persists at the post-secondary level. In Washington state, of the mere 2 percent of Native students who enroll in college, only 15 percent graduate—after six years.[8] According to a 2010 report by the Education Trust, Washington ranked among the bottom five states in narrowing its gap.[9] The persistence of a gap bodes especially ill for the region in light of shifts in student demographics. Since 1998, in Washington state, the white student population has declined by 11 percent, while nonwhite student populations have increased by 38 percent.[10] Several factors are predictive of test score performance. State reports have consistently found that the ratio between Native and white students, the percentage of teachers with master's degrees, and the number of student support personnel directly correlate to test scores.[11] Similarly, the Educational Longitudinal Study, a national dataset with only Native participants, found that socioeconomic status, the mother's education level, student attitudes toward school and participation in after-school programs, and use of resources (such as computers in math classes) are positive correlatives.[12]

But at least two data point to cultural differences in language use socialization. Statewide test scores in grade 3 among Native students living in urban, suburban, small town, and rural areas showed no difference. In grade 4, however, Native students living in small town and rural areas scored lower than their counterparts in urban and suburban areas on reading and math—but not in writing, which again showed no difference.[13] Insofar as geographic settings variously encode socioeconomic status (SES) and acquaintance with, if not acculturation to, white ways with words, the fact that all Native students in grades 1–4 statewide scored equally well in writing may suggest that they shared a similar pattern of early language socialization. That socialization most clearly reemerges in student communication, both speaking and writing.[14] In the very early grades, then, culture may outweigh SES in predicating a certain kind of performance in writing. In like manner, as cited earlier, notice that test scores of AI/AN students not from low-income homes are comparable to those of *low*-income groups. In other words, the SES of AI/AN students does not account for low test scores, for all AI/AN students regardless of income score as low as poor students of all ethnicities. Thus students' biological identities as American Indians alone seems to be predictive of low scores on writing tests.

Deconstructing the Achievement Gap

But in many ways the achievement gap is also a data gap, unwittingly participating in the discourses of Indian-ness that have framed "the Indian problem" for at least two hundred years. The statistics used to document the achievement gap are based on incomplete data, perpetrating the notion of the Vanishing Indian while also failing to recognize the complexities of Indian identity in the twenty-first century. Most obviously, data are underreported and findings overgeneralized. For example, according to state adequate yearly progress (AYP) reports required under the No Child Left Behind Act (NCLB) in 2006–7 only 6.8 percent of AI/AN students met standards for math and only 7.2 percent for reading, but these findings are based on data submitted by only twenty-two districts—fewer than 10 percent of the school districts in Washington state.[15] While the Native-enrollment range statewide is enormous—anywhere from 0 to 1,136 AI/AN students—almost half of all districts enrolled only 1–29 AI/AN students.[16] With such low numbers, districts may not report specifics of AI/AN test performance to protect student privacy, leaving those districts with high Native enrollments overrepresented in the analyses. In 19 districts of the total of 297 districts in Washington, Native enrollment exceeds 20 percent; in 8 of those 19, it exceeds 65 percent.[17] Further skewing the gap is the fact that schools do not report the number of AI/AN in gifted programs; their achievement is thus left unaccounted for and rendered invisible in overall test scores.[18] Clearly, much more research is needed on other factors, individually and in concert, that affect student performance on tests, including instructional content, classroom practices, as well as teacher, school, and community factors.[19]

Even more problematic is the very designation of AI/AN as a biologically defined category based on blood quantum rather than as a sociopolitical category necessarily in flux. Such a category would recognize both the history and the future of Indian identities as heterogeneous, multiple, intersecting, and sometimes contradictory, as defined by such vectors as geography, socioeconomic resources, and "access to . . . cultural capital."[20] The practice of defining racial categories, assessing intelligence categorically, and supporting that assessment objectively with numbers has a long and ugly history—then as now, backed by the science of metrics. Historically that science equated difference with deficiency. Because Native societies were "primitive," it was assumed they lacked legal, religious, intellectual, and educational systems. Not only were Native ways of "informal" education deficient, Native learners were also deficient in "the verbal, cognitive, and even motor skills necessary to succeed in school."[21]

Civilizing these primitives by forcing Native students to attend boarding school became the prevailing federal educational policy well into the twentieth century. In boarding schools Native learners' stoicism and silence were taken as signs of their mental, emotional, and linguistic deficiencies, not as logical and enforced responses to English-only policies and five centuries of colonial education that demanded silence as a matter of daily discipline and regimentation.[22] Thus the discourse of scientific racism conspired with nineteenth-century legal discourse infantilizing Indians as wards of the state to create the prevailing view that Indians were willful children as well as physically inferior, "racially backward, culturally deficient, and intellectually feeble."[23]

Yesterday's difference-as-deficiency is today's difference-as-deficit, the model upon which the achievement gap rests, measuring all students regardless of background against the norms of Euro-American education goals, standards, and cultural competence. For example, the Common Core State Standards (CCSS)—which will drive curricula, textbooks, and test design across the United States for the next several years—call for writing arguments

- with stated claims, supported with relevant evidence from multiple, credible print and digital sources
- that distinguish the claims from counterclaims
- that are organized and developed logically
- use words, phrases, and clauses to create cohesion
- that maintain a formal style and objective tone.[24]

These particular criteria (I have not paraphrased all of them) proceed from certain premises about what constitutes good writing: cohesion, explicitness, objectivity, logic, easy-to-follow organization, and reliance on experts other than trusting in one's own experience. In short, the author does all the work. In the Plateau Indian rhetorical tradition, as seen throughout this book, readers co-author meaning, the texts themselves often delaying or leaving unstated their theses, their arguments organized unpredictably and supported with experiential knowledge, re-created with high affect.

Interestingly, the CCSS also call for writing narrative with an emphasis not found in previous standards. In the preface to the writing section of the CCSS, this new emphasis is explained: "For students, writing is a key means of asserting and defending claims, *showing what they know about a subject, and conveying what they have experienced, imagined, thought, and felt.* . . . They need to know how to combine elements of different kinds of writing—*for example, to use narrative strategies within argument and explanation within narrative to produce complex and nuanced writing.*"[25] The preface highlights three text types that students must be adept at: arguments, informative/explanatory texts, and narrative. The Internet seems to have propelled narrative writing to this elevated status, for the CCSS also stress the role of technology across all domains. Yet the grade-level criteria spell out a very Eurocentric view of storytelling. To wit: narratives are to be as explicit, structured, and detailed as arguments.[26]

The charge that tests are culturally biased is as old as the achievement gap itself. As early as 1928, the federal Meriam Report pointed to the need for "locally developed curriculum" and use of "individually adaptive methods."[27] American Indian education scholarship today more broadly attributes the gap to cultural bias in curricular content, teaching methods, and assessment practices.[28] All of these aspects are included in the umbrella term "culturally relevant pedagogy" (CRP). Coined in 1995 and grounded originally in black feminist theory, CRP is applicable to all classrooms constituted of all kinds of identity groups, as marked by multiple identifiers such as rural, transgender, and religious designations. Like a three-legged stool, CRP has one interdependent goal: to foster the academic achievement, cultural competence, and sociopolitical consciousness of all students.[29] But how might CRP apply specifically to American Indian students and within schools with different demographics: (1) Native schools and colleges with 100 percent Native enrollments; (2) public schools on or near reservations where Native students constitute at least a substantial minority; (3) white-dominant schools with very few Native students; and (4) white-dominant institutions of higher education? Each of these contexts raises particular issues, and I have organized the following discussion accordingly. My recommendations should be read cumulatively, all of them holding applicability in all classrooms, however they may be demographically configured.

CRP in Native Schools and Colleges

The racist assumption is that academic achievement and cultural relevance are oppositional terms, as if anything "alternative" to the Euro-American schooling is less than rigorous. On the contrary, cultural relevance is a precondition for achievement. CRP builds positive Native identity by building curricula centered on cultural and place-based knowledge that integrates traditional values and practices, while CRP teaching methods use "cultural knowledge, prior experiences, frames of reference, and performance styles to make learning encounters more relevant to and effective for them. It teaches to and through the strengths of these students."[30] Thus CRP in Native schools shifts the frame of reference from a Euro-American educational paradigm to a Native one. No doubt well-intentioned, much scholarship has perpetrated the notion that Native learners learn differently, as if culture were biology. Accordingly, Native students have been stereotyped as having "less developed visual perception" and "severe linguistic inadequacy"; as coming from "cultures of poverty" that self-perpetuate intergenerational poverty; and as being observational, visual, cooperative/noncompetitive, field-dependent, right-brained, "ecological," "holistic," or "spiritual" learners.[31]

For sure, culture produces a certain orientation to learning; the problem lies in the portrait of American Indians as one-dimensional learners.[32] That picture fails to take into account the distinctiveness of tribal differences; the multiplicity of identities; the complexity of Native language, knowledge, and intellectual traditions; the nuances of communication and interaction protocols; and, yes, the multimodalities of teaching and learning preferences. And such one-dimensional stereotypes lead to one-dimensional practices in the classroom: Indians are visual; show films. Indians are nonverbal; don't do debates. Indians are oral/aural; play podcasts.[33]

With this caution in mind, how might Native education be generally described, in contradistinction to the Euro-American paradigm and the ideology of schooling? Respect for, and the responsibility of, the learner is highly valued, with the expectation that the learner will formulate her own hypotheses based on her own observation and experiences, test those hypotheses, and rethink them, and she will do so in her own time, repeating the process to plumb the multiple layers of lessons to be learned from any given story, other life forms, additional life experience, hers or that of others. The learner's progress is therefore highly individualized. Typically, too, children in and outside of school learn in language-rich environments, with daily access to multiple genres: songs, stories, lectures, scoldings, jokes. Learning is not only verbal but also operational, with hands-on activities privileged more than they are in white-dominant schooling. Ultimately life is the best teacher—and the best test.[34] Not surprisingly, Native education mirrors the same values embodied in Plateau Indian rhetoric. Learner responsibility, like listener responsibility, respects the rights of the individual, a central principle of Plateau lifeways.

To this conversation on Native education, I would add certain caveats, consistent with the propositions I have advanced throughout this book. While I agree that tribal schools and colleges need to continue to create (to recall the words of the Meriam Report back in 1928) "locally developed curriculum" and use "adaptive methods," they still need to bear in mind that Native identity is multiple. This multiplicity is rarely acknowledged in Indian education, which often takes, in indigenous studies scholar Lyons's words, "more monologic tones" that argue for teaching "Our Culture, Our Language, Our Dialect, Our Nation(s)."[35] In the words of Lyons's father, himself an Indian educator: "To understand Indian kids, you need to know Nike first, tribal culture second."[36] American Indian studies scholar and author Greg Sarris would agree. He explains how one teacher on the Kashaya Pomo reservation made this vital connection between the past and the present by having her students create a children's book for younger students based on traditional stories. The teacher gave no other directives. Students could work collaboratively or individually. They could ask family and friends for advice. They could choose any stories they wished. The finished product amply illustrated a common strategy: they recast the mythic past in terms of their real today. One story, for example, re-presented Coyote as a low-rider, ready to rumble, learning the hard way the truths of the past.[37]

In contrast, another teacher read students the story of Slug Woman, in hopes of providing culturally relevant material. Students responded with apathy, alienation, and even contempt with comments like "That's all devil worship" and "I don't want to read about no savages."[38] Sarris points out that the version that the teacher read was decontextualized, without the first-person narrative framework, without attribution to previous tellers of this story (as the original does). It was also "translated" and written in insipid English, divorced from the verb-powered Kashaya language. Just as important, though, the teacher failed to take into account that many of her students were Mormonized, while others had relatives who were historically ostracized for being related to or in affinity with Slug Woman. This reading activity implicitly required that students "shelve their personal experience."[39] It discouraged them from contextualizing or questioning the text, unwittingly replicating the confusion, frustration, and alienation of a community in painful cultural flux.[40] Modernizing the *ethnie* in terms of the curriculum, rather than eroding tradition, actually keeps tribal values alive, carrying them forward into the future.

Similarly, the *ethnie* needs to be modernized in terms of pedagogy. Native education typically valued "instruction that is operationalized through interaction with other lifeforms (such as plants and animals) and interaction with the technologies of material culture."[41] Certainly, the example of the teacher who had her students rewrite traditional stories tapped into Native ways of knowing in designing her methods. While keeping faith with traditional pedagogy, Native-run schools and colleges need to continue to make modern connections to new technologies that will strengthen, rather than erode, tribal values and group identity, just as the technology-adverse Amish nonetheless embraced cell phones because the new technology sustains their worldview in a way that land-line telephones did not.[42] Integration of new media, and the multiple genres it has fostered, is not just culturally relevant pedagogy; it is good pedagogy, period. I will have more to say about why and how later in this chapter.

CRP in Public Schools on or Near Reservations

The demographic profile of public schools on or near reservations varies depending on the region and on its proximity to urban centers. But in the public schools on or near the rural, isolated reservations on the Plateau, Latino/a and Indian students together typically comprise supermajorities. Although white students make up a minority, they nonetheless have access to cultural capital both in school and in the community that their peers do not have. Their parents are often college-educated or are employed as managers in agribusiness or might own local businesses. Not surprisingly, their discursive practices align with those privileged in schools. Typically, CRP champions place-based curriculum: teachers collect information about a community's funds of knowledge and students' cultural capital. Thus curriculum responds to students, not the other way around.[43]

But in schools such as these, where gangs are organized around cultural differences and caste-like class hierarchies have become naturalized, CRP needs to first expand students' notion of culture. Although skin color and heritage are constitutive of one kind of culture, everyone participates in multiple identity groups, including something that might be called "youth culture." Teachers can draw on such common reference points across skin-defined gangs and class-based groups, while still remaining true to CRP's overarching, interdependent goals: achievement, cultural competence, and sociopolitical consciousness. Students in isolated, rural reservation schools already have cultural competence. But this competence is grounded in a reified notion of culture, forever fixed in time, rather than a notion of culture in flux, shaped by political dynamics and socioeconomic realities. The battle lines among students of color living in poverty on or near reservations have been drawn. CRP's project in the classroom should be to unravel them, finding common ground across cultures and building sociopolitical consciousness. In short, a culturally relevant curriculum in reservation schools needs to be a critical literacy curriculum.

And what of students' cultural heritage based on nationality? In their papers collected in the Writing Across Culture project, students occasionally allude to the role of traditions in their lives, such as *quinceañera* (a Latina's fifteenth birthday celebration of her entrance into womanhood) and longhouse ceremonies (a longhouse is the site for religious and community services for American Indians). But I want to say that popular culture is the common culture of young adults across ethnic boundaries: "common" in the sense of being ordinary but also in the sense of being shared. Popular culture inhabits these students' domestic spaces as well as their social practices (i.e., choices in clothes, music, magazines, dance, banter). And their common stories now come from television and movies, which are among the most racist, sexist, and classist stories in their everyday lives outside of school. Analysis of their meaning and their meaning-making mechanisms needs to be included in every English language arts classroom. These materials can provide a base for a critical literacy curriculum on at least three levels.

At the most obvious level, attention needs to be directed at issues of representation. For example, in the Writing Across Culture project several students mentioned that Jackie Chan movies and the *Rush Hour* franchise were among their favorites. Why are these movies so funny, and to whom are they funny? How might different members of an audience view these stereotypes? In other words, what meanings do these movies, often by means of stereotypes but also by other means (i.e., casting, score, and film editing), create for different kinds of viewers, defined by race, class, gender, sexual orientation, and so forth? Young adults are among the most sophisticated readers of visual and multimedia images of any age group, so an equally sophisticated investigation of those images is well within their reach.

On a second level, students need to examine more subtle forms of representing bias. They need to be directed to explore what values are embedded in the visual narratives of movies and to what degree these values support or undermine their own. At this level, issues of meanings need to be recontextualized and critically framed in terms of the local as well as the national and global perspectives. Storytelling embodies not just the forms but also the norms of a community. Do the stories told by Hollywood serve the same social-oriented purposes of family stories that these students have heard all their lives? Do movies valorize human beings who survive humbly and miraculously? What orientations to the world, to the community, to individuals are embedded in these narratives? Besides making connections between their own collective stories and those of mainstream entertainment, they also need to widen their gaze to other genres and media. Asking tough questions of literary materials as well as tapping into community resources, such as local and state newspapers, will help students see that the ultimate aim of learning to read is reading to learn. And reading to learn is more than collecting "objective" information, no matter if that information is dressed in literary or nonliterary language.

Finally, on a third level, the genres generated by the entertainment industry can be introduced into the classroom as a bridge to academic literacy. Comparing thumbnail movie synopses written for different audiences and even in different media model different ways of handling the same information. These particular forms are precisely applicable to fiction, the genre that predominates in most language arts curricula. Such genre models abound, which students can emulate as they write about an art form that they know and care about.

Cultural relevance also takes on new meaning in these multiethnic communities now immersed in electronic media. In their writing assignments collected in the Writing Across Culture projects, students reported daily use of various media, including cell phones, video games, and computers—and that was in the early 2000s. Just ten years later, even elementary school children in reservation schools have cell phones, teachers have told me, although few have computers and Internet connectivity at home. Instead, schools and community centers have become common access points. Teachers have also told me that their students are especially adept at researching, e-mailing, tweeting, Facebooking. And young adults talking with one another—whether online or off—is a culturally congruent pattern of interaction and learning for Latino/a and Plateau Indian students alike.

Unfortunately, students in reservation public schools are generally disallowed this kind of Internet use, ironically, because of low test scores. Instead of a culturally relevant pedagogy, a pedagogy of poverty almost exclusively focused on basic skills (based on oral Standard American English and its grapholect, Edited American English) and Euro-American texts prevails, diverting attention from the real reason these students fail: social and economic inequalities systemically maintained. Literacy education need not proceed in lockstep sequence, with students having to answer *what*-questions before *why*-questions and before giving affective commentary, personalizing their learning. Actually, just the reverse may be true. The more alienated the group of students, the more important it is to address at least one of the issues at the root of that alienation in the classroom: the huge breach between home and school literateness. Heightening this alienation from school is the working-class awareness that the kind of literate behaviors required in school will not be valued or even needed in the job sectors that await them: agriculture, ranching, the trades.

All the more reason to strive for a sense of critical literateness—CRP's goal of sociopolitical consciousness—one that works from the premise that for students of color, academic literacy is an instance of interethnic communication. Students need to know the ways of the "culture of power."[44] To wit: that certain written discursive practices as well as communicative competence derive from white, middle-class ways of thinking, talking, and writing. This awareness is an important antidote to the assimilationist agenda of public schools generally; otherwise students of color will continue to drop out, or worse, they will stay in school and run the risk of losing confidence in their abilities, their ambitions, or both. Thus differences in their own ways of seeing the world need to be explicitly drawn, and the comparison should not come at the expense of students' home literacies, too often described in terms of lack.

CRP in White-Dominant Public Schools

Within the context of white-dominant public schools—schools with only a few Native students, located in multiethnic urban areas or monocultural suburban or rural areas—teachers implementing CRP face multiple challenges. Interestingly, both tribal schools and reservation public schools share some of these challenges; how they address those challenges also applies to white-dominant schools. In the white-dominated classrooms, cultural competence so often gets watered down as cultural sensitivity—or worse, cultural celebration.[45] Culture becomes an object, often an exotic object, fossilized in the past. American Indian culture, in particular, is discussed as one culture, rather than several differentiated tribes with distinct intellectual and written traditions, plural. Thus overgeneralized, American Indian narrative practices are then reduced to "the oral tradition," as if orality and literacy were mutually exclusive forms of expression, setting up the binary equations of oral = primitive and literate = civilized with their implicit hierarchy of value.

As in tribal schools, CRP in white-dominant schools would modernize the *ethnie* of tribes local to those schools and communities. While state standards currently call for a renewed emphasis—in almost jingoistic tones—on reading so-called "seminal" U.S. documents such as the Constitution and the Declaration of Independence, CRP would call for studying other seminal texts, such as treaties of local tribes. Better yet, modernize the local tribe's *ethnie* by introducing nontraditional texts, such as American Indian raps, which have found their markets in and outside of Indian Country. As illustrated in chapter 1, Indian rap draws from a genre common to youth culture worldwide; what differs are the values it advances and the consequences of the Conquest from which it draws. Just incorporating multicultural texts—no matter the genre (historical documents, speeches, poetry, fiction)—does not rise to CRP's standards of cultural competence and sociopolitical consciousness; rather, it is how such texts are read. As in reservation public schools, critical engagement of texts necessarily involves multiple perspectives, not just white and Native in binary opposition. As with the Indian rap song example, integrating popular culture within the curriculum serves all students, helping students to recognize and honor their own cultural beliefs and practices while acquiring access to the wider culture.

But cultural competence goes further still, for teachers also need "insight into the ways that speech and negotiation are used in [students'] home and community."[46] With multiple demographics in one white-dominant classroom, teachers cannot always employ culturally relevant methods, but they can at least seek out and imagine methods that converge. Assignments that call for narrative (such as autobiography or ethos-building introductions) and assignments that require primary research (such as drawing one's family tree or interviewing or doing ethnography) are all examples of "cultural congruence" between Euro-American and Native education. In fact, cultural congruence may partially explain why Native students score better in writing than they do in reading and math throughout their school years. Despite the "hidden curriculum," in education theorist Michael Apple's famous phrase, the goal of which is to homogenize all students regardless of cultural background to Euro-American norms, K–12 education has typically valued personal narrative, especially in early grades. At the secondary level, personal narrative translates into personal experience for supporting evidence; it also reemerges as "voice," or most recently on the state scoring rubric, "a sense of the person behind the words."[47] The CCSS actually adds that mode of writing—narrative—to its curricular list, although (as discussed earlier) the assessment standards for telling a story are Eurocentric. This one point of cultural congruence between Euro-American and indigenous rhetoric, however, fades out in higher education, especially in Research I institutions, which have far less tolerance for Native rhetoric and its strategies of personalization. Throughout the schooling process, Native students have to translate and negotiate these preferences, which are rarely made explicit or comparable to their own.

CRP in Higher Education

A degree of proficiency with academic discourse is necessary but not sufficient for success in college.[48] How then should educators prepare Native students to be proficient in academic discourses and at the same time honor their rhetorical sovereignty? In response to that question, at least four trends have emerged, more or less in this order historically, each with its own assumptions about students, their needs, and the corresponding goals of writing instruction.[49] The deficit model, which sees basic writers as linguistically unsophisticated or even cognitively impaired, aims to remediate and cure students of their verbal ills. The acculturation model, which sees basic writers as simply unfamiliar and unversed in academic discourse, aims to initiate students into the discursive practices of the university. The third trend, recognizing inevitability of discursive hybridization, questions the unitary, reified notion of academic discourse itself, with the goal of bridging communicative gaps between home and university literacies by encouraging students "to experiment with their own forms of hybrid discourses."[50] A fourth trend is usually not invoked in conversations about basic writing: multimodality. This trend advocates that literacy instruction for basic writing needs programmatic inclusion of multimodal writing with new media and over networks.

These four trends in literacy instruction might be succinctly contrasted this way: (1) the deficit model asks student to reproduce the university; (2) the acculturation model (in David Bartholomae's famous phrase) to invent it; (3) the hybrid model (which might be called the bridge-and-blend model) to reinvent it; and (4) the multimodal model that seeks to "re-mediate" the university—"re-mediate" in the way the new media scholars Jay David Bolter and Richard Grusin use the word in their book *Remediation:* that all media derive and evolve from earlier media (photography being re-mediated painting, film being re-mediated photography and theater, television being re-mediated film, and so on). Rather than narrowly preparing students for essayist literacy, and bearing in mind that writing on paper and writing in electronic spaces are not competing but complementary competencies, they need to be prepared more broadly in mixed media, for at least three reasons. These spaces more readily allow for and even require mixed forms of discourses. These mixed forms more closely align with many students' own homegrown literacies of negotiation. Finally, students need to be prepared not just for college writing but also writing after and outside of college.

As rhetorician Patricia Bizzell has pointed out, mixed forms are emerging and gaining legitimacy in the academy, as evidenced by scholars and students alike. The work of rhetorician Victor Villanueva and intercultural communication scholar Helen Fox, for example, has demonstrated the effectiveness and eloquence of blending personal experience and scholarship. Increasingly visible in today's composition classrooms is, in Bizzell's words, "a generation of discourses that are themselves mixed, reflecting linguistic and rhetorical resources from many and varied cultural archives."[51] These new developments might be chalked up in part to greater diversity but in larger part to the ability of mixed forms to do new kinds of intellectual work.[52] I would further argue that new media and popular culture have accelerated this blending process, exerting pressures on both home and academic discourses, separately, even before they intersect in the classroom. The web, MTV, advertising, the visual—all are leaving their fingerprints, and at least some composition textbooks acknowledge their collective impact. For just one example: rhetoric and composition scholars Gerald Graff and Cathy Birkenstein in *They Say/I Say* devote a section on mixing academic and colloquial styles, blending in popular expressions and sayings.[53]

Informal questions, the coauthors recommend, can introduce objections to one's argument (80). And if one is not sure about one's own position, expressing ambivalence may not necessarily be viewed as indecisiveness but as the writer's "deep sophistication" (61); Graff and Birkenstein go on to offer a template for showing agreement and disagreement at the same time. They even mention the "satiric summary" (35) as a way for a writer to give her own spin on someone else's argument, in the same way that cable TV host Jon Stewart does on the parody news show *The Daily Show*. Rather than approach the teaching of argumentation focusing on principles of logic (e.g., syllogisms, claims, warrants, inductive and deductive reasoning), their text takes an experiential approach, actually trying out one's argument with people who then respond (xvii). Furthermore, hypertextual arguments rely more heavily on associative arguments that require more work of readers to make connections and draw conclusions.[54] Composition textbooks increasingly include discussion and practice in visual forms, such as implicit arguments in advertisements and other graphic design messages, while others use only the visual as entrée into academic discourses. Even formatting on paper is breaking up, creating new meanings in abbreviated, telegraphic ways, with headings and subheadings common occurrences, while other visual effects such as graphs and charts are leaking out of the sciences and into the humanities.

Interestingly, these "new" directions in composition textbooks harken back to the future, as it were. Expressing ambivalence, using questions to develop refutation, supporting arguments with an array of evidence, including personal experience, and satirizing to express dissent—these discursive features align with those favored in Plateau Indian rhetoric for over seven generations. Experiential, embodied learning is the preferred learning style of the Plateau peoples—and, coincidentally, for most young people generally today. Literacy scholar James Gee argues that "learning does not work well when learners are forced to check their bodies at the school room door like guns in the old West. School learning is often about disembodied minds learning outside any context of decisions and actions. When people learn something as a cultural process their bodies are involved because cultural learning always involves having specific experiences that facilitate learning . . . [H]umans understand content, whether in a comic book or a physics text, much better when their understanding is embodied, that is, when they can relate that content to possible activities, decisions, talk, and dialogue."[55]

New media have opened up other pedagogical possibilities that are culturally congruent. Knowledge-displays in the academy—traditionally confined to the individualistic, competitive "research paper" and the essay exam—are no longer as constrained as they once were, as portfolios, presentations, and field projects now complicate the mix. While communicating over networks is not necessarily the equalitarian enterprise early practitioners once believed it would be, peer-to-peer interaction is the key communicative competence of Plateau Indian students, like many other groups who share similar childrearing practices and socialize their children to listen to adults but talk freely among their peer group. Being monitored by adults, blogs, wikis, and Facebook may seem to be too public and too self-promotional for young Native adults to express themselves at length; yet the forms themselves allow for personal expression based on experiential, embodied knowledge (sometimes embarrassing, by mainstream standards), and the public yet collaborative nature of generating these forms might prove to be an effective threshold for young people on the cusp of adulthood. Using e-mail as a response medium between teacher and a single student honors another preferred interaction channel in Plateau Indian culture specifically, and probably other cultures as well, including working-class cultures. E-mail conferencing might be less intimidating for such students than a face-to-face conference, even as the genre is another mixed form, re-mediating the old forms of the office memorandum and the personal letter. In turn, e-mail itself has been remediated by texting and tweeting. And so on, each re-mediation opening up yet more possibilities not only for writing but for collaborating and teaching—all culturally congruent with Plateau Indian ways of knowing.

Rhetorical Sovereignty in Praxis

Academic discourses are not monolithic. Nor are they strictly or necessarily oppositional to the home literacies that students bring to the university. The real problem is that we teachers and professors often portray them as if they were in basic writing classes and programs, even though such positions belie our scholarship and betray our practice in other writing classes for mainstream students and at later stages of the program. Thus we engage in "rhetorical imperialism" (to recall Lyons's term) when we do not allow students to participate in the great flowering of academic discourses, confining them to school essayist forms and formulas, such as point-counterpoint argumentation, instead of conveying a sense of argument as evolving from a complex process of "agonistic inquiry and confrontation cooperation."[56] We engage in rhetorical imperialism when we naturalize academic discourse as superior, stable, and definitive, instead of advancing an understanding of the values it embodies and the people it endows.[57] And we engage in rhetorical imperialism when we lump all nonmainstream rhetorics together for analysis and discussion; when we automatically assume that any one student writes, or should write, from an indigenous tradition; when we ask students to write with their "authentic" voices as if identity were unitary and stable. In such classrooms premised on rhetorical imperialism, Native students' "mixedblood literacies of negotiations" (to recall yet another of Lyons's phrases) are about as negotiated as those at Walla Walla in 1855. Then, as now, it is the Indian who has to do most of the negotiating, especially in first-year composition and graduate programs. As entry and exit points in higher education respectively, these tend to be even more self-conscious and susceptible to so-called academic standards than even the public schools. In fact, it is the standards in higher education that often drive the standards in public schools.

True enough: the writing of students whose communicative competence draw exclusively or derive heavily from the principles of Plateau Indian rhetoric may never conform to the standards of academic discourses. Conducting secondary research—instead of citing personal and tribal experience—seems to be especially difficult for Plateau Indian students because it is decontextualized knowledge, divorced from human relationships between and among known people. But that conflict is not insurmountable, especially for Plateau Indian students, whose tradition has always highly valued education and language pluralism as ways to preserve and propel their culture forward to future generations. It is a conflict that can be negotiated if we educators act in concert, with each other and with Native students, from a place of mutual respect, by first honoring Native students' rhetorical sovereignty. We do so when we recognize their rhetorical traditions, plural, not collectively but specific to tribe or tribal group, as a people with spiritual, historical, and physical connections to a specific land.

This book provides that evidence for one group of tribes, collectively known as the Plateau Indians, documenting a rhetorical *ethnie* that dates back at least as far as 1855 but also by modernizing it, tracing its continuity and evolution into the new millennium. Recognition of the distinctiveness of this rhetoric makes it available for comparison with the Greek tradition that informs school essayist literacy, and explicit comparison in and of itself is a powerful learning tool—and teaching tool. The burden of negotiation and translation should not fall exclusively on Native students. Teachers and faculty too need cultural competence. That competence will enable them to design culturally relevant curriculum and seek out culturally congruent ways to teach it. New media in many ways serve both aims. As a common culture among students especially, the Internet employs a rhetoric of personalization that values human connection, irreverent humor, collective action, and personal agency—just as the Plateau Indian rhetorical tradition does, and has, for at least two hundred years. The problem of assessment, of course, remains. But as our assignments evolve to embrace new genres and to employ new modes of collaboration and communication occasioned by the Internet, so will writing standards and the criteria by which those standards are measured. Like Plateau Indian activists who have worked on "the White problem" for at least seven generations and counting, we too need to take the long view.

Afterword
Kristin L. Arola

grew up in Michigan's Keweenaw Peninsula. This matters deeply to me. On
the Euro-sides of my family—mostly Finnish with a dab of Italian, German,
and French Canadian for good measure—I'm the fifth generation born within
a thirty-mile radius. On the Anishinaabe (also known as Ojibwa, also known
as American Indian) side of my family, it looks like about seventh generation,
depending on whom you ask. In a lived sense, I understand *ethnie,* what it means
to have a connection to ancestral land, a connection that shapes ways of relating
and being and writing and speaking and meaning-making. For me, growing up
thirty miles, and arguably a world away, from the tribe of which my mother is
a member, my *ethnie* is not neatly Anishinaabe, and likely more identifiable as
Yooper—people from the Upper Peninsula (the U.P.) of Michigan.

When it comes to my literacy practices, I find that left to my own devices, I
theorize through stories, I have a hard time dealing with those who resist prag-
matism, and I relate to most things through what Scott Lyons has called self-
location. Barbara Monroe describes self-location as a practice "where the speaker
identifies his kind, his kin's locale, past and present, thereby establishing possible
points of connections to his audience." In my homeland this self-location involves
identifying my grandparents, parents, cousins, people I went to high school with,
the places they lived, worked, the bars they frequent(ed), the high school sports
they played. In academe this self-location still matters greatly to me, and in that
spirit here's one important node of connection.

In the mid-1990s, courtesy of a minority scholarship and an eighteen-year-
old's sense of defiance that made me believe there just might be something revo-
lutionary for me in Ann Arbor, I traveled ten very far hours from home to attend
the University of Michigan. To this day, it remains one of the hardest things I've
ever done. I learned fairly quickly that I had very little in common with most of
my peers, most of whom came from the East Coast or affluent suburbs in the Midwest. When they talked about AP classes, high school orchestras, debate teams,
or the politics of the Middle East, I learned to smile and nod, pretending I understood. When they preached about gun laws, I learned to skip the part where
I had to take hunter's safety to pass the sixth grade (and that I'm a pretty good
shot). When they talked about the great novels they read in high school, I learned

to keep quiet that because of an extremely tight budget (new books were a scarce commodity) and a rotating cast of English teachers, I only ever read one novel in high school.

Yet despite these differences, I had a strong sense that I *could* learn to be like my peers, to know the things that they knew, to carry it off with confidence. Chalk it up to being racially white or to growing up in a solidly upper-middle-class family where education was deeply valued, but I believed I *could* learn to play by these rules. So when it became clear to my English 101 instructor that I needed a bit of extra help, I listened very closely when she taught me about thesis statements and transitions sentences. I took it to heart when she suggested that while my personal storytelling was great and oftentimes persuasive, in argumentative papers I also needed to include "expert" opinions, "outside" research. By my junior year, after eating up all of the English courses I could, and almost always earning A's in them, I chose to leave the School of Natural Resources to become an English major. I believed that my continued success in these courses was because I was handed the tools and I worked hard to use them. I believed this saved me from my Yooper *ethnie* and made me a true scholar, a real intellectual, an academic success story.

That all changed in my senior year when I began working in the peer-tutoring program. I walked into the writing center believing that if I just enacted what Monroe refers to as the pedagogy of power (focusing on the goals of assimilation), I could save other students, just as I had been saved. Very quickly I learned otherwise. In addition to our regular peer-tutor duties on campus, we participated in a special outreach project conducted largely online. We were to serve as peer-mentors for a group of inner-city Detroit high school students, helping them prepare for the essay portion of their ACT, and share with them our college experiences. Wielding my pedagogy of power and ready to spread the good news of the thesis statement and citation practices, we traveled to the school to meet our mentees.

After one hour in the school I found myself stunned silent by the layers of systemic and institutional oppression facing these students. My pedagogy of power simply could not address the myriad issues these students lived with everyday. I could not magically assimilate my mentee into Edited American English and academic writing and university culture. Nor should I. While my belief in the pedagogy of power was shattered, I was left in a space where I could more clearly see the richness in my own precollege discursive practices and the value in listening to students' lived experiences. While I could, and should, provide my mentee with tips for succeeding on the ACT, I learned more about revaluing what Monroe (with a nod to James Gee) sees as experiential, embodied learning: a peda-gogy that doesn't force learners to "check their bodies at the schoolroom door," in Gee's words. This learning was fostered both through my experience with that high school and through our meetings with the coordinator of the peer-tutoring program, who mindfully helped us unpack our cultural assumptions and savior narratives, and helped me reenter my body and revalue my Yooper *ethnie*. This coordinator who changed everything I thought I knew about literacy? It was Bar-bara Monroe.

My reentry into my body, as it were, led me down a path of graduate work that took me to my current life as an associate professor where I have the pleasure of working alongside, and learning from, Barbara. Perhaps not surprisingly, my own research works to make visible bodies and discursive practices that are often erased from university settings. What I have learned by listening to Anishinaabe women as they make or work with cultural artifacts (baskets, quills, cedar, or wild rice, for example) is that, as Monroe argues, all ways of making/composing have inherent value. These values are often different from community to commu-nity, from tribe to tribe, from small town to small town, and from *ethnie* to *ethnie*. What is distinctive about a people's rhetorical practices is often, as Monroe traces, a long-standing tradition—one that has no doubt been modernized in various ways but one that often still connects with the past, the land, the people.

Monroe reminds me that it is our job as educators to value, and to teach our students to value, the rhetorical practices—both their own and others'—that don't neatly fit into our institutional practices. My own world changed when I deeply understood that my Yooper *ethnie* was a valid way of being and communi-cating in the world, just as valid as was my mentee's *ethnie* from that Detroit high school. In valuing it, in seeing it as a deep, rich, long-standing rhetorical practice (as Monroe does in this book with the Plateau peoples), I was able to return to my body and to see more clearly the discursive practices and norms around me. In honoring the rhetorical sovereignty of Plateau Indian students, Monroe reminds me that "what counts as appropriate discursive behavior by whom is always dy-namically arbitrated by a historically situated discourse community that has both interpretive and generative power." It is our job to help our students, and each other, see this.

There is something, as Monroe shows us, distinctive about the Plateau peo-ples' writing practices, and it is a "something" that is rooted in a history, a place, and a way of being in the world. This rhetorical sovereignty is particularly im-portant to indigenous peoples, and although I take much away from Monroe's argument that helps me think through my relationship with both indigenous and nonindigenous students, we should be careful to acknowledge the specific ways both *ethnie* and *rhetorical sovereignty* matter to Native peoples. As Monroe states, rhetorical sovereignty in particular "holds special resonance for American Indians, and should be reserved for that context only, in deference not only to the Native-specific history of sovereignty but also to the Native-specific history of education." This is not to say we can't take something very powerful from this book, but let us respect the specific space of, in this case as Monroe does, the Plateau peoples' rhetorical sovereignty.

That being said, Monroe's words both implicitly and explicitly make a strong case for the power of a multimodal pedagogy, one that seeks to remediate the university through the remixing of both media and discourses. Working with multimodality in ways that the New London Group (arguably, the founders of multimodal theory) articulates them ensures that we acknowledge both "the burgeoning variety of text forms associated with information and multimedia technologies" as well as "the context of our culturally and linguistically diverse and increasingly globalized societies."[1] I often ask my own students to produce multimodal texts and to unpack their own literacy narratives. Many educators are doing the same. The Digital Archive of Literacy Narratives (DALN) provides a rich pedagogical site, one that is slowly building a historical record of literacy practices. *Stories That Speak to Us,* a digital collection of curated narratives from the DALN, is also a good starting place.

Along with exploring linguistic, words-in-a-row literacy, I find that asking students to explore how they learned to compose a nonlinguistic-based object— photographs, fishing flies, computers, chocolate chip cookies, crocheted hats, motorcycles—has also provided the class with a rich way of learning from each other's historically situated practices. Such work, I hope, helps the class to consider issues of rhetorical imperialism and to question what types of texts matter, for whom, and in what situations. As Monroe says, "We engage in rhetorical imperialism when we naturalize academic discourse as superior, stable, and definitive, instead of advancing an understanding of the values it embodies and the people it endows." I hope we might all take the time to respect both in ourselves and in our students the inherent value in rhetorical practices that don't fit neatly into our classrooms.

KRISTIN L. AROLA

Notes

Introduction

1. Wee-ah-pe-kum's speech at the third Colville council, journal entry July 3, 1870, letterbook pp. 31–33, folder 34, box 4, cage 147, William Parkhurst Winans Papers. See chapter 3 for his speech quoted in full.

2. Lyons, "Rhetorical Sovereignty," 449–50; emphasis in the original.

3. Lyons, *X-Marks*, 131.

4. Ibid.

Chapter 1. "Real Indians" Don't Rap

1. In an effort to protect the anonymity of teachers and students, I leave unspecified the names of the tribe and schools that I worked with. In chapter 6, I describe in greater detail the larger project of which this collection was a part.

2. Powell, "Rhetorics of Survivance," 397.

3. Ibid., 428.

4. V. Deloria, *Custer Died for Your Sins*, 2.

5. Lyons, "Rhetorical Sovereignty," 449–50; emphasis in the original.

6. Qtd. in Cheyfitz, "(Post)Colonial Construction of Indian Country," 50. Subsequent references to this work are noted parenthetically within the text.

7. Qtd. in Lyons, "Rhetorical Sovereignty," 452–53.

8. Ibid., 452.

9. Cheyfitz, "(Post)Colonial Construction of Indian Country," 103.

10. Murray, "Sovereignty and the Struggle for Representation in American Indian Nonfiction," 342.

11. Ibid., 319–20.

12. Qtd. in Cushman, "Toward a Rhetoric of Self-Representation," 324.

13. Ibid., 338.

14. Cheyfitz, "(Post)Colonial Construction of Indian Country," 16.

15. Cushman, "Toward a Rhetoric of Self-Representation," 321.

16. Ibid., 341.

17. Cheyfitz, "(Post)Colonial Construction of Indian Country," 19.

18. Lyons, *X-Marks*, 36.

19. Cheyfitz, "(Post)Colonial Construction of Indian Country," 19–20.

20. The term "bio-logic" is from ibid., 16.

21. Ibid.

22. Lyons, *X-Marks,* 51–54.

23. Ibid., 78.

24. Ibid., 78–79.

25. See also Hunn, *Nch'i-Wana, "The Big River,"* 58.

26. Cheyfitz, "(Post)Colonial Construction of Indian Country," 11.

27. Gee, *An Introduction to Discourse Analysis,* 24. Subsequent references to this work are noted parenthetically within the text.

28. Philips, *Invisible Culture,* 3.

29. Ibid., 3–4.

30. Holliday, Hyde, and Kullman, *Intercultural Communication,* 158.

31. Gee, *Introduction to Discourse Analysis,* 24. Subsequent references to this work are noted parenthetically within the text.

32. Lyons, *X-Marks,* 28. Subsequent references to this work are noted parenthetically within the text.

33. Cheyfitz, "(Post)Colonial Construction of Indian Country," 29, 35.

34. Lyons, *X-Marks,* 113.

35. Anthony D. Smith, qtd. in ibid., 120.

36. Ibid., 131.

37. Stromberg, "Rhetoric and American Indians," 5–6.

38. Richardson, *Hiphop Literacies,* 74.

39. I have omitted using [*sic*] here and throughout this book when quoting primary sources not only to aid readability but also to honor the author's words as written.

40. Richardson, *Hiphop Literacies,* 74–83.

41. Murray, "Sovereignty and the Struggle for Representation," 326.

42. Richardson, *Hiphop Literacies,* 72–74.

43. Ibid., 12.

44. Ibid., 79.

45. Cheyfitz, "(Post)Colonial Construction of Indian Country," 55.

46. Sarris, *Keeping Slug Woman Alive,* 19.

47. Cheyfitz, "(Post)Colonial Construction of Indian Country," 86.

48. Richardson, *Hiphop Literacies,* 83.

49. *Reel Injun: On the Trail of the Hollywood Indian,* documentary written and directed by Diamond, Bainbridge, and Hayes.

50. Konkle, *Writing Indian Nations,* 9.

51. Chief Marshall as qtd. in Cheyfitz, "(Post)Colonial Construction of Indian Country," 90.

52. Lyons, *X-Marks,* xiii.

53. Richardson, *Hiphop Literacies,* 76.

54. Cheyfitz, "(Post)Colonial Construction of Indian Country," 71.

55. Konkle, *Writing Indian Nations,* 6, 32.

56. Compare with Deyhle, "From Break Dancing to Heavy Metal," 6.

57. Konkle, *Writing Indian Nations,* 30.

58. Sarris, *Keeping Slug Woman Alive,* 198.

59. Konkle, *Writing Indian Nations,* 27.

60. Philip Deloria as qtd. in ibid., 39.

61. Lyons, *X-Marks,* 181.

62. Lomawaima and McCarty, *To Remain an Indian,* 111.

63. Murray, "Sovereignty and the Struggle for Representation," 330.

64. Lyons, "Rhetorical Sovereignty," 465.

Chapter 2. Defining Principles of Plateau Indian Rhetoric

1. Kaplan, "Foreword," ix.

2. Ibid., viii.

3. Gee, "New Literacy Studies," 180.

4. Kaplan, "Foreword," ix.

5. Gumperz, Kaltman, and O'Connor, "Cohesion in Spoken and Written Discourse," 9.

6. Bizzell, "Cognition, Convention, and Certainty," 378.

7. Tannen, "Spoken and Written Narrative in English and Greek," 33.

8. Ibid., 33, 37.

9. Ibid., 39.

10. Erickson, "Rhetoric, Anecdote, and Rhapsody," 93.

11. Ibid., 96–97.

12. Cheyfitz, "(Post)Colonial Construction of Indian Country," 66.

13. Sarris, *Keeping Slug Woman Alive,* 24.

14. Tannen, paraphrasing Scollon and Scollon, in Tannen, "Introduction," xvi.

15. Lyons, *X-Marks,* viii.

16. See Bizzell, "(Native) American Jeremiad"; Redfield, "Inside the Circle, Outside the Circle"; Lyons, "Crying for Revision"; and Krupat, *Red Matters.*

17. Murray, *Forked Tongues,* 54, 59.

18. Tannen, "Spoken and Written Narrative in English and Greek," 26.

19. Sarris, *Keeping Slug Woman Alive,* 189.

20. Bizzell, "William Perry and Liberal Education," 306.

21. Tannen, "Indirectness in Discourse," 232.

22. Leap, *American Indian English*, 253.

23. Tannen, "Relative Focus on Involvement in Oral and Written Discourse," 125.

24. Sarris, *Keeping Slug Woman Alive*, 194.

25. On the Homeric tradition, see Ong, *Orality and Literacy*; Parry, *Making of Homeric Verse*; and Havelock, *Preface to Plato*. Scollon and Scollon, "Cooking It Up and Boiling It Down," 182.

26. Ong, *Orality and Literacy*, 67.

27. On conversations, jokes, and anecdotes as speech events that Plateau Indian communicative productions can take, see Sarris, *Keeping Slug Woman Alive*, 18.

28. Tannen, "Spoken and Written Narrative in English and Greek," 32.

29. See also Rose, "Narrowing the Mind and Page"; Bizzell, "Cognition, Convention, and Certainty"; Shaughnessy, "Diving In"; and Tannen, "Relative Focus on Involvement."

30. Heath, "Protean Shapes in Literacy Events," 116.

31. Cheyfitz, "(Post)Colonial Construction of Indian Country," 60.

32. Murray, *Forked Tongues*, 44.

33. Ibid., 25.

34. Leap, *American Indian English*, 78–79.

35. Ibid., 175.

36. Ibid.

37. Nesbitt et al., "Culture and Systems of Thought," 301; emphasis in the original.

38. Tannen, describing Erickson's essay including in this collection, in Tannen, "Introduction," xvi.

39. Leap, *American Indian English*, 275.

40. Kaplan, "Cultural Thought Patterns in Intercultural Education," 16.

41. Rose, "Narrowing the Mind and Page," 326.

42. Among Native scholars see, for example, Fixico, *American Indian Mind in a Linear World*. Among non-Native scholars see, for example, Monroe, "Plateau Indian Ways with Words."

43. Rose, "Narrowing of the Mind and Page," 331.

44. Berthoff, "Is Teaching Still Possible?," 312.

45. Lev Vygotsky as qtd. in Bizzell, "Cognition, Convention, and Certainty," 376.

46. Ibid.; emphasis in the original.

47. Tannen, "Introduction," xiv.

48. Gumperz, Kaltman, and O'Connor, "Cohesion in Spoken and Written Discourse," 8.

49. Ibid., 5.

50. Ibid., 17; see also Michaels and Collin, "Oral Discourse Styles"; and Jarrett, "Pragmatic Coherence in an Oral Formulaic Tradition."

51. Halliday, "Foreword," x.

52. Bizzell, "Cognition, Convention, and Certainty," 381.

53. Glenn, *Unspoken*, 113.

54. *Invisible Culture*, 71–126.

55. Tannen, "Indirectness in Discourse," 233.

56. Ibid.

57. Ibid., 234.

58. Leap, *American Indian English*, 88.

59. Ibid.

60. Erickson, "Rhetoric, Anecdote, and Rhapsody," 93; and Ong, *Orality and Literacy*, 41.

61. Leap, *American Indian English*, 254, 245.

62. For more details on this project, see chapter 6.

63. Monroe, *Crossing the Digital Divide*, 92–97.

64. Kaplan, "Foreword," xi.

65. Weaskus, "Earthly Rhetorics of Nez Perce Peoples," 94–95.

66. Ibid.

67. Leap, *American Indian English*, 149; Tannen, "Indirectness in Discourse," 236; Scollon and Scollon, "Athabaskan-English Interethnic Communication," 276; and Philips, *Invisible Culture*, 3.

68. Mao, "Rhetorical Borderlands," 434–41.

69. Leap, *American Indian English*, 228.

70. Philips, *Invisible Culture*, 66–67.

71. Hunn, *Nch'i-Wana, "The Big River,"* 201.

72. Looking Glass as qtd. in Stevens, *True Copy of the Record of the Official Proceedings at the Council in the Walla Walla Valley,* 99. I have omitted the use of [*sic*] here and throughout this book when quoting primary material, not only to aid readability but also to honor the speaker's words as they appear in the record.

73. Scott, "Endnotes," 120.

74. Ray, *Cultural Relations in the Plateau*, 24, 35.

75. Hunn, *Nch'i-Wana, "The Big River,"* 217.

76. Ray, *Cultural Relations in the Plateau*, 24.

77. Nicandri, *Northwest Chiefs*, 9–10.

78. Chief Yoom-tee-bee's account of disciplining his son, as told to Lucullus McWhorter, 1909, folder 419, box 43, Cage 55, Lucullus Virgil McWhorter Papers.

79. Washines, "Spirit of 'Whip Man' Being Called into Action," 1.

80. Philips, *Invisible Culture*, 66–67.

81. Leap, *American Indian English*, 149.

Chapter 3. Speaking Straight in Indian Languages, 1855–1870

1. Spokan Garry as qtd. in Doty, *Journal of Operations of Governor Isaac Ingalls Stevens*, 61.

2. The phrase "mutual intelligibility" is from Murray, *Forked Tongues*, 6.

3. Ibid., 36–41.

4. Lyons, "Rhetorical Sovereignty," 458, 462.

5. Leap, *American Indian English*, 7. Subsequent references to this work are noted parenthetically within the text.

6. Ibid., 149; Philips, *Invisible Culture*, 3; Tannen, "Indirectness in Discourse," 236; and Scollon and Scollon, "Athabascan-English Interethnic Communication," 276.

7. Richards, *Isaac I. Stevens*, 192.

8. Ibid., 121.

9. Trafzer and Scheuerman, *Renegade Tribe*, 41.

10. Ibid., 42.

11. Richards, *Isaac I. Stevens*, 198.

12. Trafzer and Scheuerman, *Renegade Tribe*, 31.

13. Beckham, "History since 1846," 155.

14. Ibid.

15. Scott, "Introduction," 8.

16. Trafzer and Scheuerman, *Renegade Tribe*, 43.

17. Beckham, "History since 1846," 151.

18. Ibid., 152.

19. Ibid.

20. Splawn, *Ka-mi-akin, Last Hero of the Yakimas*, 59. The spelling of "Yakima" varies, depending on the period. In the Treaty of 1855, it is spelled "Yakama" but the federally recognized tribe is spelled "Yakima." In 1994 the tribe officially changed the spelling of its name to "Yakama," in keeping with the Treaty of 1855 but also to distinguish the Yakama Nation from a nearby city, Yakima. To be consistent and to forestall confusion, throughout this book I have normalized the spelling to "Yakama," with two exceptions: when quoting primary sources that use the spelling "Yakima" and when referring to the Yakima War.

21. Trafzer and Scheuerman, *Renegade Tribe*, 41.

22. Richards, *Isaac I. Stevens*, 206.

23. Ibid., 220.

24. Pevar, *Rights of Indians and Tribes*, 5.

25. Richards, *Isaac I. Stevens*, 192.

26. Scott, "Introduction," 6.

27. Trafzer and Scheuerman, *Renegade Tribe*, 50.

28. Stevens, *Official Proceedings at the Council in the Walla Walla Valley*, 95; Scott, "Endnotes," 111; and Richards, *Isaac I. Stevens*, 418.

29. Stevens, *Official Proceedings at the Council in the Walla Walla Valley*, 418.

30. About five thousand Indians were encamped on the grounds, with two thousand attending daily sessions. As it was, many sitting in the back had trouble hearing the proceedings.

31. Nicandri, *Northwest Chiefs*, 13; Scott, "Introduction," 20; and Stevens, *Official Proceedings at the Council in the Walla Walla Valley*, 9.

32. Richards, *Isaac I. Stevens*, 206.

33. As in Stevens, *Official Proceedings at the Council in the Walla Walla Valley*, 61.

34. Ibid., 60.

35. Spellings of all Indian names have been standardized here and throughout the book to avoid confusion and to aid readability.

36. Peo-peo-mox-mox's speech as in Stevens, *Official Proceedings at the Council in the Walla Walla Valley*, 55–57.

37. I am reappropriating Bizzell's term "appropriative history," which she has identified as a common feature of hybrid academic discourses and defines as "a creative retelling of traditional history in which the writer's agenda for needed new research is highlighted" (Bizzell, "Hybrid Academic Discourses," 14). I have altered that name and notion from "appropriative" to "appropriated" to highlight the differences between academic discourses today (the context of Bizzell's essay) and Plateau Indian discourse in the period 1855–70.

38. Brown, *The Indian Side of the Story*, 101–2.

39. Tip-pee-il-lan-ah-cow-pook's speech as in Stevens, *Official Proceedings at the Council in the Walla Walla Valley*, 61–63.

40. Nicandri, *Northwest Chiefs*, 78–79.

41. Lawyer's speech as in Stevens, *Official Proceedings at the Council in the Walla Walla Valley*, 72–77. I have omitted the use of [*sic*] here and throughout this book when quoting primary material, not only to aid readability but also to honor the speaker's words as they appear in the record.

42. For a detailed look at the causes, the course, and the outcomes of this war, see Trafzer and Scheuerman, *Renegade Tribe*; and Richards, *Isaac I. Stevens*. For accounts based strictly on Indian sources, see Brown, *Indian Side of the Story*; and McWhorter, *Tragedy of the Wahk-Shum*.

43. Doty, *Journal of Operations of Governor Isaac Ingalls Stevens*, 37.

44. Kowrach, "Introduction," 11.

45. Trafzer and Scheuerman, *Renegade Tribe*, 158.

46. Doty, *Journal of Operations of Governor Isaac Ingalls Stevens*, 46. Subsequent references to this work are noted parenthetically within the text. I have omitted Doty's quotation marks that he used when quoting speeches; I do so to avoid using double quotation marks throughout.

47. Quin-quim-moe-so's speech as in ibid., 58–59.

48. Sho-homish's speech as in ibid., 56–57.

49. The distinctions I draw regarding singular and plural pronouns may not be valid, given that they rest on a close reading of translated text. I make them nonetheless because "we" so seldom appears in these early translated texts.

50. This unnamed chief's speech is in Doty, *Journal of Operations of Governor Isaac Ingalls Stevens*, 52. Translation is also at issue in the passage above. "We" in the first paragraph may just as well refer to the whites and the Indians, together, both sides failing to know each other's hearts, but today finding some way to communicate accurately and negotiate fairly with each other.

51. The Coeur d'Alene chief's speech is in ibid., 53.

52. Scott, "Endnotes," 118.

53. Beckham, "History since 1846," 158.

54. Letter to superintendent of Indian affairs, August 1, 1870, letterbook p. 44, folder 34, box 4, cage 147, William Parkhurst Winans Papers.

55. Garry as qtd. in Doty, *Journal of Operations of Governor Isaac Ingalls Stevens*, 49. Subsequent references to this work are noted parenthetically within the text. I have omitted Doty's quotation marks, which he used when quoting speeches; I do so to avoid using double quotation marks throughout. Emphasis in the original.

56. Spokan Garry as qtd. in ibid., 61.

57. Ibid., 61–62.

58. Lahren, "Reservations and Reserves," 492.

59. Letter to superintendent of Indian affairs, August 7, 1870, letterbook p. 65, folder 34, box 4, cage 147, William Parkhurst Winans Papers. Qua-tal-i-kun was also known as Chief Moses (Mid-Columbia), while the Moses that Winans refers to here was a headsman for the Sanpoil.

60. Trafzer and Scheuerman, *Renegade Tribe*, 64; and Brown, *Indian Side of the Story*, 93.

61. Ray, "Columbia Indian Confederacy," 783.

62. Qua-tal-i-kun's speech at the first Colville council, journal entry of June 26,

1870, letterbook pp. 17–18, folder 34, box 4, cage 147, William Parkhurst Winans Papers.

63. Journal entry of June 30, 1870, letterbook p. 23, folder 34, box 4, cage 147, William Parkhurst Winans Papers.

64. Wilson's speech at the first Colville council, June 26, 1870, letterbook p. 19, folder 34, box 4, cage 147, William Parkhurst Winans Papers.

65. Wee-ah-pe-kum's speech at the third Colville council, journal entry of July 3, 1870, letterbook pp. 31–33, folder 34, box 4, cage 147, William Parkhurst Winans Papers.

66. For references to the proceedings as "stormy," see Doty, *Journal of Operations of Governor Isaac Ingalls Stevens*, 32. For "philippic" references, see Kip, *Indian War in the Pacific Northwest*, 17. For references to them as "bold and frank," see Stevens, *Official Proceedings at the Council in the Walla Walla Valley*, 98.

67. Richards, *Isaac I. Stevens*, 217.

68. Doty, *Journal of Operations of Governor Isaac Ingalls Stevens*, 3.

69. Kip, *Indian War in the Pacific Northwest*, 18.

70. General O. O. Howard as qtd. in Trafzer and Scheuerman, *Renegade Tribe*, 57.

71. Brown, *Indian Side of the Story*, 133.

72. Trafzer and Scheuerman, *Renegade Tribe*, 67–69; Scott, "Introduction," 19; and Ruby and Brown, *Indians of the Pacific Northwest*, 150.

73. Trafer and Scheduerman, *Renegade Tribe*, 90–91.

74. Kamiakin as qtd. in Brown, *Indian Side of the Story*, 398.

75. Ibid., 126.

76. Kowrach, "Introduction," 12.

77. Ibid., 8.

78. Stevens, *Official Proceedings at the Council in the Walla Walla Valley*, 98.

79. Pevar, *Rights of Indians and Tribes*, 40.

80. Ibid.

81. Ibid.

82. "Congress OKs Millions to Settle Colville Tribes' Land Claims."

Chapter 4. Writing in English, 1910–1921

1. "Indians Defy Park Hunting Regulations," clipping from unidentified newspaper, September 1915, folder 356, box 37, cage 55, Lucullus V. McWhorter Papers.

2. Ibid.

3. Olson, "Introduction," 1.

4. Murray, *Forked Tongues*, 26.

5. Chief Sluiskin as qtd. in "Sluiskin Tells True Story of Mountain," clipping from the *Tacoma Daily News,* n.d., folder 356, box 37, cage 55, Lucullus V. McWhorter Papers.

6. Murray, *Forked Tongues,* 42.

7. For a thoroughgoing ethnography of Yakama activism, see Jacob, *Yakama Rising.*

8. See Lucullus Virgil McWhorter Papers, 1848–1945, cage 55, online at http://ntserver1.wsulibs.wsu.edu/masc/mcwhortr/Mcwh1.htm.

9. Louis Mann's "History life of a bad Injun," March 25, 1880, folder 120, box 15, cage 55, Lucullus Virgil McWhorter Papers.

10. Louis Mann's "Indian View of Registration," clipping from the *Yakima Morning Herald,* June 17, 1917, folder 357b, box 37, cage 55, Lucullus Virgil McWhorter Papers. I have omitted using [*sic*] here and throughout this book when quoting primary sources, not only to aid readability but also to honor the author's words as they appear in the record.

11. Cheyfitz, "(Post)Colonial Construction of Indian Country," 51.

12. Louis Mann's letter to L. M. Holt, July 10, 1920, folder 338a, box 35, cage 55, Lucullus Virgil McWhorter Papers.

13. "Why Indians Aren't Registering," clipping from the *Yakima Morning Herald,* June 17, 1917, folder 368, box 38, cage 55, Lucullus Virgil McWhorter Papers.

14. Telegram to Hon. Cato Sells, 1915, folder 2, box 1, cage 55, Lucullus Virgil McWhorter Papers.

15. Antiliquor petition, c. 1910, folder 382a, box 40, cage 55, Lucullus Virgil McWhorter Papers.

16. Second antiliquor petition, c. 1910, folder 338a, box 35, cage 55, Lucullus Virgil McWhorter Papers.

17. Leap, *American Indian English,* 52.

18. See ibid., 93–111.

19. "Indian of Today Writes Grievance on Typewriter," clipping from the *Seattle Intelligencer,* May 15, 1921, folder 458, box 47, cage 55, Lucullus Virgil McWhorter Papers. Quotation marks as printed in the newspaper.

20. "Indian Lecturer Praises Yakimas," clipping from the *Yakima Morning Herald,* November 8, 1927, folder 458, box 47, cage 55, Lucullus Virgil McWhorter Papers.

21. "Nipo T. Strongheart Biography."

22. "'Give the Indian a Chance,' Pleads Chief Strongheart; Decries School Segregation," *Christian Science Monitor,* August 7, 1924, folder 354, box 37, cage 55, Lucullus Virgil McWhorter Papers.

23. Nipo Strongheart's Chautauqua lecture, July 3, 1921, folder 383, box 40, cage 55, Lucullus Virgil McWhorter Papers. Quotation marks in the original typescript.

24. Relander, *Strangers on the Land*, 85.

25. Chief Meninick's speech before the state Supreme Court, 1921, folder 18, box 55, Relander Collection.

26. This empathetic reenactment is strikingly like the one used by a student to make his point, eighty years later, as I point out in chapter 6.

27. Cheyfitz, "(Post)Colonial Construction of Indian Country," 44.

28. Ibid., 43–44.

29. "Indians Refused Old Game Rights," clipping from the *Yakima Morning Herald*, July 8, 1927, folder 356, box 37, cage 55, Lucullus Virgil McWhorter Papers.

Chapter 5. Deliberating Publicly, 1955–1956

1. Burdette Kent's opening remarks at General Council meeting, January 13, 1956, folder 15, box 111, Relander Collection. I have omitted using [*sic*] here and throughout this book when quoting primary sources, not only to aid readability but also to honor the speaker's words as they appear in the record.

2. Rankin, *Relander Collection*, 2–3 (guide to the collection).

3. Because there are so many varieties of Sahaptin, Native as well as white people on the Plateau generically used the term "Indian" to refer to all varieties of the language. That usage occurs both in the unofficial minutes that constitute the primary material in this chapter as well as among my own Native contacts.

4. Cheyfitz, "(Post)Colonial Construction of Indian Country," 43.

5. Ibid., 16.

6. Ibid., 42–43; and Philips, *Invisible Culture*, 28–29.

7. Philips, *Invisible Culture*, 38.

8. Ibid., 29; and Leap, *American Indian English*, 171.

9. Philips, *Invisible Culture*, 30.

10. Cheyfitz, "(Post)Colonial Construction of Indian Country," 42.

11. Murray, *Forked Tongues*, 349.

12. Cheyfitz, "(Post)Colonial Construction of Indian Country," 43.

13. "$3B to End Royalty Dispute with Indian Tribes."

14. Cheyfitz, "(Post)Colonial Construction of Indian Country," 42.

15. Ibid.; and Pevar, *Rights of Indians and Tribes*, 57.

16. Pevar, *Rights of Indians and Tribes*, 57.

17. Hunn, *Nch'i-Wana, "The Big River,"* 280.

18. Relander, *Strangers on the Land*, 85; and Philips, "Warm Springs 'Indian Time,'" 105.

19. Walter Cloud's remarks at General Council meeting, December 5, 1955, folder 15, box 111, Relander Collection.

20. Philips, *Invisible Culture*, 54–55.

21. Lawrence Goudy's remarks at General Council meeting, January 13, 1956, folder 15, box 111, Relander Collection.

22. Louis Sohappy's testimony at federal hearing, February 16, 1956, folder 1, box 111, Relander Collection.

23. Relander, *Strangers on the Land*, 95.

24. Philips, *Invisible Culture*, 3–7.

25. Leap, *American Indian English*, 80.

26. Ibid., 81; and Philips, "Warm Springs 'Indian Time,'" 105.

27. Ambrose Smartlowit's testimony at federal hearing, February 16, 1956, folder 1, box 111, Relander Collection.

28. Philips, "Warm Springs 'Indian Time,'" 105.

29. Otis Shilow's remarks at General Council meeting, December 5, 1955, folder 15, box 111, Relander Collection.

30. Dick Walker's remarks at General Council meeting, January 13, 1956, folder 15, box 111, Relander Collection.

31. Kiutus Jim's remarks at General Council meeting, January 13, 1956, folder 15, box 111, Relander Collection.

32. Frank Sohappy's comment at General Council meeting, December 7, 1955, folder 15, box 111, Relander Collection.

33. Minne Whitefoot's testimony at federal hearing, February 14, 1956, folder 1, box 111, Relander Collection.

34. Rosie Jack's testimony at federal hearing, February 16, 1956, folder 1, box 111, Relander Collection.

35. Ruby Parks's testimony at federal hearing, February 14, 1956, folder 1, box 111, Relander Collection.

36. Relander's notes in ibid.

37. Alice Wyenoke's comments at General Council meeting, December 5, 1955, folder 15, box 111, Relander Collection.

38. Ackerman, *Necessary Balance*, 114.

39. Wilson Charley's speech at General Council meeting, December 5, 1955, folder 15, box 111, Relander Collection.

40. Alex Saluskin's comments at General Council meeting, December 5, 1955, folder 15, box 111, Relander Collection.

41. Marguerite Vivette's testimony at federal hearing, February 16, 1956, folder 1, box 111, Relander Collection.

42. George Umtuch's remarks at General Council meeting, December 6, 1955, folder 15, box 111, Relander Collection.

43. Maggie Syyou's comments at General Council meeting, January 13, 1956, folder 15, box 111, Relander Collection.

44. Burdette Kent's closing remarks at General Council meeting, January 13, 1956, folder 15, box 111, Relander Collection.

45. Relander, *Strangers on the Land*, 96–97.

46. Ferolito, "Tribal Members Urged New Ballot Voting System."

47. Ferolito, "Yakama Chief Balances Old, New."

48. Washines as qtd. in ibid.

49. Ibid.

Chapter 6. Writing in School, 2000–2004

1. Beckham, "History since 1846," 153.

2. See Nicandri, *Northwest Chiefs*, for Gustav Sohon's eyewitness sketches.

3. Scott, "Endnotes," 113.

4. Lomawaima and McCarty, *To Remain an Indian*, 158.

5. Ibid., 152.

6. Ibid., 154, 165, 153.

7. The NCLB's stated goal as qtd. in ibid., 155.

8. Ibid., 150–69.

9. NALA as qtd. in ibid., 134.

10. Nixon as qtd. in ibid., 116.

11. Ibid.

12. Bureau of Indian Education, "Reports," online at http://www.bie.edu/HowAre WeDoing/index.htm.

13. Lomawaima and McCarty, *To Remain an Indian*, 133.

14. Ibid., 5–8.

15. I have used pseudonyms for the three towns and have left the reservation unnamed in an effort to protect the anonymity of the schools and the human subjects who participated in this research project. For the same reason I am intentionally vague in describing the specific schools, their distinctive relationship and histories, and the degree of their involvement with the Writing Across Cultures project. All figures are taken from the 2010 United States Census and have been rounded off simply to aid readability.

16. Renamed in 2002 to the more neutral-sounding Secondary School Student Writing, the Writing Across Cultures project was just one of many sponsored under the umbrella of CO-TEACH (Collaboration on Teaching Education for Children with

High Needs), a multimillion-dollar grant from the U.S. Department of Education to the College of Education at Washington State University (WSU) from 2000 through 2006. The overarching goal of CO-TEACH was to improve WSU's teacher education program by building partnerships: first, on campus among colleges and content areas with teacher education tracks; second, with community colleges around the state; and third, with schools serving high-poverty areas, including Indian reservations. I served as the liaison between the College of Liberal Arts and the College of Education, and between the College of Education and one reservation. My role in both connections was largely administrative. With reservation schools I was mainly responsible for identifying common needs and goals with partner schools, working out and executing action plans, and managing funds and personnel at WSU. The substantial geographic distance between my assigned reservation and WSU constrained frequent physical contact; on average, I visited once a month, winter roads permitting. E-mail sustained our collaboration between visits.

It was within this context that the Writing Across Cultures project took place. As approved and then exempted by Institutional Review Board, the research protocol proceeded this way. Teachers secured parental permission for students to participate; participating students then filled out background questionnaires, identifying their age, gender, grade, ethnicity, and first and other languages spoken at home. With each writing assignment, participating students returned their papers, after they had been graded, back to their teachers. Teachers would then send the graded set to me, complete with a cover sheet providing some minimal context for reading the set, including the assignment, prewriting activities, curricular context, the number of students completing the assignment, and any other impressions they wanted to share, usually their general assessment of students' response to the assignment.

Either a graduate student assistant or I would pick up the set of papers. For each set—a "set" defined as one class's papers on one assignment—the teacher (or school, depending on local requirements) was paid one hundred dollars, to be spent as the teacher saw fit: books, supplies, field trips, disposable cameras, and so on. Meanwhile, graduate student assistants processed the papers. After creating a master list of participating students and schools, graduate students matched student names with assigned numbers and logged in their writing assignments as they came in. After labeling each paper with the student's assigned number, which could only be referenced by the master list, they also masked any identifying personal information from each piece before scanning for our archive. The original papers were then returned to the teacher. In addition to this research protocol, I received papers on two other occasions: before the project was even conceived, a teacher at the tribal school sent me a set of papers via disk in 2000; and at the very end of the project, the tribal school released several boxes of students' Learning Record portfolios. The superintendent gave me written permission to include these additions in the project.

17. See Sarris, *Keeping Slug Woman Alive,* 152–53.

18. I have randomly assigned gender to student writers, in an additional effort to protect their anonymity. In quoting from students' work, I have not used [*sic*] for the sake of readability and to honor their words as written.

19. I have omitted using [*sic*] here when quoting students' writing, not only to aid readability but also to honor their words as written.

20. Tannen, "Indirectness as Discourse," 234.

21. After thirteen years of litigation, a settlement of 3.4 billion dollars was reached in 2009, far less than the 47 billion dollars the plaintiffs sought and far more than the low millions the defendants claimed. "$3B to End Royalty Dispute with Indian Tribes."

22. Talhelm, "Federal Judge Removed from Tribal Trust Case."

23. Leap, *American Indian English,* 183.

24. "Schaffer Paragraph," online at http://en.wikipedia.org/wiki/Schaffer_paragraph.

25. Leap, *American Indian English,* 276.

26. Ibid., 183.

27. Lareau, *Unequal Childhoods,* 1.

28. Gee, *Introduction,* 26.

29. For a more comprehensive analysis of the writing produced by these students, as well as more detailed analysis of divergent language socialization practices in the home, see Monroe, *Crossing the Digital Divide,* chapter 4.

30. Leap, *American Indian English,* 254.

31. Philips, *Invisible Culture,* 71–126.

32. Lyons, "Captivity Narrative," 107.

33. Ibid.

Chapter 7. Reassessing the Achievement Gap

1. Stevens, *Official Proceedings at the Council in the Walla Walla Valley,* 52.

2. For a comprehensive history of federal Indian education policy from 1900 to the present, see Lomawaima and McCarty, *To Remain an Indian.*

3. Clearinghouse on Native Teaching and Learning, *From Where the Sun Rises,* 47.

4. Ibid., 4.

5. Burke, "Historical Review on Opportunity Gap," 21–26. Subsequent references to this work are cited parenthetically within the text.

6. Clearinghouse on Native Teaching and Learning, *From Where the Sun Rises,* 16.

7. OSPI, *Closing Opportunity Gaps in Washington's Public Education System* (January 2011), 11.

8. Clearinghouse on Native Teaching and Learning, *From Where the Sun Rises*, 8.

9. OSPI, *Closing Opportunity Gaps in Washington's Public Education System* (January 2011), 6.

10. Ibid., 1.

11. Clearinghouse on Native Teaching and Learning, *From Where the Sun Rises*, 72.

12. Ibid., 143.

13. Ibid., 71.

14. See chapter 4 in Monroe, *Crossing the Digital Divide,* for a full discussion of the culture-marked differences in language use socialization in the preschool years for white and Latino-of-Mexican-descent students.

15. Clearinghouse on Native Teaching and Learning, *From Where the Sun Rises,* 57.

16. Ibid., 82.

17. Ibid., 8.

18. Ibid., 82.

19. Ibid., 57.

20. Ibid., 64.

21. Lomawaima and McCarty, *To Remain an Indian,* 16.

22. Ibid., 18.

23. Ibid., 48.

24. OSPI, *Common Core State Standards,* 45.

25. Ibid., 41; emphasis mine.

26. Examination of narrative lies outside the scope of this book, but I do so in another context: chapter 4 of Monroe, *Crossing the Digital Divide.*

27. The Meriam Report as qtd. in Lomawaima and McCarty, *To Remain an Indian,* 71.

28. Clearinghouse on Native Teaching and Learning, *From Where the Sun Rises,* 25.

29. Laughter, "Cultural Relevant Pedagogy," 2.

30. Clearinghouse on Native Teaching and Learning, *From Where the Sun Rises,* 81.

31. Qtd. in Lomawaima and McCarty, *To Remain an Indian,* 20–21.

32. For a comprehensive literature review of Native students as one-dimensional learners, see Lomawaima and McCarty, *To Remain an Indian,* 20–21.

33. Ibid., 22–23.

34. Ibid., 25–26, 36–37.

35. Lyons, "Captivity Narrative," 89.

36. Qtd. in ibid., 96.

37. Sarris, *Keeping Slug Woman Alive*, 197–99.

38. Qtd. in ibid., 190.

39. Ibid., 189.

40. Ibid., 190.

41. Lomawaima and McCarty, *To Remain an Indian*, 37.

42. Rheingold, "Look Who's Talking," 1.

43. Payne and Laugher, "Your Colleagues Weigh In," 15.

44. Delpit, "Silenced Dialogue," 282.

45. Payne and Laughter, "Culturally Relevant Pedagogy in ELA," 3.

46. Ibid., 4.

47. OSPI, *High School Content, Organization, and Style Scoring Guide.*

48. Gee, *Introduction to Discourse Analysis*, 94.

49. Bizzell, "Basic Writing and the Issue of Correctness," 4–5.

50. Bizzell, "Hybrid Academic Discourses," 17.

51. Ibid.

52. Bizzell, "Basic Writing and the Issue of Correctness," 11.

53. Graff and Birkenstein, *They Say/I Say,* 116. Subsequent references to this work are noted parenthetically within the text.

54. Monroe, "'Compromising' on the Web."

55. Gee, *Introduction to Discourse Analysis*, 39.

56. Lynch, George, and Cooper, "Moments of Argument," 61.

57. Royster, "Academic Discourses or Small Boats on a Big Sea," 25.

Afterword

1. New London Group, "Pedagogy of Multiliteracies," 9.

Bibliography

Archival Sources

Lucullus Virgil McWhorter Papers, 1848–1945. Cage 55. Manuscripts, Archives, and Special Collections, Washington State University Libraries, Pullman, WA.

Relander Collection. Yakima Central Library, Yakima Valley Libraries. Yakima, WA.

William Parkhurst Winans Papers, 1815–1917. Cage 147. Manuscripts, Archives, and Special Collections, Washington State University Libraries, Pullman, WA.

Published Sources

Ackerman, Lillian. *A Necessary Balance: Gender and Power among Indians of the Columbian Plateau.* Norman: University of Oklahoma Press, 2003.

Apple, Michael W. *Ideology and Curriculum* (Twentieth-Fifth Anniversary Edition). London: Routledge, 2004.

Bartholomae, David. "Inventing the University." In *Cross-Talk in Comp Theory: A Reader,* 3rd ed., edited by Victor Villanueva and Kristin L. Arola, 523–53. Urbana, IL: National Council of Teachers of English, 2011.

Basso, Keith. *Wisdom Sits in Places: Landscape and Language among the Western Apache.* Albuquerque: University of New Mexico Press, 1996.

Beckham, Stephen Dow. "History since 1846." In *Plateau.* Vol. 12 of *Handbook of North American Indians,* edited by Deward E. Walker, 149–73. Washington, DC: Smithsonian Institution Press, 1998.

Berthoff, Ann E. "Is Teaching Still Possible? Writing, Meaning, and Higher Order Reasoning." In *Cross-Talk in Comp Theory: A Reader,* 3rd ed., edited by Victor Villanueva and Kristin L. Arola, 309–23. Urbana, IL: National Council of Teachers of English, 2011.

Bizzell, Patricia. "Basic Writing and the Issue of Correctness, or, What to Do with Mixed Forms of Academic Discourse." *Journal of Basic Writing* 19 (2000): 4–12.

———. "Cognition, Convention, and Certainty: What We Need to Know about Writing." In *Cross-Talk in Comp Theory: A Reader,* 3rd ed., edited by Victor Villanueva and Kristin L. Arola, 367–91. Urbana, IL: National Council of Teachers of English, 2011.

———. "Hybrid Academic Discourses: What, Why, How." *Composition Studies* 7 (1999): 7–21.

———. "(Native) American Jeremiad: The 'Mixedblood' Rhetoric of William Apess." In *American Indian Rhetorics: Word Medicine, Word Magic*, edited by Ernest Stromberg, 34–49. Pittsburgh: University of Pittsburgh Press, 2006.

———. "William Perry and Liberal Education." In *Cross-Talk in Comp Theory: A Reader*, 3rd ed., edited by Victor Villanueva and Kristin L. Arola, 299–308. Urbana, IL: National Council of Teachers of English, 2011.

Bolter, Jay David, and Richard Grusin. *Remediation: Understanding New Media*. Cambridge: Massachusetts Institute of Technology Press, 1999.

Brooks, Joanna, ed. *The Collected Writings of Samson Occom, Mohegan: Literature and Leadership in Eighteenth-Century Native America*. New York: Oxford University Press, 2006.

Brown, William Compton. *The Indian Side of the Story*. Spokane, WA: C. W. Hill Printing Co., 1961.

Bureau of Indian Education. "Reports." Online at www.bie.edu/HowAreWeDoing /index.htm.

Burke, Alan. "Historical Review on Opportunity Gap." October 16, 2012. Appended to "Closing Opportunity Gaps in Washington's Public Education System: Annual Report by the Educational Opportunity Gap Oversight and Accountability Committee (EOGOAC)." Office of the Superintendent of Public Instruction. January 31, 2013. Online at www.k12.wa.us/AchievementGap/pubdocs/EOGOAC_Final_ Report2013.pdf.

Cheyfitz, Eric. "The (Post)Colonial Construction of Indian Country." In *The Columbia Guide to American Indian Literatures of the United States since 1945*, edited by Eric Cheyfitz, 3–124. New York: Columbia University Press, 2006.

Clearinghouse on Native Teaching and Learning. *From Where the Sun Rises: Addressing the Educational Achievement of Native Americans in Washington State*. Pullman, WA: Clearinghouse on Native Teaching and Learning, 2008. Online at www .goia.wa.gov/Links-Resources/NativeAmericanAchievementReport.pdf.

Clements, William M. "This Voluminous Unwritten Book of Ours: Early Native Writers and the Oral Tradition." In *Early Native American Writing*, edited by Helen Jaskoski, 122–35. Cambridge: Cambridge University Press, 1996.

"Congress OKs Millions to Settle Colville Tribes' Land Claims." *Seattle Times*. October 11, 1994.

"Contemporary Indian Reservations of Northwest Coast and Plateau Cultural Groups." Digital Collections, University Libraries, University of Washington. Online at http://content.lib.washington.edu/aipnw/pnw.html.

Cushman, Ellen. "Toward a Rhetoric of Self-Representation: Identity Politics in Indian Country and Rhetoric and Composition." *College Composition and Communication* 60, no. 2 (2008): 321–65.

Deloria, Philip J. *Playing Indian*. New Haven, CT: Yale University Press, 1998.

Deloria, Vine. *Custer Died for Your Sins: An Indian Manifesto*. London: Macmillan Press, 1969.

Delpit, Lisa. "The Silenced Dialogue: Power and Pedagogy in Educating Other People's Children." *Harvard Educational Review* 58, no. 3 (1988): 280–98.

Deyhle, Donna. "From Break Dancing to Heavy Metal: Navajo Youth, Resistance, and Identity." *Youth and Society* 30, no. 3 (1998): 3–31.

Digital Archive of Literacy Narratives. Ohio State University Libraries. Online at http://daln.osu.edu/handle/2374.DALN/1.

Doty, James. *Journal of Operations of Governor Isaac Ingalls Stevens of Washington Territory in 1855*, edited by Edward J. Kowrach. Fairfield, WA: Ye Galleon Press, 1978.

Erickson, Frederick. "Rhetoric, Anecdote, and Rhapsody: Coherence Strategies in a Conversation among Black American Adolescents." In *Coherence in Spoken and Written Discourse*, edited by Deborah Tannen, 81–154. Norwood, NJ: Ablex, 1984.

Ferolito, Phil. "Tribal Members Urged New Ballot Voting System." *Yakama Nation Review*. March 17, 2006.

———. "Yakama Chief Balances Old, New." *Spokesman Review*. May 6, 2007.

Fixico, Donald L. *The American Indian Mind in a Linear World: American Indian Studies and Traditional Knowledge*. New York: Routledge, 2003.

Fox, Helen. *Listening to the World: Cultural Issues in Academic Writing*. Urbana, IL: National Council of Teachers of English, 1994.

Gee, James. *An Introduction to Discourse Analysis: Theory and Method*. New York: Routledge, 2005.

———. "The New Literacy Studies: From 'Socially Situated' to the Work of the Social." In *Situated Literacies: Theorising Reading and Writing in Context*, edited by David Barton, Mary Hamilton, and Roz Ivanic, 180–96. New York: Routledge, 2000.

Glenn, Cheryl. *Unspoken: A Rhetoric of Silence*. Carbondale: Southern Illinois Press, 2004.

Graff, Gerald, and Cathy Birkenstein. *They Say/I Say: The Moves That Matter in Academic Writing*. New York: Norton, 2006.

Gumperz, John J., Hannah Kaltman, and Mary Catherine O'Connor. "Cohesion in Spoken and Written Discourse: Ethnic Style and the Transition to Literacy." In *Coherence in Spoken and Written Discourse*, edited by Deborah Tannen, 3–20. Norwood, NJ: Ablex, 1984.

Halliday, M.A.K. Foreword to *Class, Codes and Control*. Vol. 3 of *Towards a Theory of Educational Transmission*, by Basil Bernstein, ix–xiv. London: Routledge and Kegan Paul, 1973. Reprint, New York: Routledge, 2003.

Havelock, Eric A. *Preface to Plato*. Cambridge, MA: Belknap Press, 1963.

Heath, Shirley Brice. "Protean Shapes in Literacy Events: Ever-Shifting Oral and Literate Traditions." In *Spoken and Written Language: Exploring Orality and Literacy*, edited by Deborah Tannen, 91–118. Norwood, NJ: Ablex, 1982.

———. *Ways with Words: Language, Life, and Work in Communities and Classrooms*. London: Cambridge University Press, 1986.

Holliday, Adrian, Martin Hyde, and John Kullman. *Intercultural Communication: An Advanced Resource Book*. London: Routledge, 2004.

Hunn, Eugene S. *Nch'i-Wana, "The Big River": Mid-Columbia Indians and Their Land*. Seattle: University of Washington Press, 1990.

Jacob, Michelle M. *Yakama Rising: Indigenous Cultural Revitalization, Activism, and Healing*. Tucson: University of Arizona Press, 2013.

Jarrett, Dennis. "Pragmatic Coherence in an Oral Formulaic Tradition: I Can Read Your Letters/Sure Can't Read Your Mind." In *Coherence in Spoken and Written Discourse*, edited by Deborah Tannen, 155–71. Norwood, NJ: Ablex, 1984.

Kaplan, Robert B. "Cultural Thought Patterns in Intercultural Education." *Language Learning* 16 (1966): 1–20.

———. "Foreword: What in the World Is Contrastive Rhetoric?" In *Contrastive Rhetoric Revisited and Redefined*, edited by Clayann Gilliam Panetta, vii–xx. Mahwah, NJ: Lawrence Erlbaum Associates, 2001.

"Key to Tribal Territories." Digital Collections, University Libraries, University of Washington. Online at http://content.lib.washington.edu/aipnw/hnai12.html.

Kip, Lawrence. *Indian War in the Pacific Northwest: The Journal of Lieutenant Lawrence Kip*. Lincoln: University of Nebraska Press, 1999.

Konkle, Maureen. *Writing Indian Nations: Native Intellectuals and the Politics of Historiography, 1827–1863*. Chapel Hill: University of North Carolina Press, 2004.

Kowrach, Edward J. "Introduction." In *Journal of Operations of Governor Isaac Ingalls Stevens of Washington Territory in 1855*, by James Doty, edited by Edward J. Kowrach. Fairfield, WA: Ye Galleon Press, 1978.

Krupat, Arnold. *Red Matters: Native American Studies*. Philadelphia: University of Pennsylvania Press, 2002.

Lahren, Sylvester L., Jr. "Reservations and Reserves." In *Plateau*. Vol. 12 of *Handbook of North American Indians*, edited by Deward E. Walker, 484–98. Washington, DC: Smithsonian Institution Press, 1998.

Lareau, Annette. *Unequal Childhoods: Class, Race, and Family Life.* Berkeley: University of California Press, 2003.

Laughter, Judson. "Cultural Relevant Pedagogy." *English Leadership Quarterly* 35, no. 3 (February 2013): 1–2.

Leap, William L. *American Indian English.* Salt Lake City: University of Utah Press, 1993.

Lomawaima, K. Tsianina, and Teresa L. McCarty. *To Remain an Indian: Lessons in Democracy from a Century of Native American Education.* New York: Teachers College Press, 2006.

Lynch, Dennis A., Diana George, and Marilyn M. Cooper. "Moments of Argument: Agonistic Inquiry and Confrontational Cooperation." *College Composition and Communications* 48, no. 1 (1997): 61–85.

Lyons, Scott. "A Captivity Narrative: Indians, Mixedbloods, and 'White' Academe." In *Outbursts in Academe: Multiculturalism and Other Sources of Conflict*, edited by Kathleen Dixon, 87–108. Portsmouth, NH: Boynton, 1998.

———. "Crying for Revision: Postmodern Indians and Rhetorics of Tradition." *Making and Unmaking the Prospects for Rhetoric: Selected Papers from the 1996 Rhetoric Society of America Conference*, edited by Theresa Enos, 123–32. Mahwah, NJ: Lawrence Erlbaum, 1997.

———. "Rhetorical Sovereignty: What Do American Indians Want from Writing?" *College Composition and Communication* 51, no. 3 (2000): 447–68.

———. *X-Marks: Native Signatures of Assent.* Minneapolis: University of Minnesota Press, 2010.

Mao, LuMing. "Rhetorical Borderlands: Chinese American Rhetoric in the Making." *College Composition and Communications* 56, no. 3 (2005): 426–69.

McWhorter, Lucullus. *Tragedy of the Wahk-shum: The Death of Andrew J. Bolon, Indian Agent to the Yakima Nation, in Mid-September, 1855.* Fairfield, WA: Ye Galleon Press, 1968.

Michaels, Sarah, and James Collin. "Oral Discourse Styles: Classroom Interaction and the Acquisition of Literacy." In *Coherence in Spoken and Written Discourse*, edited by Deborah Tannen, 219–44. Norwood, NJ: Ablex, 1984.

Monroe, Barbara. "'Compromising' on the Web: Evolving Standards for an Evolving Genre." *Kairos: A Journal for Teachers of Writing in Webbed Environments* 4, no. 1 (1999). Online at http://english.ttu.edu/kairos/4.1.

———. *Crossing the Digital Divide: Race, Writing, and Technology in the Classroom.* New York: Teachers College Press, 2004.

———. "Plateau Indian Ways with Words." *College Composition and Communication* 61, no. 1 (2009): W321–W342.

Mourning Dove [Quintasket, Christine]. *Cogewea, the Half-Blood: A Depiction of the Great Montana Cattle Range,* 1927. Reprint, Lincoln: University of Nebraska Press, 1981.

———. *Mourning Dove: A Salishan Autobiography.* Lincoln: University of Nebraska Press, 1990.

Murray, David. *Forked Tongues: Speech, Writing, and Representation in North American Indian Texts.* Bloomington: Indiana University Press, 1991.

———. "Sovereignty and the Struggle for Representation in American Indian Nonfiction." In *The Columbia Guide to American Indian Literatures of the United States since 1945,* edited by Eric Cheyfitz, 319–56. New York: Columbia University Press, 2006.

Nesbitt, Richard E., Kaiping Peng, Incheol Choi, and Ara Norenzayan. "Culture and Systems of Thought: Holistic versus Analytic Cognition." *Psychological Review* 108 (2001): 291–310.

New London Group. "A Pedagogy of Multiliteracies: Designing Social Futures." In *Multiliteracies: Literacy Learning and the Design of Social Futures,* edited by Bill Cope and Mary Kalantzis, 9–37. New York: Routledge, 2000.

Nicandri, David L. *Northwest Chiefs: Gustav Sohon's Views of the 1855 Stevens Treaty Councils.* Tacoma: Washington State Historical Society, 1986.

"Nipo T. Strongheart Biography." Online at www.imdb.com/name/nm0835072/bio.

Office of the Superintendent of Public Instruction (OSPI). *Closing Opportunity Gaps in Washington's Public Education System: Annual Report by the Educational Opportunity Gap Oversight and Accountability Committee (EOGOAC).* January 31, 2013. Online at www.k12.wa.us/AchievementGap/pubdocs/EOGOAC_Final_Report2013.pdf.

———. *Closing Opportunity Gaps in Washington's Public Education System: A Report by the Achievement Gap Oversight and Accountability Committee.* January 2011. Online at www.k12.wa.us/AchievementGap/pubdocs/AgapLegReport2011.pdf.

———. *Common Core State Standards for English Language Arts and Literacy in History/Social Studies, Science, and Technical Subjects.* June 2, 2010. Online at www.k12.wa.us/CoreStandards/ELAstandards/pubdocs/CCSSI_ELA_Standards.pdf#3.

———. *High School Content, Organization, and Style Scoring Guide.* October 2009. Online at www.k12.wa.us/Writing/Assessment/resources.aspx.

Olson, David R. "Introduction." In *Literacy, Language, and Learning: The Nature and Consequences of Reading and Writing,* edited by David R. Olson, Nancy Torrance, and Angela Hildyard, 1–15. Cambridge: Cambridge University Press, 1985.

Ong, Walter. *Orality and Literacy: The Technologizing of the Word.* London: Methuen, 1982.

Parry, Milman. *The Making of Homeric Verse: The Collected Papers of Milman Parry.* Edited by Adam Parry. Oxford: Clarendon Press, 1971.

Payne, Emily, and Judson Laughter. "Culturally Relevant Pedagogy in ELA." *English Leadership Quarterly* 35, no. 3 (February 2013): 2–5.

———, eds. "Your Colleagues Weigh In." *English Leadership Quarterly* 35, no. 3 (February 2013): 15.

Pevar, Stephen L. *The Rights of Indians and Tribes.* Carbondale: Southern Illinois University Press, 1992.

Philips, Susan Urmston. *The Invisible Culture: Communication in Classroom and Community on the Warm Springs Indian Reservation.* New York: Longman, 1983.

———. "Warm Springs 'Indian Time': How the Regulation of Participation Affects the Progression of Events." In *Explorations in the Ethnography of Speaking,* 92–109, edited by Richard Bauman and Joe Sherzer. London: Cambridge University Press, 1974.

Powell, Malea. "Rhetorics of Survivance: How American Indians *Use* Writing." *College Composition and Communication* 53, no. 3 (2002): 396–434.

Rankin, Del. *Relander Collection.* Yakima, WA: Yakima Valley Regional Library, n.d.

Ray, Verne F. "The Columbia Indian Confederacy: A League of Central Plateau Tribes." In *Culture in History: Essays in Honor of Paul Radin,* edited by Stanley Diamond, 771–89. New York: Columbia University Press, 1960.

———. *Cultural Relations in the Plateau of Northwestern America.* Los Angeles: Southwest Museum Administrator of the Fund, 1939.

Redfield, Karen. "Inside the Circle, Outside the Circle: The Continuance of Native American Storytelling and the Development of Rhetorical Strategies in English." In *American Indian Rhetorics: Word Medicine, Word Magic,* edited by Ernest Stromberg, 149–64. Pittsburgh: University of Pittsburgh Press, 2006.

Reel Injun: On the Trail of the Hollywood Indian. Documentary written and directed by Neil Diamond, Catherine Bainbridge, and Jeremiah Hayes. Rezolution Pictures production in association with the National Film Board of Canada, 2009.

Relander, Click. *Strangers on the Land.* Yakima, WA: Franklin Press, 1961.

Rheingold, Howard. "Look Who's Talking." *Wired* 7 (January 1999): 1–6.

Richards, Kent. *Isaac I. Stevens: Young Man in a Hurry.* Pullman: Washington State University Press, 1993.

Richardson, Elaine. *Hiphop Literacies.* London: Routledge, 2006.

Robertson, William. *History of the Discovery and Settlement of North America.* London, 1777. Reprint, New York: J. & J. Harper, 1828.

Rose, Mike. "Narrowing the Mind and Page: Remedial Writers and Cognitive Reductionism." In *Cross-Talk in Comp Theory: A Reader*, 3rd ed., edited by Victor Villanueva and Kristin L. Arola, 325–65. Urbana, IL: National Council of Teachers of English, 2011.

Royster, Jacqueline Jones. "Academic Discourses or Small Boats on a Big Sea." In *Alt Dis: Alternative Discourses and the Academy*, edited by Christopher Schroeder, Helen Fox, and Patricia Bizzell, 23–30. Portsmouth, NH: Boynton-Heinemann, 2002.

Ruby, Robert H., and John A. Brown. *Indians of the Pacific Northwest*. Norman: University of Oklahoma Press, 1981.

Sarris, Greg. *Keeping Slug Woman Alive: A Holistic Approach to American Indian Texts*. Berkeley: University of California Press, 1993.

Scollon, Ronald, and Suzanne Wong Scollon. "Athabaskan-English Interethnic Communication." In *Cultural Communication and Intercultural Contact*, edited by Donal Carbaugh, 259–86. Hillsdale, NJ: Erlbaum, 1990.

———. "Cooking It Up and Boiling It Down: Abstracts in Athabaskan Children's Story Retellings." In *Coherence in Spoken and Written Discourse*, edited by Deborah Tannen, 173–97. Norwood, NJ: Ablex, 1984.

Scott, Darrell. "Introduction" and "Endnotes." In *A True Copy of the Record of the Official Proceedings at the Council in the Walla Walla Valley, 1855*, by Isaac Ingalls Stevens, edited by Darrell Scott. Fairfield, WA: Ye Galleon Press, 1985.

Shaughnessy, Mina P. "Diving In: An Introduction to Basic Writing." In *Cross-Talk in Comp Theory: A Reader*, 3rd ed., edited by Victor Villanueva and Kristin L. Arola, 291–97. Urbana, IL: National Council of Teachers of English, 2011.

Splawn, A. J. *Ka-mi-akin, Last Hero of the Yakimas*. Portland, OR: Binfords & Mort, 1944.

Stevens, Isaac Ingalls. *A True Copy of the Record of the Official Proceedings at the Council in the Walla Walla Valley, 1855*. Edited by Darrell Scott. Fairfield, WA: Ye Galleon Press, 1985.

Stromberg, Ernest. "Rhetoric and American Indians: An Introduction." In *American Indian Rhetorics of Survivance: Word Medicine, Word Magic*, edited by Ernest Stromberg, 1–14. Pittsburgh: University of Pittsburgh Press, 2006.

Talhelm, Jennifer. "Federal Judge Removed from Tribal Trust Case." Associated Press. *Yakama Nation Review*. July 14, 2006.

Tannen, Deborah. "Indirectness in Discourse: Ethnicity as Conversational Style." *Discourse Processes* 4 (1981): 221–38.

———. "Introduction." In *Coherence in Spoken and Written Discourse*, edited by Deborah Tannen, xiii–xvii. Norwood, NJ: Ablex, 1984.

———. "Relative Focus on Involvement in Oral and Written Discourse." In *Literacy, Language, and Learning: The Nature and Consequences of Reading and Writing*, edited by David R. Olson, Nancy Torrance, and Angela Hildyard, 124–47. Cambridge: Cambridge University Press, 1985.

———. "Spoken and Written Narrative in English and Greek." In *Coherence in Spoken and Written Discourse*, edited by Deborah Tannen, 21–44. Norwood, NJ: Ablex, 1984.

"$3B to End Royalty Dispute with Indian Tribes." *Seattle Times*. December 8, 2009.

Trafzer, Clifford, and Richard Scheuerman. *Renegade Tribe: The Palouse Indians and the Invasion of the Inland Pacific Northwest*. Pullman: Washington State University Press, 1986.

Ulman, H. Lewis, Scott Lloyd DeWitt, and Cynthia Selfe, eds. *Stories That Speak to Us: Exhibits from the Digital Archive of Literacy Narratives*. Utah University State Press, Computers and Composition Digital Press, 2011. Online at http://ccdigital press.org/sites/default/files/STSTUflier.pdf.

Vizenor, Gerald. *Manifest Manners: Postindian Warriors of Survivance*. Hanover, NH: Wesleyan University Press, 1994.

Washines, Ronnie. "Spirit of 'Whip Man' Being Called into Action." *Yakama Nation Review*. June 14, 2002.

Weaskus, Jeanette. "Earthly Rhetorics of Nez Perce Peoples—Past, Present, Future." PhD diss., Washington State University, 2011.

Wieder, D. Lawrence, and Steven Pratt. "On Being Recognizably Indian among Indians." In *Cultural Communication and Intercultural Contact*, edited by Donal Carbaugh, 45–64. Hillsdale, NJ: Erlbaum, 1990.

Index